# Lecture Notes in Computer Science

*Commenced Publication in 1973*
Founding and Former Series Editors:
Gerhard Goos, Juris Hartmanis, and Jan van Leeuwen

T0238509

## Editorial Board

Twittie Senivongse   Rui Oliveira (Eds.)

# Distributed Applications and Interoperable Systems

9th IFIP WG 6.1 International Conference, DAIS 2009
Lisbon, Portugal, June 9-12, 2009
Proceedings

 Springer

Volume Editors

Twittie Senivongse
Chulalongkorn University, Department of Computer Engineering
Phyathai Road, Pathumwan, Bangkok 10330, Thailand
E-mail: twittie.s@chula.ac.th

Rui Oliveira
Universidade do Minho, Departamento de Informática
Campus de Gualtar, 4710-057 Braga, Portugal
E-mail: rco@di.uminho.pt

Library of Congress Control Number: Applied for

CR Subject Classification (1998): C.2.1, C.2.4, D.3.2, D.4.7, H.3.4, C.3

LNCS Sublibrary: SL 6 – Image Processing, Computer Vision, Pattern Recognition, and Graphics

ISSN  0302-9743

ISBN  978-3-642-02163-3 Springer Berlin Heidelberg New York

springer.com

© Springer-Verlag Berlin Heidelberg 2009

Typesetting: Camera-ready by author, data conversion by Scientific Publishing Services, Chennai, India
Printed on acid-free paper      SPIN: 12689385      06/3180      5 4 3 2 1 0

# Foreword

This year's edition of the international federated conferences on Distributed Computing Techniques took place in Lisbon during June 9–11, 2009. It was hosted by the Faculty of Sciences of the University of Lisbon and formally organized by Instituto de Telecomunicações.

The DisCoTec conferences jointly cover the complete spectrum of distributed computing subjects ranging from theoretical foundations to formal specification techniques to practical considerations. The event consisted of the 11th International Conference on Coordination Models and Languages (COORDINATION), the 9th IFIP International Conference on Distributed Applications and Interoperable Systems (DAIS), and the IFIP International Conference on Formal Techniques for Distributed Systems (FMOODS/FORTE). COORDINATION focused on languages, models, and architectures for concurrent and distributed software. DAIS emphasized methods, techniques, and system infrastructures needed to design, build, operate, evaluate, and manage modern distributed applications in any kind of application environment and scenario. FMOODS (11th Formal Methods for Open Object-Based Distributed Systems) joined forces with FORTE (29th Formal Techniques for Networked and Distributed Systems), creating a forum for fundamental research on theory and applications of distributed systems.

In an effort for integration, each of the three days of the event started with an invited talk suggested by one of the conferences in a plenary session, and, furthermore, one of the technical sessions was composed of the papers from the three conferences. The common program also included the first tutorial series on Global Computing, a joint initiative of the EU projects Mobius (Mobility, Ubiquity and Security) and Sensoria (Software Engineering for Service-Oriented Overlay Computers), which contributed to a very interesting program. I would like to thank all the invited speakers for accepting to give talks at the event, and all the authors for submitting papers.

As satellite events, there were two workshops; the Second Workshop on Context-Aware Adaptation Mechanisms for Pervasive and Ubiquitous Services (CAMPUS 2009), focusing on approaches in the domain of context-aware adaptation mechanisms supporting the dynamic evolution of the execution context, and the Third Workshop on Middleware-Application Interaction (MAI 2009), focusing on middleware support for multiple cross-cutting features such as security, fault tolerance, and distributed resource management. Co-located with DisCoTec were the 10th International Conference on Feature Interactions in Telecommunications and Software Systems (ICFI) and meetings of the EU COST action on Formal Verification of Object-Oriented Software and the Sensoria project.

I hope this rich program offered every participant interesting and stimulating events. It was only possible thanks to the dedicated work of the members of the Organizing Committee—Ana Matos, Carla Ferreira, Francisco Martins,

João Seco and Maxime Gamboni—and to the sponsorship of the Center of Informatics and Information Technology (CITI), the Portuguese research foundation Fundação para a Ciência e a Tecnologia (FCT), the Instituto de Telecomunicações (IT), and the Large-Scale Informatics Systems Laboratory (LaSIGE).

June 2009                                                    António Ravara

# Preface

This volume contains the proceedings of DAIS 2009, the 9th IFIP WG. 6.1 International Conference on Distributed Applications and Interoperable Systems. The conference was held in Lisbon, Portugal during June 9-11, 2009 as part of the federated event on Distributed Computing Techniques (DisCoTec), together with the 11th International Conference on Coordination Models and Languages (CO-ORDINATION) and the IFIP International Conference on Formal Techniques for Distributed Systems (FMOODS/FORTE). The conference was organized by the Instituto de Telecomunicações and hosted by the Faculty of Sciences of the University of Lisbon.

The conference program presented the state of the art in research on various aspects of distributed and interoperable application systems. Significant hardware and software developments and advances in communications and global networking have made distributed application systems an integral part of the socio-economic ecosystem of our everyday environment. The confluence of these technological developments and emerging usage modes provides motivation for evolving such systems into ones with seamless provision of services to heterogeneous user domains and requirements. Challenging issues include service orientation, interoperability, autonomy, and dependability of distributed architectures, models, technologies, and platforms.

The papers at DAIS 2009 addressed service orientation, quality of service and service contracts, business processes, Web services, service components, algorithms and protocols supporting dependability, fault tolerance, data replication, group communication, adaptive and collaborative systems, context awareness, model-driven development, middleware for ubiquitous computing and sensor networks, ad hoc network protocols, peer-to-peer systems, and overlays. This year the technical program of DAIS drew 32 submissions. From these, 12 regular papers were accepted for presentation. All submitted papers were reviewed by at least four reviewers, coordinated by our International Program Committee. The conference program also included three keynote addresses, in conjunction with the other two DisCoTec conferences, from Raghu Ramakrishnan, Research Fellow at Yahoo! Research and Professor of Computer Sciences at the University of Wisconsin-Madison, USA, titled "Data Management in the Cloud," Manuel Serrano of INRIA Sophia-Antipolis, France, titled "Semantics and Implementation of the HOP Programming Language," and Jayadev Misra, Professor and Schlumberger Centennial Chair in Computer Sciences at the University of Texas at Austin, USA, titled "Structured Application Development over Wide-Area Networks."

We would like to take this opportunity to thank numerous people whose work made this conference possible. We wish to thank the Instituto de Telecomunicações and the Faculty of Sciences, University of Lisbon, for organizing and hosting the conference, and also António Ravara for acting as the General Chair of DisCoTec. Many thanks go to António's team for organizing the event and to Hartmut König and Martin Steffen for their help with the publicity tasks. Useful advice from DAIS Steering Committee on many occasions is truly appreciated. Finally, we wish to express our gratitude to the authors of all submitted papers and to all Program Committee members as well as external reviewers for their technical contributions towards another successful DAIS.

June 2009

Twittie Senivongse
Rui Oliveira

# DAIS 2009 Organization

## Executive Committee

Program Chairs      Twittie Senivongse (Chulalongkorn University, Thailand)

Rui Oliveira (University of Minho, Portugal)

Publicity Chair      Hartmut König (BTU Cottbus, Germany)

## Steering Committee

| | |
|---|---|
| Frank Eliassen | University of Oslo, Norway |
| Kurt Geihs | University of Kassel, Germany |
| Jadwiga Indulska | University of Queensland, Australia |
| Hartmut König | BTU Cottbus, Germany |
| Lea Kutvonen | University of Helsinki, Finland |
| René Meier | Trinity College Dublin, Ireland |
| Alberto Montresor | University of Trento, Italy |
| Elie Najm | ENST, France |
| Kerry Raymond | Queensland University of Technology, Australia |
| Sotirios Terzis | University of Strathclyde, UK |

## Sponsoring Institutions

IFIP WG 6.1

## Program Committee

| | |
|---|---|
| N. Alonistioti | University of Athens, Greece |
| M. Aoyama | Nanzan University, Japan |
| J. E. Armendáriz-Íñigo | Universidad Pública de Navarra, Spain |
| D. Bakken | Washington State University, USA |
| Y. Berbers | Katholieke Universiteit Leuven, Belgium |
| A. Beresford | University of Cambridge, UK |
| A. Beugnard | TELECOM Bretagne, France |
| G. Blair | Lancaster University, UK |
| A. Casimiro Costa | University of Lisbon, Portugal |
| I. Demeure | ENST, France |
| S. Dobson | University College Dublin, Ireland |
| D. Donsez | Université Joseph Fourier, France |
| N. Dulay | Imperial College London, UK |
| F. Eliassen | University of Oslo, Norway |

| | |
|---|---|
| P. Felber | Université de Neuchâtel, Switzerland |
| K. Geihs | University of Kassel, Germany |
| N. Georgantas | INRIA, France |
| K. Göschka | Vienna University of Technology, Austria |
| R. Grønmo | SINTEF ICT, Norway |
| D. Hagimont | INP Toulouse, France |
| S. Hallsteinsen | SINTEF ICT, Norway |
| P. Herrmann | NTNU Trondheim, Norway |
| J. Indulska | University of Queensland, Australia |
| R. Kapitza | University of Erlangen-Nuremberg, Germany |
| H. König | BTU Cottbus, Germany |
| R. Kroeger | University of Applied Sciences, Wiesbaden, Germany |
| L. Kutvonen | University of Helsinki, Finland |
| W. Lamersdorf | University of Hamburg, Germany |
| M. Lawley | Queensland University of Technology, Australia |
| P. Linington | University of Kent, UK |
| C. Linnhof-Popien | University of Munich, Germany |
| K. Lund | Norwegian Defence Research Establishment (FFI), Norway |
| R. Macêdo | Federal University of Bahia, Brazil |
| R. Meier | Trinity College Dublin, Ireland |
| A. Montresor | University of Trento, Italy |
| E. Najm | ENST, France |
| N. Narasimhan | Motorola Labs, USA |
| R. Oliveira | University of Minho, Portugal (Co-chair) |
| P. Pietzuch | Imperial College London, UK |
| A. Puder | State University San Francisco, USA |
| K. Raymond | Queensland University of Technology, Australia |
| D. Schmidt | Vanderbilt University, USA |
| T. Senivongse | Chulalongkorn University, Thailand (Co-chair) |
| K. Sere | Åbo Akademi University, Finland |
| E. Tanter | University of Chile, Chile |
| S. Terzis | University of Strathclyde, UK |
| J. Xu | Hong Kong Baptist University, Hong Kong |
| H. Yokota | Tokyo Institute of Technology, Japan |

## Distributed Computing Techniques 2009 Organizing Committee

| | |
|---|---|
| António Ravara | Technical University of Lisbon, Portugal (General Chair) |
| Carla Ferreira | New University of Lisbon, Portugal |
| Maxime Gamboni | Technical University of Lisbon, Portugal |
| Ana Almeida Matos | Technical University of Lisbon, Portugal |

João Costa Seco          New University of Lisbon, Portugal
Martin Steffen           University of Oslo, Norway (Publicity Chair)
Francisco Martins        University of Lisbon, Portugal
                         (Workshops Chair)

## Additional Referees

T. Abdessalem          H. Gjermundrod          M. Schmid
M. Alia                F. Gschwandtner         M. Segarra
D. Bade                S. Jiang                C. Spielvogel
N. Ben Lakhal          F. Liu                  J. Sudeikat
S. Bleul               M. Migliavacca          A. Taherkordi
L. Braubach            J. Pereira              A. Vilenica
L. Broto               E. Riviere              M. Zapf
D. Comes               R. Rouvoy               Z. Zhan
G. Da Costa            P. Ruppel
I. Dionysiou           R. Sanders
M. Dixit               J. Schaefer

# Table of Contents

# Exploiting Synergies between Coexisting Overlays

Shen Lin, François Taïani, and Gordon Blair

Computing Department
Lancaster University, UK
{s.lin,f.taiani,gordon}@comp.lancs.ac.uk

**Abstract.** Overlay networks have emerged as a powerful paradigm to realise a large range of distributed services. However, as the number of overlays grows and the systems that use them become more interconnected, overlays must increasingly *co-exist* within the same infrastructure. When this happens, overlays have to compete for limited resources, which causes negative interferences. This paper takes an opposite view, and argues that coexisting overlays may also introduce positive *synergies* that can be exploited to benefit a distributed system. Unfortunately, and in spite of some pioneering work, this phenomenon is still poorly understood and has yet to be investigated systematically. To address this problem, this paper proposes *a principled classification* of synergies, and illustrates how it can be used to exploit synergies in a typical overlay platform targeting gossip protocols (GOSSIPKIT). We review in detail the risks and benefits of each identified synergy; we present experimental data that validate their added value, and finally discuss the lessons we have learnt from our implementation.

**Keywords:** coexistence, synergy, gossip, overlay framework.

## 1 Introduction

An overlay network creates a virtual topology that is built on top of another virtual or physical topology. Over the past decade, overlay networks have emerged as a popular paradigm to offer more tailored services to specific classes of application such as multicasting, inter-domain routing, distributed file sharing and storage, and multimedia streaming [5,6,9,21].

As more overlays are being developed, and as the systems that support them become more interconnected, overlays must increasingly *co-exist* in the same infrastructure. Because overlays are typically domain specific, a given node needs to support a growing number of overlays for different functions (e.g. a personal computer user might be making a Skype call over a VoIP overlay while downloading videos from a BitTorrent overlay). Furthermore, one overlay often depends on other overlays in intricate patterns, and must co-exist with them: for instance, T-Man [9] relies on overlays that maintain random graph to build

T. Senivongse and R. Oliveira (Eds.): DAIS 2009, LNCS 5523, pp. 1–15, 2009.
© IFIP International Federation for Information Processing 2009

various structured network topologies. Finally, changing requirements in long-running systems will lead deployed overlays to be replaced, adding a dynamic dimension to the co-existence of overlays.

When overlays coexist in the same infrastructure, they may affect each other adversely: they must compete for node and network resources; they may also interact in unexpected ways, causing inconsistencies [3,4]. In this paper we take an opposite view, and look instead at the cases when coexisting overlays might benefit from each other through potential *synergies* — i.e. when a set of mutually collaborating protocols perform more efficiently than the individual protocols operating in isolation.

Specific cases of synergies have been studied in a number of pioneering works [1,2,5]. Unfortunately, and in spite of these works, the general phenomenon of synergies remains poorly understood, and has never been studied systematically. This lack of analytical framework in turn limits the ability of overlay developers to analyse and exploit synergies, and prevent users of complex distributed systems to receive the full benefits that coexisting overlays can bring.

As a first step towards addressing these challenges, this paper presents a principled classification of synergies (Section 2), and illustrates its value by demonstrating how it can be used to identify and exploit synergies in GOSSIPKIT [8], a representative component framework that supports coexisting gossip overlays. More precisely, we discuss four concrete examples of synergies that demonstrate the main categories of our classification, and highlight their potential risks and benefits (Section 3). We then present experimental data based on a prototype implementation based on GOSSIPKIT that validate the added values of these synergies (Section 4). We finally discuss the lessons learnt from this work (Section 5), before discussing related work and concluding (Sections 6 and 7).

## 2   A Classification of Synergies between Coexisting Overlays

We define synergy as the *beneficial emergent behaviour* of a set of *coexisting and collaborating overlays* that achieves a higher efficiency than when they operate in isolation. Synergies provide a *global* benefit through the *local* adaptation of each overlay's behaviour, thus delivering a high payoff at a minimum cost.

Since synergies result from the interactions of coexisting overlays, they depend on the *orientation* of these overlays in a system's physical architectural space, i.e. on how overlays coexist with respect to each other. In addition, and because of their nature, synergies must involve the collaboration of some key elements of each overlay. We have termed these key elements *facets*. *Orientation* and *facets* provide the two main dimensions of our classification (Fig. 1).

Communication protocols in general, and overlays in particular, are very often layered in stacks [14,18]. In terms of *orientation*, this translates into two classic forms of coexistence (Fig 1): The *horizontal orientation* indicates overlays that execute in parallel at the same layer of a system, but do not normally require each other to deliver their individual service, in the same way that say TCP

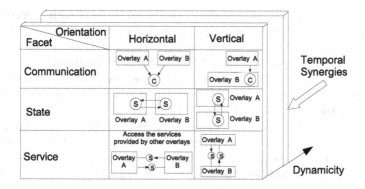

**Fig. 1.** A Classification of Synergies

and UDP reside above IP. Meanwhile, the *vertical orientation* occurs when an overlay uses the functionality of an overlay located in a lower layer to provide its services. For instance, Ghodsi et al. [2] discuss how gossip-based unstructured overlays can be built on top of a structured overlay such as Chord [21].

In terms of *facets*, three key elements are likely to introduce synergies between overlays: their patterns of communication (*communication facet*), their states (*state facet*), and the possible external services they rely on (*service facet*). The *communication facet* refers to how the nodes of an overlay maintain a particular virtual topology by selecting neighbours according to specific control algorithms. When overlays coexist, their *communication facets* can often be coordinated locally to cause them to communicate with the same destination in a way that does not degrade the original service. When this happens, the network traffic can be reduced through piggybacking [22,23] by merging together the data and control messages of multiple overlays to the same destination.

The *state facet* denotes the local data such as sensor readings, routing tables or unstable message buffers that an overlay maintains on a node. The *state facets* of coexisting overlays can often be shared to improve the overall performance of a distributed system through *state synergies* [1,5]. For instance, the Synergy [5] networking platform enables co-existing overlays to share their local routing information. As a result, the messages of a given overlay can utilise the routes maintained by another overlay if those are shorter. This kind of cooperation is analogous to code sharing between airlines: a customer with a ticket from airline *A* might use airline *B*'s flight on part of his journey if the two companies have agreed to share certain routes. Another example of state synergy is the joint overlay proposed by Maniymaran et al. [1]. In this work, the structured overlay Pastry [12] organises nodes in a ring topology. It coexists with an unstructured Clustering overlay that brings together nodes with close interests (e.g. similar videos or games on the node). When operating independently, both overlays need to maintain a list of virtual neighbours along with a "pool" of random peers. This pool acts as a shortcut for joining nodes to quickly discover their neighbours.

Maniymaran et al. point out that the virtual neighbours of each overlay can be used as a pool of random peers by the other. Doing so significantly reduces the network messages (2/3 of the overall messages) used by both overlays.

Finally, the *service facet* denotes the combination of distributed services that an overlay may provide. For instance, the prime functionality of a structured overlay such as Pastry is a standard key-based routing mechanism. However, Pastry's ring topology can also be used to broadcast messages or to aggregate data. Recognising this particular mix of services can allow an overlay that requires *both* routing and broadcast to use Pastry alone instead of a combination of two different overlays [2]. This in turn saves both computing and network resources. We refer to this kind of overlay "consolidation" as *service synergies*.

As mentioned in our introduction, long-running systems means overlays need to be reconfigurable at run-time. This dynamicity adds a third *temporal* dimension to the orientations and facets we have just discussed (Fig. 1). *Temporal synergies* refer to the situation when the initialisation of a newly loaded overlay can benefit from pre-existing overlays, in particular from those being replaced.

## 3    Case Study: Identifying Synergies within GOSSIPKIT

The classification of synergies that we have just presented provides a space of potential synergy types, which can serve as a guideline for developers to identify and exploit synergies between coexisting overlays. To evaluate this point, we apply here this classification to GOSSIPKIT [8], a representative component framework that supports coexisting gossip overlays, and discuss four synergy examples that illustrate the key categories of Figure 1.

### 3.1    Background: Gossip Overlays and GOSSIPKIT

Gossip algorithms allow information to spread over a network in the way a rumour is randomly gossiped amongst a group of people. Gossip-based overlays have been widely applied to provide highly scalable communication in both IP-based networks [9,10,16,17] and mobile adhoc environments [19]. To deliver scalable communication in a large fixed network, a gossip algorithm repeatedly exchanges limited data with a fixed number of randomly selected peers during gossip rounds. The random selection of peers can itself be implemented as a gossip overlay (e.g. RPS [10]). Gossip overlays in mobile adhoc networks differ in that they favour a probabilistic broadcast mechanism rather than a random selection of neighbours, and tend to be reactive rather than periodic, but their probabilistic and scalable approach remains unchanged [19].

Gossip overlays offer many classic examples of coexistence and hence are ideal candidates for the concrete study of synergies: they are often composed of simpler gossip overlays to achieve more complex tasks [11] (vertical coexistence); they are frequently employed to maintain various aspects of structured and unstructured overlays [9] (vertical/horizontal coexistence); and because they are built on randomised mechanisms and behave stochastically, are sometimes replicated to improve reliability (horizontal coexistence) [17].

GOSSIPKIT [8] is a fine-grained component framework that we have developed to ease the development of (re)configurable gossip overlays. In particular, it provides a toolkit to develop middleware platforms that support the coexistence of multiple gossip overlays. To illustrate its value, we have used GOSSIPKIT to implement eight different gossip-based overlays[1]. We have shown that GOSSIPKIT promotes code reuse, simplifies the configuration of gossip-based middleware, and supports the concurrent execution of multiple gossip overlays [8].

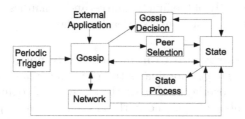

**Fig. 2.** GOSSIPKIT's Common Interaction Model

GOSSIPKIT's design follows a component model that captures the key elements of most gossip overlays [8] (Fig. 2). The `Gossip` component orchestrates the dissemination of data to random peers selected by the `Peer Selection` component via the `Network` component. The `Network` component supports inter-node interactions by encapsulating different communication mechanisms (TCP, UDP, or another overlays). The `Gossip` component can either be triggered reactively by events from external applications or periodically by the `Periodic Trigger` component. The `State` component maintains the data (e.g. a temperature reading, a list of temporary network packets or a set of neighbouring nodes) that is gossiped between nodes and is updated by the `State Process` component. Finally, the `Gossip Decision` component captures the conditions that trigger a gossip dissemination. This component model is recursive — each component can itself be implemented as a gossip overlay that follows the same component model. For instance, the `Peer Selection` component that provides topological maintenance can itself be a membership overlay such as RPS [10]. GOSSIPKIT provides different implementations for each of the above components, and thus allows users to realise a wide range of gossip-based overlays by simple composition.

## 3.2   Synergy Identification

To explore synergies within GOSSIPKIT, we first need to map each of three facets of our classification (Fig. 1) onto the components of GOSSIPKIT's model. In Figure 2, the `State` component directly matches the *state facet* in Figure 1. The `Peer Selection` component decides the communication target of individual

---

[1] The source code of these overlays and of GOSSIPKIT is available on line: www.lancs.ac.uk/postgrad/lins6/GossipKit.html

nodes, and is therefore a prime candidate for potential *communication* synergies. The `Network` component can itself be implemented as an overlay, and may thus provide additional services (*service facet*) that are exploitable by the gossip overlays. The remaining four components in Fig. 2 do not directly match any of our three overlay facets: they encapsulate processes that are limited to local computations, and are thus unlikely to provide exploitable synergies.

In the following we use this mapping to analyse four scenarios of overlay coexistence, both horizontal and vertical, and we investigate their potential for synergies through a study of the functionalities and semantics of the `State`, `Peer Selection` and `Network` components of each overlay.

### 3.2.1   Potential Horizontal Communication Synergy

A *Communication Synergy* coordinates the *communication facets* of coexisting overlays so that these overlays can share the same set of communication targets and reduce the number of their network messages through piggybacking (see Section 2).

This situation may occur for instance when a distributed file storage system uses two gossip overlays for different parts of its functionalities: a *failure detection* overlay [16] to aggregate evidence of failed nodes; and *a data aggregation overlay* [17] to calculate the average data storage on overlay nodes and assist with load-balancing of the system. The impacts of a communication synergy between these two overlays can be analysed as follows.

**Benefit (Network Usage):** When operating independently, these two overlays must both select a constant number of $M$ random peers to communicate with. The probability of a given node to be selected in a gossip round is $\frac{M}{N}$, and these two overlays will on average have $M \times \frac{M}{N} = \frac{M^2}{N}$ communication targets in common, thus contacting an overall average of $2M - \frac{M^2}{N}$ peers at each round. In large-scale networks ($N \gg M$), the number of messages sent during each round will thus approaches $2M$, and more generally the total number of messages will increase linearly with the number of coexisting overlays.

In contrast, using communication synergy, both overlays can consolidate their communication needs and invoke the `Peer Selection` component only once during each round. This allows both overlays to communicate with the same set of $M$ random peers during the same round. With the exploitation of piggybacking mechanism, this approach limits the number of peers to be contacted to a constant $M$, regardless of the number of coexisting gossip overlays, and correspondingly reduces the number of network messages.

**Risk (Aggregation Speed):** Despite the above benefit, communication synergy raises a potential risk as the randomised exchange of information (e.g. through random peer selection) is crucial for a data aggregation gossip overlay to achieve a high convergence speed (typically $O(logN)$ rounds). *Communication Synergies* might therefore jeopardise an overlay's overall efficiency by introducing interferences in its peer selection process.

### 3.2.2    Potential Horizontal State Synergy

A *State Synergy* considers that coexisting overlays can benefit from sharing the data they maintain. We have already mentioned the work of Maniymaran et al. [1]. As a further example, consider the coexistence of T-MAN [9] and Clustering [1]. T-MAN constructs various logical topologies (e.g. a ring) from any initial random graph, and maintains a set of peers that are closer to the local node's coordinates (i.e. the *neighbour set* state). In addition to its *neighbour set* state, T-MAN also relies on the RPS protocol (see Section 3.1) to provide a *random* set of nodes that act as shortcuts for joining nodes to quickly discover their neighbours. Clustering (Section 2) is a gossip overlay that maintains nodes with close interests (e.g. similar videos or games on the node) in its *cluster* state. Similarly to T-MAN, Clustering also use RPS to obtain a *random* state. Because T-MAN uses random node coordinates, its *neighbour set* and Clustering's *cluster* state are not strongly correlated. One overlay's neighbour set can thus be viewed as random by the other overlay. By sharing their states, Clustering can use T-MAN's *neighbour set* as its *random* state and T-MAN can access Clustering's *cluster* set for the same purpose, thus eliminating the need to maintain the RPS overlay.

**Benefit (Network Usage):** Without state synergy, the combination of T-MAN, Clustering, and RPS generates a total number of $3 * M$ messages at each gossip round, where $M$ is the number of peers contacted by each overlay. The state synergy eliminates RPS from the system, hence potentially reducing the total number of network messages to $2 * M$.

**Risk (Convergence Speed):** Both Clustering and T-MAN aim for convergence: T-MAN converges from any random topology to a predefined structure, while Clustering converges to an unstructured topology where nodes with close interests are linked. Both overlays eventually reach a stable situation, where the contents of T-MAM's *neighbour set* and Clustering's *cluster* state remain unchanged. As a result, when they approach convergence, each overlay might fail to provide enough random peers to the other, thus reducing the effectiveness of shortcuts, and slowing down both overlays' convergence speed. Therefore, to safely exploit this synergy type, developers must ensure that the state contents of two overlays are actually uncorrelated.

### 3.2.3    Potential Temporal State Synergy

GOSSIPKIT supports the reconfiguration of gossip-based overlays at runtime, introducing the opportunity of temporal synergies (see Section 2). For instance, consider the case where the SCAMP overlay [15] is being replaced by T-MAN/RPS [9] because of changes in application requirements. SCAMP is a light-weight membership overlay that maintains a random partial membership with maximal entropy to ensure an optimal propagation of broadcast messages. Compared with SCAMP, T-MAN/RPS constructs various logical topologies from any initial random graph to provide a number of services that are not limited to broadcasting. It does so by updating each node's local membership view with the closest logical neighbours (i.e. as defined by a ranking function) on receipt of periodically exchanged random membership information. In order to bootstrap its topological construction, T-MAN normally relies on RPS. This bootstrapping stage requires each joining peer to contact some well-known starting peers, which then propagate join messages to the rest of the overlay.

**Benefit (Stabilisation Speed):** Using state synergy, T-MAN/RPS can work more efficiently by reusing the random partial view previously maintained by SCAMP. Intuitively, SCAMP already contains a lists of nodes belonging to the system. By using this lists, RPS can speed up its joining process, and directly interact with multiple other group members, rather than a limited set of well-known peers, and thus stabilise more rapidly to a stable global state.

### 3.2.4   Potential Vertical Service Synergy

As introduced in Section 3.1, the `Network` component of GOSSIPKIT can be implemented by an underlying overlay that provides a communication service (e.g. Pastry). Such overlays often exhibit properties in addition to communication (e.g. Pastry's ring topology). These properties can be leveraged to provide additional distributed services to the stacked overlays that use them, and thus *consolidate* services.

For instance, consider some gossip overlays that run atop a structured overlay such as Chord [21] to exploit its efficient broadcasting mechanism [2]. In this case, Chord can also provide a random peer sampling service, thus eliminating the need for an explicit sampling overlay such as RPS. This can be done by generating random identifiers from Chord's identifier space, followed by a distributed lookup with Chord's *find_successor* API [21].

**Benefit (Flexibility):** In contrast with gossip-based membership overlays that can only provide a fixed number of random peers in any gossip round, structured overlays can provide a set of random peers of any size.

**Benefit (Network Usage):** Chord's *find_successor* algorithm only requires a worst case of $\log N$ network messages to find a random peers in a network of N nodes, which is potentially much more efficient than the periodic $2 * N$ messages (2 indicates the bi-directional exchange of information) used by a gossip-based membership overlay such as RPS.

**Risk (Network Usage):** A periodic gossip overlay typically requires every node to select a random peer to gossip at each gossip round. Since each random peer selection takes $\log N$ messages, the global number of messages will reach $N * \log N$ per gossip round for a network of N nodes with Chord, which is less efficient than the $2 * N$ messages of RPS.

# 4    Quantitative Evaluation

The four synergies that we have just presented provide both potential benefits and potential risks. To validate their actual value, and assess how difficult they are to realise, we have implemented each of them in GOSSIPKIT. We first present below a quantitative evaluation based on this implementation and a network simulation. We will then move on (in Section 5) to discuss the lessons we learnt from this implementation.

In the experiments that follow, we used the network simulator Jist/SWANS [20] underneath GOSSIPKIT to provide a virtual network environment. In particular, this experimental set-up maintained GOSSIPKIT's ability to insert and remove overlays at run-time, thus allowing us to study temporal synergies.

## 4.1    Horizontal Communication Synergy (Failure Detection and Data Aggregation)

As explained in Section 3.2.1, the reduction in network messages that this synergy provides might come as the cost of an increased number of gossip rounds for the data aggregation of both protocols. To investigate this drawback, we perform the following experiment.

We execute both the failure detection overlay and the data aggregation overlay within GOSSIPKIT. In our implementation, both overlay protocols are configured to periodically send their local states (i.e. part of the global information that must be aggregated) to one randomly selected peer. A simulation run terminates when both overlays have converged — i.e. when the data aggregation overlay has reached a global average and the failure detection overlay has gathered liveness information about all the system's nodes. Each simulation run can be parameterised to exploit the communication synergy (i.e. by selecting the same random peer) or not. The corresponding simulation results, averaged over 20 simulation runs, are shown in Fig. 3 and Fig. 4 for various network sizes.

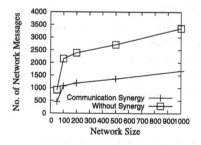
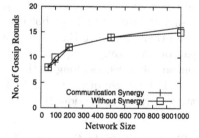

**Fig. 3.** Less network messages with the communication Synergy (ave. -50%)

**Fig. 4.** Gossip rounds not degraded with the communication synergy

**Benefit (Network Usage):** Fig. 3 indicates that network messages are reduced by 50% when both overlays select the same peer at each gossip round and then merge their messages to be sent to this peer (piggybacking). This shows that communication synergy can significantly save network resources.

**Risk (Aggregate Speed):** Fig. 4 shows that the expected $O(logN)$ convergence rate remains as the network size grows, thus demonstrating that in this case the communication synergy does not affect the scalability of either overlays, and does not come at a cost of a slower convergence rate. This result can be generalised to any pair of independent gossip overlays who have identical randomness requirements.

### 4.2  Horizontal State Synergy (T-MAN and Clustering)

We have seen in Section 3.2.2 how some gossip overlays can share each other's state to obtain random links, and thus eliminate the need for an explicit peer sampling overlay such as RPS. To evaluate this type of synergy, we execute T-MAN and Clustering in parallel (see Section 3.2.2), and run two types of simulations. In the first type, T-Man and Clustering rely on RPS to select random peers, while in the second, they share each other's state to obtain random links (state synergy).

**Benefit (Network Usage):** The number of messages required by both types of simulation, averaged over 20 runs, is shown in Fig. 5 for various network sizes. On average, the state synergy reduces network messages by 35% across all network sizes.

**Risk (Convergence Speed):** As mentioned in Section 3.2.2, T-MAN and Clustering might not be able to provide each other with peers that are "random enough" to maintain their speed of convergence. We look at this risk in Fig. 6 which plots the number of rounds needed for both T-MAN and Clustering to converge for various network sizes. This number remains unchanged with or without state synergy. The reasons for this is because the main topologies maintained by T-MAN and Clustering are not correlated. (T-Man maintains peers that are close in a virtual coordinate space while Clustering maintains peers who share similar interests.) Thus both overlays can provide enough random peers for each other even once they have stabilised. In fact, this reasoning applies to any pair of coexisting gossip overlays that maintain both a main topology and a random set of peers, as along as their main topologies are uncorrelated. Maniymaran's [1] joint use of Pastry and Clustering is a similar example of this type of state synergy (see Section 2).

### 4.3  Temporal State Synergy (SCAMP Replaced by T-MAN)

In Section 3.2.3, we explained how nodes running T-MAN/RPS could potentially reduce their bootstrapping overhead by reusing the membership information maintained by a preexisting SCAMP overlay. The following experiment

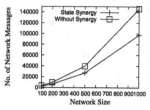 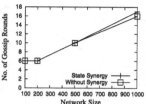 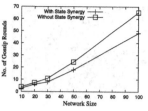

**Fig. 5.** Network messages are reduced with a state synergy (ave. -35%)

**Fig. 6.** Convergence remains unchanged with a state synergy

**Fig. 7.** Bootstrap speed improved with a temporal synergy (ave. -26%)

quantifies this reduction by using T-MAN/RPS to construct a ring topology in two sorts of simulation. In the first sort, T-MAN/RPS starts on each node with a empty local view (i.e. a bootstrap is required), while in the second, SCAMP is executed first and used to initialise T-MAN/RPS with a resulting set of random peers. We terminate both types of runs when T-MAN/RPS converges to a ring.

In all these experiments, T-MAN maintains a local state of size 2, and exchanges messages with both neighbours during every round; RPS maintains a local view of size 4 and communicates with only one random peer per round. SCAMP, as per construction, does not limit the size of its local view. Instead its sample size approximates $\log N$ for a network of $N$ nodes. In the simulations in which T-MAN/RPS initialises its state with SCAMP's, RPS only keeps four random peers from SCAMP's view if SCAMP has more than four.

**Benefit (Stabilisation Speed):** Fig. 7 shows the number of gossip rounds needed by T-MAN to converge (averaged over 20 runs), with and without temporal state synergy. As expected, the synergy helps reduce the number of gossip rounds (an average of 26% reduction) needed to construct a ring topology on various network sizes.

### 4.4 Vertical Service Synergy (Gossiping Over Chord)

In Section 3.2.4, we have analysed that gossip overlays can exploit the *find_successor* service of a structured overlay such as Chord to select random peers on demand, and have discussed the potential risks of doing so for periodic gossip overlays. To evaluate the actual benefits and risks, we carry out the follow experiment with Chord configured to use an identifier space between 0 and 159.

**Benefit (Flexibility):** The RPS overlay can only return a limited number of random peers per round: calling the service repeatedly in the same round will return the same peers. In contrast, Chord can support an unlimited number of queries over any period of time. Fig. 8 illustrates this by plotting the distribution of 1000 random queries made by the same node on a Chord ring.

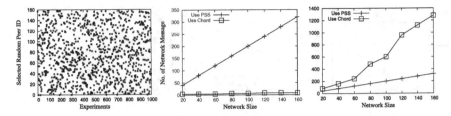

**Fig. 8.** 1000 Uniformly Random Peers are Selected for a Random Node on Chord

**Fig. 9.** The Network Usage for Selecting Random Peers on Demand

**Fig. 10.** The Network Usage for Selecting Random Peers Periodically on All Nodes

**Benefit (Network Usage):** Fig. 9 shows the average number of messages used by a single invocation of Chord's *find_successor*. The graph shows that Chord is indeed much more efficient than RPS if random peer selection is only needed occasionally, because it avoids the periodic flooding generated by RPS. Chord is thus a perfect candidate to maintain a static random graph, e.g. to broadcast probabilistic messages, and only occasionally select some random peers when a node joins or leaves the network (i.e. on demand).

**Risk (Network Usage):** However, our experiments (Fig. 10) have also confirmed that our case study of service synergy uses more network messages if it is used to support gossip overlays that require all nodes to gossip periodically.

## 5   Discussion

Fig. 11 summarises the results of the previous section for the synergies we have presented. In the remainder of this section, we discuss the lessons we learnt from this implementation and from our experimental evaluation.

1. We have demonstrated the existence of synergies for each of the four synergies we identified in Section 3.2, based on the classification we proposed in Section 2. The fact that GOSSIPKIT is a fine-grained component-based framework played a major role in this identification. This is because fine-grained component frameworks often clearly separate the key functional facets of an overlay, and hence help analyse these facets' potential for synergies. They also simplify the implementation of synergies by facilitating collaboration between facets.

2. Our *temporal synergy* example shows that synergies do not only exist between overlays executing in parallel, but also between overlays that coexist transiently during a reconfiguration. We think this directly impacts the design of future reconfigurable middleware, which should ideally support the automatic exploitation of synergies. Towards this aim, it seems that an overlay's state structure should be made explicitly manipulable by the middleware to support automatic reasoning.

3. To be exploitable, potential synergies should not violate the "good properties" of existing overlays. For instance, a main advantage of gossip overlays

| Facets (within GossipKit) \ Orientation | Horizontal | Vertical | Temporal Synergies |
|---|---|---|---|
| **Communication** (Peer Selection) | Failure Detection & Data Aggregate: <br> Network Messages ⬇ <br> Convergence Speed = | | SCAMP replaced by T-MAN: <br> Stablisation Speed ⬆ |
| **State** (State) | T-Man & Clustering: <br> Network Messages ⬇ <br> Aggregate Speed = | | |
| **Service** (Network) | | Gossiping on Chord: <br> Flexibility ⬆ <br> Network Messages ⬇ ⚠ | |

⬇ decrease    ⬆ increase    ⚠ risk    = same

**Fig. 11.** A Summary of the Synergy Examples within GOSSIPKIT

is their ability to converge in logarithmic rounds. Synergies, in particular those that limit the amount of entropy present in a platform, should maintain this.

4. Finally, while implementing the above four synergies, we found GOSSIP-KIT's reflection mechanisms to be particularly helpful. For instance reflection allowed us to easily expose internal interfaces to other overlays. The use of a component model also opens the path for adaptor components that can resolve incompatible interfaces between different overlays.

## 6   Related Work

The iOverlay [6] framework was one of the earliest attempts to support overlay networks. It is essentially a low-level software cross-connect that forwards messages according to a script that embodies the semantics of a particular overlay. Macedon [7] provides a high-level domain specific language to facilitate the configuration of overlays. Both iOvelay and Macedon provide generic platforms for overlays, but do not focus on the coexistence of multiple overlays. GridKit [18] is a reflective middleware framework that supports the coexistence and cooperation of multiple of overlays in the same system. ODIN-S [4] addresses resource contention between coexisting overlays, and provides a scheduling mechanism to optimise resource usage. Very few studies have considered exploiting the potential synergies amongst coexisting overlays, and most of them only considered a particular instance of synergies. We have already discussed many of these works [1,2,5]. In addition, Ucan et al. [22] proposed a piggybacking mechanism to reduce overheads between multiple gossip broadcasts in a wireless sensor network.

## 7   Conclusion

In this paper, we have shown that coexisting overlays can introduce a wide range of potential synergies to benefit a distributed system. More precisely, as an early approach towards the systematic study of synergies, we have proposed a *principled classification* of synergies and demonstrated how this classification can help identify exploitable synergies within GOSSIPKIT, a representative component framework for gossip overlays. We have discussed the benefits and risks of each identified synergies, and provided an experimental evaluation on each of them, before discussing the lessons learnt from our experiments.

This paper opens up several exciting avenues of research. First, our *classification* could be further refined by studying a broader range of overlays. Second, because synergies are fraught with risks, an assessment mechanism seems inevitable to ensure that the exploitation of synergies does not cause negative side-effects to overlay systems. Finally, since new overlays will emerge and might need to be dynamically deployed into a distributed system without restart (e.g. a long-life system), we think that new (re)configuration mechanisms will be needed that directly support the dynamic exploitation of synergies.

**Acknowledgement.** This work has been partially supported by ESF MiNEMA Project and by the EU FP7 ICT Project WISEBED n. 224460.

# References

1. Maniymaran, B., Bertier, M., Kermarrec, A.-M.: Build One, Get One Free: Leveraging the Coexistence of Multiple P2P Overlay Networks. In: Proc. of 27th International Conference on Distributed Computing Systems (2007)
2. Ghodsi, A., Haridi, S., Weatherspoon, H.: Exploiting the Synergy Between Gossiping and Structured Overlays. In: Proc. of ACM SIGOPS Op. Sys. Review (2007)
3. Steinhauer, S., Okanda, P., Blair, G.: Virtual Overlays: An Approach to the Management of Competing or Collaborating Overlay Structures. In: Meier, R., Terzis, S. (eds.) DAIS 2008. LNCS, vol. 5053, pp. 112–125. Springer, Heidelberg (2008)
4. Cooper, B.: Trading Off Resources Between Overlapping Overlays. In: van Steen, M., Henning, M. (eds.) Middleware 2006. LNCS, vol. 4290, pp. 101–120. Springer, Heidelberg (2006)
5. Kwon, M., Fahmy, S.: Synergy: An Overlay Internetworking Architecture. In: Proc. of 14th Inter. Conf. on Computer Communications and Networks (2005)
6. Li, B., Guo, J., et al.: iOverlay: A Lightweight Middleware Infrastructure for Overlay Application Implementations. In: Proc. of IFIP/ACM Middleware Conf. (2004)
7. Rodriguez, A., Killian, C., Bhat, C., et al.: MACEDON: Methodology for automatically creating, evaluating, and designing overlay networks. In: Proc. of USENIX/ACM Symposium on Networked Systems Design (2004)
8. Lin, S., Taiani, F., Blair, G.: Facilitating Gossip Programming with the GossipKit Framework. In: Meier, R., Terzis, S. (eds.) DAIS 2008. LNCS, vol. 5053, pp. 238–252. Springer, Heidelberg (2008)
9. Jelasity, M., Babaoglu, O.: T-Man: Gossip-based overlay topology management. In: EngineeringSelf-Organising Systems: 3rd International Workshop (2005)
10. Jelasity, M., Guerraoui, R., Kermarrec, A., et al.: The Peer Sampling Service: Experimental Evaluation of Unstructured Gossip-Based Implementations. In: Proc. of the 5th ACM/IFIP/USENIX international conference on Middleware (2004)
11. Riviere, E., Baldoni, R., Li, H., et al.: Compositional gossip: a conceptual architecture for designing gossip-based applications. In: ACM SIGOPS Op. Sys. Review (2007)

12. Rowstron, A., Druschel, P.: Pastry: Scalable, decentralized object location and routing for large-scale peer-to-peer systems. In: Guerraoui, R. (ed.) Middleware 2001. LNCS, vol. 2218, p. 329. Springer, Heidelberg (2001)
13. Kermarrec, A.-M., Massoulie, L., Ganesh, A., et al.: Probabilistic Reliable Dissemination in Large-Scale Systems. IEEE Trans. Parallel Distrib. Syst. (2003)
14. Birman, K., Abbadi, A., Dietrich, W., et al.: An Overview of the ISIS Project. IEEE Distributed Processing Technical Committee Newsletter (January 1985)
15. Ganesh, A., Kermarrec, A.-M., Massoulie, L.: SCAMP: Peer-to-Peer Lightweight Membership Service for Large-Scale Group Communication. In: Crowcroft, J., Hofmann, M. (eds.) NGC 2001. LNCS, vol. 2233, p. 44. Springer, Heidelberg (2001)
16. Renesse, R., Minsky, Y., Hayden, M.: A gossip-style failure-detection service. In: Proc. Distributed Systems Platform and Open Distributed Processing (1998)
17. Jelasity, M., Montresor, A., Babaoglu, O.: Gossip-based aggregation in large dynamic networks. ACM Trans. Comput. Syst. 23(3), 219–252 (2005)
18. Grace, P., Coulson, G., Blair, G., et al.: GRIDKIT: Pluggable Overlay Networks for Grid Computing. In: Proc. Int. Symp. on Distributed Objects and Applications (2004)
19. Friedman, R., Gavidia, D., Rodirgues, L., et al.: Gossiping on MANETs: the Beauty and the Beast. ACM Operating Systems Review (2007)
20. Barr, R., Haas, Z., van Renesse, R.: JiST: an efficient approach to simulation using virtual machines: Research Articles. Software Practical Experiments (2005)
21. Stoica, I., Morris, R., Liben-Nowell, D., et al.: Chord: A Scalable Peer-to-peer Lookup Protocol for Internet Applications. In: Proc. of ACM SIGCOMM (2001)
22. Ucan, E., Thompson, N., Gupta, I.: A Piggybacking Approach to Reduce Overhead in Sensor Network Gossiping. In: 2nd International Workshop on Middleware for Sensor Networks (MidSens 2007) (2007)
23. Ananthanarayana, V., Vidyasankar, K.: Dynamic Primary Copy with Piggy-Backing Mechanism for Replicated UDDI Registry. In: Madria, S.K., Claypool, K.T., Kannan, R., Uppuluri, P., Gore, M.M. (eds.) ICDCIT 2006. LNCS, vol. 4317, pp. 389–402. Springer, Heidelberg (2006)

# D-Praxis : A Peer-to-Peer Collaborative Model Editing Framework

Alix Mougenot[1,*], Xavier Blanc[2], and Marie-Pierre Gervais[1]

[1] LIP6, Paris Universitas, France
[2] INRIA Lille-Nord Europe, LIFL CNRS UMR 8022,
Université des Sciences et Technologies de Lille, France

**Abstract.** Large-scale industrial systems involve nowadays hundreds of developers working on hundreds of models representing parts of the whole system specification. Unfortunately, few tool support is provided for managing this huge set of models. In such a context of collaborative work, the approach commonly adopted by the industry is to use a central repository and to make use of merge mechanisms and locks.

In this article we present a collaborative model editing framework, peer-to-peer oriented, that considers that every developer has his own partial replication of the system specification and that makes use of messages exchange for propagating changes made by developers. Our approach has the advantage not to be based on a single repository, which is more and more the case in large-scale industrial projects.

## 1 Introduction

Global specifications of large scale systems are more and more composed of multiple models that are distributed in different locations [5]. During the whole system life cycle, those multiple models are continuously and concurrently edited by developers who work asynchronously on their local copy and who commit from time to time the result of their work to the rest of their team [13]. In such a context, the main problem is to keep the local copies and the global specification consistent. To face this well known problem, conflicts that may arise while developers commit their changes have to be identified and resolved [1].

While the approach commonly adopted by the industry for managing conflicts is to use a central repository and to make use of merge mechanisms and locks [15], another approach, more peer-to-peer oriented, considers that every developer has his own partial replication of the global specification and makes use of messages exchange for propagating changes [14]. The former approach seems to be more robust to deal with model consistency, the later one has the advantage not to be based on a single repository which is more and more the case in large-scale industrial projects.

---

* This work was partly funded by the french DGA.

T. Senivongse and R. Oliveira (Eds.): DAIS 2009, LNCS 5523, pp. 16–29, 2009.

Peer-to-peer approaches for collaborative editing already exist, which are dedicated to text or tree based documents (XML) [6]. To our knowledge, none of them deals with models (typed graphs). Thus our aim is to propose such an approach for models.

Reviewing peer-to-peer approaches for collaborative data editing, we concluded that, whatever the nature of data (e.g, text or tree based), all of them are based on two concerns. The first concern is the conflict identification that requires a clear definition of the data structure and data changes. The second concern is a definition of a protocol required to propagate the changes as well as a mechanism for resolving conflicts that may arise after the propagation of changes.

In this paper, we deal with these two concerns by proposing D-Praxis, a peer-to-peer collaborative model editing framework. Our approach is based on message exchanges between developers for propagating changes. Conflict detection and resolution are done by each site when receiving changes messages.

This article is structured as follows. Section 2 deals with conflict identification and proposes formal specifications for models, model changes and collaborative model editing. Thanks to those specifications, a validation of conflict identification is presented. Section 3 presents the change propagation protocol and the mechanism that has been selected in order to resolve conflicts. Section 4 presents the implementation we have done, which is a decentralized peer-to-peer UML editor. Section 5 then presents related work and the last section presents our conclusion.

## 2   Conflicts Identification

In this section, we present the formal definitions required for conflict identification. Since our concern is collaborative model editing, we propose four basic definitions: models, groups, sites and views (section 2.1). Based on them, we then define change semantics (section 2.2) and conflicts management (section 2.3). All our definitions are written in Alloy which is a lightweight specification language based on first-order relational logic [7].

### 2.1   Basic Formal Definitions: Models, Groups, Sites and Views

Various formalizations of models have been proposed in the literature [8,2,11]. For the sake of simplicity, we propose our own definition in Alloy that is compliant with those existing definitions but considers only a subset of MOF$^{\text{TM}}$[11]. In particular, we consider models to be a finite set of model elements where each model element is typed by a meta-class and can own values for properties and references (complex concepts such as opposite references, derived property and subset values are not supported). The definitions we provide are however sufficient for the purpose of this paper.

In this section, we use the following syntactic domains, represented as sets of atoms: ME for model elements, MC for meta-classes, P for properties, R for references and V for property values. Definition 1 presents the Alloy signature of the considered domains. In Alloy, a set of atoms is specified by a signature (**sig** keyword).

Definition 2 presents the Alloy specification of models where mes represents the set of model elements owned by the model (the keyword **set** means more than one), class the function that assigns one meta-class to each element, valueP the function that assigns one value to each property owned by model elements and valueR the function that assigns reference values. It should be noted that, in this formalization, all properties and references are single-valued.

A model can be included in another one if all its model elements, property values and reference values are included in the other one. Definition 2 gives, as an Alloy predicate, the formal specification of model inclusion. This definition will be used in the following sections.

**Definition 1.**
```
sig ME {} //model element
sig MC {} //metaclass
sig P {} //property
sig R {} //reference
sig V {} //value
```

**Definition 2.**
```
sig Model {
   mes: set ME, //elements of the model
   class: mes -> one MC, //metaclass
   valueP: (mes -> P) -> one V, //property values
   valueR: (mes -> R) -> one mes, //reference values
}

pred include[sub : Model , m : Model] {
   sub.mes in m.mes
   sub.class in m.class
   sub.valueP in m.valueP
   sub.valueR in m.valueR
}
```

Our definitions of group, site and view are based on [14,12]. We consider that a group is composed of several sites that collaborate in the elaboration of one single global model. The global model is an intellectual artifact, it should not exist in the implementation. Each site has a partial view of the global model. Definition 3 presents the Alloy specification of a Group where members represents the set of sites and globalModel represents the global model that is shared between the sites. This definition also represents the specification of a Site where view represents the part of the global model that is viewed by the site.

**Definition 3.**
```
sig Group {
   members: set Site,
   globalModel : one Model,
}

sig Site {view: one Model,}
```

Definition 4 presents two Alloy facts that specify that (1) all the views of group members are models that are included in the global model of the group, and (2) all elements of the global model are in at least one view. According to those definitions, the intersection of two members' views can be empty or not. Figure 1 presents an example of a global model with two views. The left part of the figure presents the global model and the right part presents two views of it.

**Definition 4.**
```
fact allMembersOfAGroupeHaveAViewIncludedInTheGlobalModel{
   all g:Group, m:g.members | include[m.view,g.globalModel]
}

fact allModelElementOfAGlobalModelAreInViews {
   all g:Group | g.globalModel in g.members.view
}
```

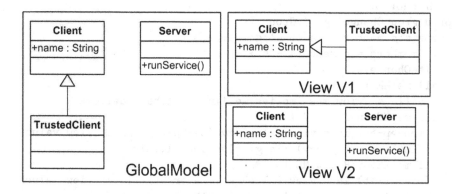

**Fig. 1.** A global model and 2 views

## 2.2   Change Semantics

In a group, each site can locally perform changes (in its view). Then, each site can decide to commit its local changes to the group. But changes made on a site view may impact the other site views. Thus it is necessary to define the semantics of a change and the impact it may have on other members of the same group.

In Alloy, such a semantics is specified thanks to predicates that have, by convention, two input parameters representing the same object but into two different states; respectively before and after the occurrence of the changes.

Definition 5 presents the semantics of a model change and of a site change. A model m is modified, and becomes a model m', if some of its elements, property or reference values are either modified or removed or if some new elements, properties or references are created (change of class are not allowed). A site s is modified, and becomes a site s' if its view is modified.

**Definition 5.**
```
pred modelChange[m , m' : Model] {
 m.mes != m'.mes || m.valueP != m'.valueP || m.valueR != m'.valueR
}

pred siteChange[s,  s':Site] {
    modelChange[s.view ,s'.view]
}
```

Definition 6 then presents the semantics of a group change. A group g is modified, and becomes a group g' if some of its sites are modified. Moreover, the specification defines that g', the modified group, contains all the model elements, properties and references of g minus all those that have been removed, plus all the ones that have been newly created by the site changes.

**Definition 6.**
```
pred groupChange[ g,g':Group ]{
  some s:g.members | some s':g'.members {
    g'.members = g.members - s + s'
    siteChange[s,s']
    all me:ME |
    me !in s'.view.mes implies me !in g'.globalModel.mes
    all me:ME, p:P , v:V |
    ((me->p->v) in s.view.valueP && (me->p->v) !in s'.view.valueP)
       implies (me->p->v) !in g'.globalModel.valueP
    all me:ME, r:R , t:ME |
    ((me->r->t) in s.view.valueR && (me->r->t) !in s'.view.valueR)
       implies (me->r->t) !in g'.globalModel.valueR
      } }
```

Definition 6 clearly specifies the semantics of group evolution. In particular, it defines that all elements deleted from a site view have to be deleted from the global model and then have to be deleted from all of the sites view that share them. For example, if the Client class is deleted from view V2, then it has to be deleted from the global model and therefore has to be deleted from the view V1.

## 2.3  Conflicts Management

The main known main difficulty for keeping consistency between a global model and its views is to deal with edition conflicts. In [10], Mens defines a conflict as "A pair of operations that lead to an inconsistency is called a conflict". More formally, in our context, a conflict occurs when two sites of a group g perform changes that cannot be integrated into a single changed group g'.

We used Alloy in order to validate our conflicts identification. We used the following approach: (1) specify the changes with Alloy and (2) ask Alloy to find a configuration where there is a group g with two sites performing the changes and a changed group g' integrating both of them. If no configuration can be found by Alloy or if Alloy returns more than one configuration, then the two changes are said to be a conflict.

For sake of brevity, we present this approach in definition 7, but for only one kind of change because of space limitation. It consists of the addition of a new value (v) to the model element (m) for the property (p). This change applied on a site (s) returns the site (s').

**Definition 7.**
```
pred addProp[s , s' : Site , m:ME , p : P , v:V] {
  s.view.mes = s'.view.mes
  m in s.view.mes
  s.view.class = s'.view.class
  m->p->v !in s.view.valueP
  m->p->v in s'.view.valueP
  no m':ME, p':P, v':V |
    m'->p'->v' in s.view.valueP && m'->p'->v' !in s'.view.valueP
  s.view.valueR = s'.view.valueR
}
```

Thanks to this definition, we have asked Alloy for an example of a changed group with two sites performing the change we just presented, on a same shared model element, on a same property but with two different values. This question, specified in the Alloy assert presented in definition 8.

**Definition 8.**
```
assert conflict1 {
  no s1,s1',s2,s2':Site , g,g':Group, m:ME, p:P   {
    s1+s2 in g.members
    s1'+s2' in g'.members
    some disjoint v1,v2:V |
      addProp[s1,s1',m,p,v1] && addProp[s2,s2',m,p,v2]
    groupChange[g,g']
  }
}
```

Asking this question to Alloy returns that no example can be provided. This means that Alloy cannot find a group g' that integrates those changes. Even if this answer cannot be considered as a proof, it is a validation that those changes are a potential conflict. Actually, as specified by definition 2, all model elements can own a single value for each property. Therefore, the two different values added by the two changes cannot be integrated into the global model. It should be noted that, if we change definition 2 in order to support multi-value property, Alloy returns an example.

We have used the same approach to validate the following conflicts:

1. **different property values:** If two sites change the property value of one shared model element and if they provide different values.
2. **add and remove property value:** If one site changes a property value of one shared model element and if another one removes the value.
3. **different reference values:** If two sites change the reference value of one shared model element and if they provide different values.
4. **add and remove reference value:** If one site changes a reference value of one shared model element and if another one removes the value.
5. **delete a model element and add a reference value that targets it:** If one site deletes a shared model element and if another one adds a reference that targets it.
6. **delete a model element and add a reference value from it:** If one site deletes a shared model element and if another one adds a reference from it.
7. **delete a model element and add a property value to it:** If one site deletes a shared model element and if another one adds a property value to it.

It should be noted that this use of Alloy does not validate the fact that we have identified all possible conflicts. It only validates the conflicts that we have identified.

## 3    D-Praxis Protocol and Conflict Resolution

The second concern of any peer-to-peer collaborative editing is the propagation of changes and the conflict resolution. We then propose a protocol responsible for the propagation of changes and a mechanism to resolve conflicts between concurrent changes. Changing a model in our context means that a site modifies its own view. To represent such a change, a representation of models is required (subsection 3.1). Subsection 3.2 then explains how a global model is distributed among the different sites of a group. Subsection 3.3 explains how changes made by sites are propagated among other sites in order to update their views. Subsection 3.4 finally explains how conflicts are identified and resolved.

### 3.1    Representation of Models

In [3], we propose to represent models as sequences of elementary operations needed to construct each model element. We reuse this approach and propose the six following elementary construction operations to represent any model. The six elementary operations we propose are inspired by the MOF reflective API [11]:

- **create***(me,mc)* creates a model element *me* instance of the meta-class *mc*. A model element can be created if and only if it does not already exist in the model (we use UUID to avoid two model elements with a same id);
- **delete***(me)* deletes a model element *me*. A model element can be deleted if and only if it exists in the model and it is not referenced by any other model element. When an element is removed, all its property values are automatically removed;
- **addProperty***(me,p,v)* assigns a value *v* to the property *p* of the model element *me*;
- **remProperty***(me,p)* remove the value, if any, to the property *p* of the model element *me*;
- **addReference***(me,r,met)* assigns a target model element *met* to the reference *r* of the model element *me*.
- **remReference***(me,r)* remove the target model element, if any, to the reference *r* of the model element *me*.

To illustrate this model representation, the left part of Table 1 presents a sequence of unitary actions corresponding to the class model of Figure 1 (Tx parameters are time stamp).

**Table 1.** Distributed representation of the example model (see figure 1)

| GlobalModel | View V1 | View V2 |
|---|---|---|
| create(c1,class,T1) | X | X |
| addProperty(c1,name, 'Client',T2) | X | X |
| create(a1,attribute,T3) | X | X |
| addProperty(p1,name,'name',T4) | X | X |
| addProperty(p1,type, 'String',T5) | X | X |
| addReference(c1,attribute,a1,T6) | X | X |
| create(c2,class,T7) | X | |
| addProperty(c2,name,'TrustedClient',T8) | X | |
| addReference(c2,super,c1,T9) | X | |
| create(c3,class,T10) | | X |
| addProperty(c3,name,'Server',T11) | | X |
| create(o1,operation,T12) | | X |
| addProperty(o1,name,'runService',T13) | | X |
| setReference(c3,operation,o1,T14) | | X |

## 3.2 Representation of a Global Model and Its Views

As we presented in section 2, in D-Praxis, a group of sites collaborates to the elaboration of one single virtual global model. We consider the global model and the site's views to be represented by sequences of construction operations, respectively named the global sequence and the site sequences. All operations sequence are completely ordered thanks to a Lamport clock [9]. As each site's view is included in the global model, each site's sequence is a subpart of the global sequence. Moreover, as different site's views may share some model elements, their corresponding site sequences may share operations.

In D-Praxis, the global sequence is not to be completely owned by one particular site. However, its operations have to be distributed in the site's sequences. Table 1 presents the example model distributed within two sites. Each operation has a time stamp (the discriminator, which is the site's ID, is not represented here), represented by the last parameter of the operation. A cross in the table means that the site sequence owns a copy of the operation.

## 3.3   Changes Propagation

As site views are represented by site sequences, changes made on site views are additions of new operations in the corresponding site sequences. Change propagation consists then in propagating those operations to the other sites, which may need to incorporate them in their own sequence to comply with the definition of the group semantics (see Definition 6).

In order to optimize change propagation and not to broadcast every change to all the sites of a group, we propose to define subgroups of sites that share one same set of model elements (publish/subscribe strategy for each model element). When a change concerns a model element, it is only propagated to sites that share it.

The following list defines our changes propagation protocol (conflict handling is discussed in the next section):

- **create***(me,mc)*: When a site adds a new model element in its view, the model element is automatically considered to be part of the global model because views are included in the global model (see definition 4). Moreover, this creation has no impact on other views (definition 6). Finally, as we use UUID, two sites cannot create two different model elements with a same id. This operation is not propagated.
- **delete***(me)*: When a site deletes a model element from its view, the model element is automatically considered to be deleted from the global model and from views that share it (definition 6). This operation has to be propagated to all the sites that share *me*.
- **addProperty***(me,p,v)*: When a site adds a new property value for a model element of its view, the global element is automatically changed as well as the views that share it (definition 6). This operation has to be propagated to all the sites that share *me*.
- **remProperty***(me,p)*: When a site removes the property value of a model element of its view, the global element is automatically changed as well as the views that share it (definition 6). This operation has to be propagated to all the sites that share *me*.
- **addReference***(me,r,met)*: When a site adds the reference value of a model element of its view, the global element is automatically changed as well as the views that share it (definition 6). This operation has to be propagated to all the sites that share *me* and *met*.

- **remReference***(me,r)*: When a site removes the reference value of a model element of its view, the global element is automatically changed as well as the views that share it (definition 6). This operation has to be propagated to all the sites that share *me*.

Change propagation does not prevent the conflicts identified in section 2.3. The next section presents how the propagated changes are integrated in the sequences of the sites that receive the changes and how conflicts are detected and resolved.

## 3.4   Conflict Resolution

Conflicts are detected and resolved by sites when they receive changes propagation. As said by Saito in [14], "Conflict resolution is usually highly application specific". Indeed, many strategies can be used to resolve them. The one we use is based on two principles: (1) the Lamport clock [9] and (2) the delete semantics of Praxis [3]. We consider that when two operations are in conflict, then the later one is kept and the former one is canceled unless it is a delete operation.

It is obvious to say that such a strategy may not be suitable to all developers' needs. Nevertheless, it has the advantage to be very simple, quite efficient and fits the objective of this work. Moreover, it should be noted that any other strategy can replace it.

The following list presents how conflicts (see section 2.3) are identified and resolved:

1. **different property values:** This conflict is detected if a site receives a new property value for one of its model element, which already owns another property value. Then, if the received operation is older than its own operation, the received operation is added to its site sequence, else it is ignored.
2. **add and remove property value:** This conflict is detected if a site receives a new property value for one of its model element where the property's value was already removed. This conflict is resolved like the previous one.
3. **different reference values:** This conflict is detected if a site receives a new reference value for one of its model element, which already owns another reference's assignment. This conflict is resolved like the previous one.
4. **add and remove reference value:** This conflict is detected if a site receives an addReference (resp remReference) for one of its model element, where this reference's assignment was already removed (resp added). This conflict is resolved like the previous one.
5. **delete a model element and add a reference value that targets it:** This conflict is detected if a site receives a delete operation of one of its model element that is locally referenced (definition 2 prevents model element to be deleted if they are referenced). Then, operations that remove all existing known references to the element from the current view are added to the site sequence (and won't be propagated) before the delete operation is added.

6. **delete a model element and add/remove a reference value from it:** This conflict is detected if a site receives a delete operation of one of its model element, and this site has some operations that assign/remove references from this model element. This conflict is resolved by ignoring the reference changes that occur after the delete operation.

7. **delete a model element and add/remove a property value to it:** This conflict is detected if a site receives a delete operation of one of its model element, and this site has some operations that add/remove property values to this model element. Then, if some of those operations are older than the delete one, they are ignored.

# 4   Validation

## 4.1   Architecture

The validation we have done of our approach, named D-Praxis/UML, is a peer-to-peer collaborative editor for UML models. D-Praxis/UML is conceptually composed of the following three components that run on each developer site.

**GroupMemberShip** is the component that controls groups of developers. Thanks to this component, a developer can (1) create a new group, (2) join an existing group, (3) list the members of a group and (4) look at the view of a member in order to declare interest to some of its model elements. When a developer creates or joins a group, the GroupMemberShip component creates an empty UML model that corresponds to the developer's view. When a developer looks at the view of a member and declares interest at some of its elements, the GroupMemberShip component asks this member site for a propagation of operations corresponding the editing of those elements.

**ChangePropagation** is the component that controls messages propagation. Thanks to this component, a developer can change his view and commit his changes. The ChangePropagation component is responsible for setting the time stamps and propagating them to the interested developers. The ChangePropagation component is then responsible for the Lamport clock and for the interest groups that are used as routing tables for change propagation.

**ConflictManager** is the component that controls remote view editing. It receives changes and automatically integrates them in the developer's view. This component listens for change propagation and then is responsible for detecting conflicts and resolving them.

## 4.2   Sample Scenario

As a validation scenario we present how two developers collaborate to the elaboration of a single global UML model. We consider that the group is composed of two developers: Bob and Alice. Thanks to the GroupMembership facility provided by D-Praxis/UML, Alice starts the creation of a new group. As a result, D-Praxis/UML creates an empty model on the Alice site. Alice then elaborates this model by adding the class Client of Figure 1. Those changes have time stamps that correspond to the Alice's clock. They don't have to be propagated as there is no member who has declared an interest to them. Bob, who knows the IP address of Alice's site, uses the GroupMembership facility of D-Praxis/UML to join the group created by Alice. As a result, D-Praxis creates an empty model on the Bob's site. Bob then uses again the GroupMembership facility in order to look at Alice's view and to declare interest in the model elements representing the class Client and its attributes. As a result, the ChangePropagation component of Alice's site propagates corresponding operation to Bob's site. The first part of table 2 represents Alice's and Bob's views at this stage.

Alice and Bob then decide to change their view in parallel. Alice adds the TrustedClient class and Bob the Server class. Those changes have time stamps that correspond to Alice's and Bob's clocks. They don't have to be propagated as they do not target shared model elements.

**Table 2.** Bob and Alice views

| Alice | Bob |
|---|---|
| create(c1,class,A1) | create(c1,class,A1) |
| addProperty(c1,name, 'Client',A2) | addProperty(c1,name, 'Client',A2) |
| create(a1,attribute,A3) | create(a1,attribute,A3) |
| addProperty(p1,name,'name',A4) | addProperty(p1,name,'name',A4) |
| addProperty(p1,type, 'String',A5) | addProperty(p1,type, 'String',A5) |
| addReference(c1,attribute,a1,A6) | addReference(c1,attribute,a1,A6) |
| create(c2,class,A7) | create(c3,class,B7) |
| addProperty(c2,name,'TrustedClient',A8) | addProperty(c3,name,'Server',B8) |
| addReference(c2,super,c1,A9) | delete(c1,B9) |
| addProperty(c1,abstract,'true',A10) | create(o1,operation,B10) |
| | addProperty(o1,name,'runService',B11) |
| | setReference(c3,operation,o1,B12) |
| remReference(c2,super,c1,A11) | Ignore:addProperty(c1,abstract,'true',A10) |
| delete(c1,B12) | |

Finally, Alice and Bob decide to change the Client class in parallel. Alice decides to make it abstract (addProperty(c1,abstract,'true')) while Bob decides to delete it (delete(c1)). As their changes target a shared model element, they are propagated. The Lamport clock states that the delete operation (B9) is before the addProperty one (A10). As we presented in section 2.3, those two changes make a conflict which is resolved by the rules we presented in section 3.4. Indeed, the delete operation is considered to be priority. As a consequence the operation remReference(c2,super,c1) is added to the Alice's view and the addProperty(c1,abstract,'true') is tagged as ignored in the Bob's view as shown in the last part of figure 1.

### 4.3 Implementation

D-Praxis/UML has been developed on top of Eclipse as a set of Eclipse plugins[1]. The GroupMembership component is designed as a classic Group Membership framework but is very simple and does not support member disconnection. The ChangePropagation component is built on top of the EMF model editor that is used by developers for editing graphically their models. The ConflictManager component listens for propagation messages and, when it receives a message, automatically updates the site sequence and the corresponding model in the editor.

## 5   Related Works

Collaborative editing has been already used for text and tree based documents but not for models [6]. Our approach follows principles defined by those approaches. In particular, it reuses the main idea of [4] which is to use operations for data and change representation.

In [12], the authors present a roadmap for building development environments that support multiviews editing and stress four points that have to be addressed: view initialization, view sharing, view change and view integration. Our proposal supports all of those four points by following a peer-to-peer decentralized approach.

Model editing conflicts have been presented in [10,15]. Our approach identifies the same conflicts but provides a formal approach to validate conflicts identification.

## 6   Conclusion

In this article we proposed D-Praxis, a peer-to-peer collaborative model editing framework with which developers of a same team can collaborate to the elaboration of one single virtual global model. D-Praxis, is based on our previous proposal that is to represent model, and hence any view, by a sequence of construction operations. Changes propagation and conflicts detection and resolution are based on this representation.

As a first contribution, we have provided a formal validation of the identification of conflicts that may arise when changes are made on some views and lead to inconsistent model.

As a second contribution, we have provided a mechanism, peer-to-peer oriented, that handles changes propagation and conflicts detection and resolution. The change propagation protocol we propose is optimized in order to only target sites that share changed model elements. The conflicts resolution strategy we propose is based on an order computed by Lamport clocks and on the delete semantics of our model representation.

---

[1] http://meta.lip6.fr

Those two contributions have been implemented in D-Praxis/UML, peer-to-peer UML class editor. This implementation is currently stress tested by students of our university in order to better measure its advantages and its limits.

This kind of peer-to-peer oriented approach does offer solutions for dealing with collaborative work in a context where it is not possible to have a single repository.

# References

1. Adams, E.W., Honda, M., Miller, T.C.: Object management in a case environment. In: Proc. Int'l Conf. Software Engineering (ICSE 1989), pp. 154–163. ACM, New York (1989)
2. Alanen, M., Porres, I.: A metamodeling language supporting subset and union properties. Software and System Modeling 7(1), 103–124 (2008)
3. Blanc, X., Mougenot, A., Mounier, I., Mens, T.: Detecting model inconsistency through operation-based model construction. In: Robby (ed.) Proc. Int'l Conf. Software engineering (ICSE 2008), vol. 1, pp. 511–520. ACM, New York (2008)
4. Ellis, C.A., Gibbs, S.J.: Concurrency control in groupware systems. SIGMOD Rec. 18(2), 399–407 (1989)
5. Feiler, P., Gabriel, R., Goodenough, J., Linger, R., Longstaff, T., Kazman, R., Klein, M., Northrop, L., Schmidt, D., Sullivan, K., et al.: Ultra-large-scale systems: The software challenge of the future. Technical report, Software Engineering Institute, Carnegie Mellon University (2006) ISBN 0-9786956-0-7
6. Ignat, C.-L., Oster, G., Molli, P., Cart, M., Ferrié, J., Kermarrec, A.-M., Sutra, P., Shapiro, M., Benmouffok, L., Busca, J.-M., Guerraoui, R.: A comparison of optimistic approaches to collaborative editing of wiki pages. In: Proceedings of the 3rd International Conference on Collaborative Computing: Networking, Applications and Worksharing, White Plains, New York, USA, November 12-15, 2007, pp. 474–483 (2007)
7. Jackson, D.: Software Abstractions: Logic, Language, and Analysis. The MIT Press, Cambridge (2006)
8. Kühne, T.: Matters of (meta-) modeling. Software and System Modeling 5, 369–385 (2006)
9. Lamport, L.: Time, clocks, and the ordering of events in a distributed system. Commun. ACM 21(7), 558–565 (1978)
10. Mens, T.: A state-of-the-art survey on software merging. IEEE Trans. Softw. Eng. 28(5), 449–462 (2002)
11. OMG. Meta Object Facility (MOF) 2.0 Core Specification (Januray 2006)
12. Ossher, H., Harrison, W., Tarr, P.: Software engineering tools and environments: a roadmap. In: ICSE 2000: Proceedings of the Conference on The Future of Software Engineering, pp. 261–277. ACM, New York (2000)
13. Perry, D.E., Siy, H.P., Votta, L.G.: Parallel changes in large scale software development: An observational case study. In: Proc. Int' Conf. Software Engineering (ICSE 1998), pp. 251–260 (1998)
14. Saito, Y., Shapiro, M.: Optimistic replication. ACM Computing Surveys 37(1), 42–81 (2005)
15. Sriplakich, P., Blanc, X., Gervais, M.-P.: Supporting collaborative development in an open mda environment. In: ICSM, pp. 244–253. IEEE Computer Society, Los Alamitos (2006)

# A Reflective Middleware to Support Peer-to-Peer Overlay Adaptation

Gareth Tyson[1], Paul Grace[1], Andreas Mauthe[1], Gordon Blair[1],
and Sebastian Kaune[2]

[1] ComputingDepartment, InfoLab21, Lancaster University, Lancaster, UK
{g.tyson,p.grace,andreas,gordon}@comp.lancs.ac.uk,
[2] KOM Multimedia Communications, Technishe Universität Darmstadt, Germany
kaune@kom.tu-darmstadt.de

**Abstract.** As peer-to-peer systems are evolving from simplistic application specific overlays to middleware platforms hosting a range of potential applications it has become evident that increasingly configurable approaches are required to ensure appropriate overlay support is provided for divergent applications. This is exacerbated by the increasing heterogeneity of networked devices expected to host the overlay. Traditional adaptation approaches rely on simplistic design-time isolated fine-tuning of overlay operations. This, however, cannot fully support the level of configurability required by next generation peer-to-peer systems. To remedy this, a middleware overlay framework is designed that promotes the use of architectural reconfiguration for adaptive purposes. Underpinning this is a generic reusable component pattern that utilises software reflection to enable rich and extensible adaptation of overlays beneath divergent applications operating in heterogeneous environments. This is evaluated through a number of case-study experiments showing how overlays developed using the framework have been adapted to address a range of application and environmental variations.

**Keywords:** Adaptation, peer-to-peer, reflective middleware.

## 1 Introduction

As distributed computing has moved towards increasingly decentralised models it has become evident that responsive and extensible adaptation mechanisms are integral for real-world deployment. Peer-to-peer networking is a prominent example of such a technology. By pushing functionality to the edge of the network it is possible to utilise the extensive resources available at end-hosts. However, by doing so it means that it is necessary to execute system functionality in increasingly uncontrolled and diverse environments, ranging from stable and well-connected desktop computers to low-power embedded devices.

This increasing diversity raises the question of how a system can be expected to effectively adapt in continually evolving operating environments. Early peer-to-peer systems were strongly bound to their application, however, recently there has been a move towards utilising peer-to-peer overlays as a middleware platform for a variety

T. Senivongse and R. Oliveira (Eds.): DAIS 2009, LNCS 5523, pp. 30–43, 2009.

of applications to operate over e.g. [12][13]. This means that overlays now must not only adapt to their environment but also to the requirements of any applications built over them. Whereas traditional mechanisms (e.g. parametric adaptation) have proved adequate in earlier peer-to-peer overlays that are restricted to a single application, it is clear that they are severely limited in their scope (e.g. file sharing). This becomes evident when deploying such overlays in diverse operating environments below various applications e.g. performing video streaming in MANETs.

This paper designs and evaluates a middleware overlay framework that promotes and utilises extensible architectural adaptation. Central to this design is the use of *abstraction, reconfigurable component-based engineering* and *reflection* to facilitate the convenient and extensible adaptation of node behaviour in both local and distributed settings. The rest of the paper is structured as follows. Section 2 offers a background to the work. Section 3 then describes the overlay middleware framework alongside the key principles of its operation. Subsequently in Section 4, a component pattern is described to show how overlays can be developed in the framework. Section 5 evaluates the overlay framework primarily using case-study experiments to highlight the capabilities of architectural adaptation. Lastly, Section 6 concludes the paper outlining areas of future work.

## 2  Background and Motivation

There has been a large body of work carried out into peer-to-peer networking. This has focussed on the construction of increasingly sophisticated and novel designs addressing application areas such as video streaming [25], distributed searching [6] and distributed object location [22]. These systems have generally been developed using 'ad-hoc' overlay-specific approaches to adaptation, focussing on adaptation for maintenance purposes [17][21][22] as well as optimisation purposes [1][2][4].

These adaptation approaches can be separated into two primary groups (although other categorisations also exist e.g. [14]). The first category we term *parametric adaptation*. This is discrete parameter adaptation based on variable inputs to a fixed algorithm. For instance, GIA [6] utilises parametric adaptation when constructing its topology. This is done by selecting different neighbourhood sizes based on node capabilities. The second category we term *policy adaptation*. This is performed using variable sets of algorithms that are exchanged during runtime. For instance, BitTorrent [2] uses policy adaptation by utilising different chunk selection algorithms based on the current download status.

Whereas these mechanisms have proved adequate in traditional peer-to-peer systems (e.g. file sharing) it is evident that their potential is limited in next generation applications and networks. This is because both mechanisms require the design-time isolation and implementation of adaptive functionality. This limits flexibility when deployed in diverse environments possessing unpredictable characteristics. For instance, an unstructured search overlay might adapt its resilience algorithms by parametrically altering the number of neighbours it utilises. This, whilst adequate in a traditional deployment, does not sufficiently support adaptation if ported to a mobile ad-hoc network (MANET). This is because it would also be necessary to adapt a number of alternate concerns. A new localised neighbour selection policy would be required to limit egress communications. Similarly the forwarding algorithms would require adaptation to exploit the broadcast nature of the MANET environment. Further, the maintenance procedures would require modification to respond to the high latency, transient nature of peers.

These criticisms were first provided by Oreizy et al [19]. This seminal paper promoted the use of well-defined software architectures for supporting system evolution. Later work such as [3][12] further identified the advantages of software architectures in adaptive system design. This work dictates that entire systems are built from well-defined independent software entities called *components* [8] that possess fixed capabilities (interfaces) alongside well-defined dependencies (receptacles). Through this, specialised and adaptive systems can be built by dynamically interconnecting optimal component interfaces and receptacles during runtime. The complete construction of systems from abstracted components further opens up adaptation to any aspect of the system rather than limited sets of functionality identified at design time.

In the last decade a number of adaptive systems have been developed using these principles. To support these, a number of lightweight *component models* have emerged e.g. Fractal [5] and OpenCOM [8]. These component models support adaptation by managing such things as component dependencies and runtime reconfiguration. Notably these two examples further support the concept of *reflection* [16]. This is the ability for a system to gain introspection to the capabilities and behaviour of its constituent components. This allows a system to match its requirements to its available components to build new and extensible *configurations*.

A range of reflective middleware has been developed for such things as QoS [7], remote method invocation [3] and sensor networking [12]. However, only limited work has been carried out into the architectural adaptation of overlays. The Open Overlays project [12] carried out initial work in the area, however, this takes a coarse grained approach. RaDP2P [15] and AdaPtP [14] look at standardised adaptation for peer-to-peer systems. These, however, focus on adaptation strategies rather than the underlying platform for adaptation i.e. parametric, architectural etc. PROST [20] utilises abstraction for overlay adaptation (specifically for structured overlays). It does this by using a standardised API (e.g. Dabek et al [9]) and using different overlay networks behind it. This, however, only offers very simplistic adaptation strategies that do not offer sufficiently fine-grained, rich adaptation for real-world usage.

## 3  Principles behind Reflective Overlay Adaptation

This section introduces the principles behind architectural reconfiguration and how they can be exploited by peer-to-peer system to achieve flexible adaptation.

### 3.1  Abstraction and (Re)Configurable Software Design

Abstraction is an important concept in software engineering. It forms a platform for both software evolution and system adaptation. It involves the modularization of system functionality into well-defined abstractions, shown as small boxes in Fig. 1; these each represent one abstracted aspects of the overlay's functionality. This can be done in a very coarse sense (e.g. the overlay as one unit) or alternatively in a very fine grained sense (e.g. placing every method behind an independent abstraction). By taking a finer-grained approach the entire system is opened up to adaptation by supporting the modification of any system aspect behind its interface. This therefore allows multiple implementations of the same interface to be dynamically exchanged on a node to react to context variations in the operating environment; these individual implementations are termed *pluggable components*.

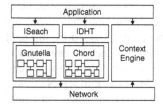

**Fig. 1.** Overview of Framework Configured with ISearch and IDHT

An important design concern is the way that system functionality is separated into these independent components. A standardised approach to functional separation is termed a *component pattern*. The framework's default component pattern for implementing overlays is described in Section 4. As well as these internal abstractions, however, the framework also exploits an external abstraction. This is the provision of standardised access to the overlay allowing the application to seamlessly operate with the overlay, even during adaptation. This can be seen in Fig. 1 with the ISearch and IDHT abstractions being offered to the application. These abstractions, in turn, are mapped to the underlying functionality of supporting overlays (in this example, Gnutella [6] and Chord [22]). This allows alternative overlays (or adapted configurations of the same overlay) to be interchanged behind the abstractions e.g. exchanging Chord for KAD [18] in unreliable environments. A number of other abstractions are also currently available in the framework, including: multicast, group messaging and stored distribution. Lower level native abstractions are also provided to support access to the base overlay operations i.e. routing messages.

### 3.2  Reflection and Context-Aware Configuration

To perform architectural adaptation it is necessary for a node to be aware of its own software structure. Reflection is the enabling technology behind this; it allows a piece of software to inspect and manipulate its own implementation. This allows the node to explicitly state which components are operating and how they interact. Importantly, it further allows the node to dynamically replace such components to best serve the host. To enable this selection process, components are associated with meta-tags describing particular attributes of their behaviour in name-value pairs.

Composites of components are further constructed to build more sophisticated bodies of functionality (for example, in Section 4 it is described how a control component is composed of finer-grained components). These composites are represented by *configuration scripts*. Simple scripts can dictate the interconnection of two components whilst more sophisticated scripts can describe the construction of a fully functioning node. Importantly, each script is required to offer meta-information that describes its characteristics in the same way that components are.

When an application is initiated it must provide the middleware with two sets of information. This first set is its *functional requirements*; these are all the application's overlay interface requirements (e.g. IDHT, ISearch etc). At runtime, this information is passed to the middleware's context engine. This is a decision engine that selects the optimal configuration for a particular set of requirements. It iterates through all available components and scripts to locate ones that offer the desired interfaces.

Once a set of compatible configurations have been selected, the context engine inspects the next set of requirements provided by the application: the *behavioural requirements*. These are rules that define the preferred meta-values of the overlay's constituent components. For instance, a behavioural requirement could be that a forwarding algorithm must be able to route in $\log(N)$ time. This would indicate that the IRouting component attached to the interface must achieve $\log(N)$ efficiency. This would be represented through the rule:

[Time_complexity=='log(N)']

Due to the distributed nature of peer-to-peer systems it is often necessary to provide coordinated reconfiguration between multiple peers. To support this, the middleware utilises a *just-in-time* approach that exploits reflection to allow nodes to dynamically adapt as and when other peers require them to. One reflective attribute provided by components and configuration scripts is the protocol messages that they can process. If a message is received at the transport layer of the framework that the current configuration cannot handle then it is reconfigured to process the message. This is done by constructing a new behavioural requirement that includes the ability to handle the unknown protocol message identifier e.g.

[Protocol_support=='LB_Routing:LoadUpdate']

This rule is then passed to the context engine which reconfigures the node based on the new requirements. This results in communities of dynamically adapting peers cooperating within the same configuration. By utilising the middleware's fine-grain component pattern (described in Section 4) this can be performed in a low-overhead fashion through the adaptation of small aspects of functionality.

### 3.3 Adaptation Policies

The ability to define behavioural requirements allows convenient specialisation of node behaviour. However, it is also beneficial to define explicit situations in which a particular adaptation should take place. The reflective nature of the design means that adaption policies can be externally defined rather than within the overlay code. Developers (or third parties) therefore provide adaptation rule-sets which dictate that a particular configuration should be executed if a node enters a certain state. To do this during runtime, the context engine correlates environmental measurements from various context sources e.g. bandwidth monitors, processor monitors, user behaviour profilers. This information is then compared against the adaptation rules; if a rule is triggered it can then dictate a certain configuration script is executed. This will be explored in more detail in Section 5.

# 4  Overlay Component Pattern

The previous section has introduced the middleware and its general mechanisms. However, as well as this, suitable software patterns are also required to optimally build overlays. This section present a generic, reusable component pattern in which overlays can be effectively developed for the purposes of adaptation. Fig. 2 provides an overview using Pastry [21] as an example. It is also important to state that the framework can operate with any component pattern. Details of alternate patterns can be found in our past work [12][[23][24].

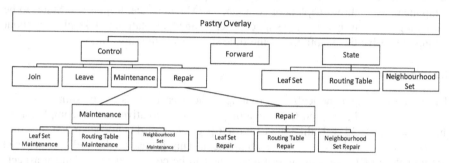

**Fig. 2.** A Pastry Implementation in the Framework's Default Component Pattern

## 4.1  Control

The Control aspects of the pattern deal with managing the overlay. There are four composite components in this branch of the tree: Join, Leave, Maintenance and Repair. These are generic concepts present in all overlays; alongside DHTs these Control aspects have been implemented in a number of other overlays including unstructured search [6], gossip communications [11] and overlay multicast [17].

The *Join* component deals with the joining procedure for a node. In terms of Pastry this refers to locating its position in the topology, collecting the necessary leaf set and routing table members then informing all interested nodes of its arrival. It is important to modularise this concern as the joining procedure largely dictates the structure of the network. Therefore by allowing independent access to the joining process, a developer can conveniently modify the topology of the overlay. For example, the ring topology of the Pastry network can be easily configured to also create links between logically distant peers in order to improve reliability, load balancing or routing.

The *Leave* component handles the removal of a node from the network. This is an effective modularisation as it allows peers in different environments, with different higher level applications to easily perform separate leaving procedures e.g. silent, elegant and daemon leaves.

The *Maintenance* component manages the monitoring of the overlay for changes. This can be for optimisation or alternatively just to ensure the overlay's integrity. There must be an individual maintenance component for each State component in the system. This maintenance component therefore monitors the necessary factors that are essential for its particular state's integrity. A wide range of possible reconfigurations can occur involving the maintenance procedures. For example, one node might use low overhead keep-alive messages whilst another would employ secure and resilient procedures involving frequent state broadcasts, certificate exchange and encryption.

The *Repair* component deals with repairing (or optimising) any problems located by related Maintenance components. Therefore, if the Leaf Set Maintenance component discovers the loss of a leaf set member then the Leaf Set Repair component is required to correct the issue. Similarly, if the Routing Table Maintenance component locates a superior routing entry then the Routing Table Repair component is responsible for implementing the state changes. In a similar vein to the Maintenance component, it is necessary for individual Repair components to be developed for each State component. This allows triplets of components (Maintenance, Repair and State) to be reused together. Further, it allows much finer-grained adaptation to take place without having to involve the adaptation of multiple state sets at the same time.

## 4.2 Forward

The Forward component deals with routing in the overlay. This can be simplistic as in the case of Gnutella [6] and CoolStreaming [25] or alternatively quite complex as in the case of Pastry [21]. Unlike the Control aspects, Forward is not separated into sub-components but is left as a single component. This is due to the well-defined and simple nature of forwarding algorithms. This can be contrasted with Control aspects which contain a wide range of diverse functionality. The Forward component is a very important modularization; this is because its reconfiguration allows rich variations in behaviour. For example, our Gnutella implementation can conveniently adapt to utilise gossip-based, random walk or semantic searching.

## 4.3 State

The State components embody the data structures required by each node in the overlay. Each data structure is embodied in its own component to improve the reusability and portability of such entities. It thus becomes possible to permanently associate the State components with their respective Control components. This therefore allows reconfiguration to occur without the need to move state data between new and old components.

## 5 Evaluative Case Studies

The framework has been implemented in Java using the OpenCOM (v1.4) component model [8]. It is part of a larger architecture called Juno [24]; this is a configurable middleware designed to address the heterogeneity of next-generation content distribution. It does this by underpinning services and delivery mechanisms with the overlay framework. A number of overlays have been implemented using this component-based approach. These include Chord [22], SCAMP [11], BitTorrent [2], TBCP [17] and Pastry [21]. Using these implementations a number of case-studies are described to highlight the capabilities and limitations of the framework. An overhead study is also provided for completeness. This evaluation, however, does not provide a quantitative study of individual overlay implementations. This is because such a study would evaluate the performance of an individual overlay or algorithm. Instead, we show how a number of systems can perform adaptation through the reflective, architectural reconfiguration of the framework. Performance details of the individual adaptation algorithm are provided in the references.

## 5.1 Case-Study Experiments

### 5.1.1 Experiment A: Local and Community Adaptation

This experiment investigates the community based adaptation of peers; first in a local sense then in a distributed one. Specifically, it looks at adapting a Pastry node to distribute load balancing information amongst routing neighbours. This adaptive mechanism (outlined in [1]) has been designed to alleviate the load on certain areas of the network. It further enables peers with low resources to contribute less, therefore improving routing performance. When a node reaches a certain load it begins to attach load tags to any sent messages. These are then read by downstream routing neighbours that, in turn, show preference to less-loaded routing choices. Further, the maintenance algorithms adapt to propagate live load information about the node. This allows nearby routing peers to maintain an accurate, real-time view of the vicinity's routing loads. This rich adaptation cannot be natively supported by a conventional Pastry implementation without redevelopment.

The framework implements adaptation through externalised adaptation rule-sets. The following rule is added to the rule-set to define the load balancing adaptation:

**if** [load > max_load] **do** config *load_balance*
      **else do** config *standard_pastry*

This indicates that a node should execute the load_balance script if its current load exceeds the maximum load. Similarly, if this load decreases it should initiate the standard_pastry script. To do this, the rule-set configuration file is therefore required to define the max_load threshold alongside the calculation of the load variable.

Due to the nature of the adaptation it is identifiable that two aspects are involved: *maintenance* and *forwarding*. The load_balancing script therefore dictates the replacement of the existing maintenance and forwarding components with their load balancing equivalents. By separating these aspects as independent pluggable components it is therefore possible to dynamically alter their behaviour by replacing them in the architecture. This simplifies the adaptation process by building well-defined algorithms embodied in components that are open to third-party coordination through reflection, configuration and later development.

During the reconfiguration process the peer is placed in a quiescent state. The framework achieves this by completing all component interactions before buffering all future interactions. Similarly, remote interactions are queued. Once the reconfiguration is complete, the peer is reactivated. At this point, the software architecture has the new LB_Maintenance and LB_Forward components attached. Due to abstracted component interaction, it is possible to continue the node's operation without changes to other existing components in the architecture.

Once the new components begin execution it is necessary to utilise protocol messages that are not natively understood by other load balancing unaware peers. To overcome this, the framework exploits *just-in-time* distributed adaptation. When an unknown protocol message is received by the remote host, the node's context engine inspects the protocol handling capabilities of all its available components and configuration scripts to locate configurations capable of understanding the message. In this scenario this obviously results in the execution of the *load_balance* script which dictates the installation of the LB_Forward and LB_Maintenance components. Once the two components have been installed, the Transport layer resumes execution from the initial receipt of the load balancing message. This results in the message being passed to the LB_Forward component and being correctly processed.

This lightweight process (c.f. Section 5.2) is carried out for every neighbour that receives the load balancing information. This allows the peers to perform coordinated adaptation in small communities; further, by dynamically acquiring new components it becomes possible to extend adaptation mechanisms at run-time.

This experiment highlights the framework's ability to dynamically install rich new adaptive functionality on a node. Particularly, this shows how the (re)configurable approach can extend the adaptive model beyond that of 'fine-tuning' by allowing entire bodies of functionality to be dynamically modified behind abstracted interfaces. Importantly this process has shown to be possible in a distributed sense. Conventional adaptive approaches are limited to well-defined strategies that are ubiquitous to all member nodes at design-time. The experiment shows, however, that it is possible to deploy adaptive strategies dynamically between subsets of peers at run-time.

### 5.1.2 Experiment B: System-Wide Adaptation

The previous experiment has shown how individual nodes can adapt in communities to improve performance. This experiment shows how system-wide adaptation strategies can further improve performance. This indicates that all peers operate the same adaptation to create system-wide behaviour. Specifically, in this experiment the Pastry overlay is separated into two groups of peers based on their capabilities. Reliable peers perform the traditional role of Pastry peers and form the *routing set,* whilst unreliable peers that do not contribute to the routing procedure form the *client set.* This separation significantly improves resilience and performance by removing transient peers from the system [4].

A new peer joining the system is initially configured as a client node by executing the pastry_client script. Once a burn-in time has been reached, the peer then adapts itself by installing the necessary routing components. A node is reconfigured to operate as a client again if its environment becomes unreliable. This is represented in the adaptation rule-set using the rules:

> **if** [online_time > burn_in && isReliable()==true]
> > **do** config *pastry_router*
> **else do** config *pastry_client*

The rule set contains the method isReliable(). This allows the rule-set to ascertain whether the peer is currently considered reliable. This script can either utilise default framework implementations or alternatively a specialised overlay implementation.

The pastry_client script contains instructions to install two components: Client_Join and Client_Forward. It is evident that the pastry_client script does not need to instantiate all the components dictated in the software pattern outlined in Section 4. This is because the simplicity of the client peers reduces the actual number of required components. Through the provision of a fine-grained architecture it therefore becomes easy to use subsets of functionality required for particular configurations. The Client_Join component simply creates a point-to-point connection with a node from the routing set whilst the Client_Forward component, in turn, forwards all messages through this proxy.

Once a peer is considered eligible for membership of the routing set, it is reconfigured by executing the pastry_router script. This involves detaching the Client_Join and Client_Forward components and attaching a full set of Pastry components. Once this reconfiguration process has completed the Join component executes the standard joining algorithm.

This case-study has shown the framework's ability to support system-wide adaptive strategies beyond the local and neighbourhood scope of the previous experiment. To facilitate this it exploits independent access to the joining and routing mechanisms. This represents an adaptive process that exceeds the capabilities of existing Pastry implementations (e.g. FreePastry [10]). This is because traditional adaptive mechanisms are restricted to adapting aspects that are isolated at design-time. The join mechanism is not utilised in conventional Pastry adaptation and is in general rarely isolated for adaptation. Therefore, by constructing nodes from open component patterns that provide access to all functionality, it becomes possible to implement adaptive strategies during run-time that exceed original design plans.

### 5.1.3  Experiment C: Application-Driven Adaptation

The previous experiments have shown how environmental factors can drive the adaptive configuration of overlay behaviour. This experiment investigates the adaptation of the middleware when operating beneath divergent applications. We define a divergent application as one that has a range of distributed interaction requirements. Specifically, this experiment looks at an application that offers stored and streamed video delivery alongside a search facility. Such a system requires at least three types of overlay, creating significant complexities for developers.

When the application is initialised over the middleware it provides a list of its required abstractions (i.e. ISearch, IStreaming and IStoredDelivery); these are termed *functional requirements*. The middleware's context engine then locates all the overlay configuration scripts that offer at least one of these interfaces. Once this has been done it is important to differentiate between overlays offering the same interface but possessing different characteristics. This is achieved through the construction of *behavioural requirements*. To investigate this, three different uses of the video application are investigated; firstly, the use of the application for distributing lectures on a campus; the second is distributing movies in an Internet-scale situation; and the third is distributing corporate videos amongst a number of offices.

This case-study obviously requires that different search mechanisms are utilised when the application is operating in different environments. When the application is bootstrapped, it defines its behavioural requirements by describing the required characteristics of any overlay operating behind the ISearch abstraction e.g.

**Abstraction**::overlays.interfaces.ISearch
      **1**: [Size > 1000]
      **2**: [Multi_Keyword==true]
      **3**: [Fuzzy==false]

This example indicates that the ISearch overlay configuration selected must be able to support a user group greater than 1000 and support multiple keyword searching whilst not requiring fuzzy matching. Any attributes can be attached to components/scripts allowing highly extensible application driven configuration to take place. This process therefore encourages the use of a domain specific ontology.

Table 1 shows the behavioural requirements of the three scenarios. The lecture scenario instantiates a Gnutella [6] overlay network due to its small size; the movie scenario instantiates a server based search mechanism as it supports large-scale fuzzy searching; lastly, the corporate scenario utilises Pastry [21] as it requires up to 50,000 users but without fuzzy search support.

**Table 1.** Behavioural Requirements of ISearch and Selected Overlay

|  | Size | Keyword | Fuzzy | Overlay |
|---|---|---|---|---|
| **Lectures** | <2000 | TRUE | TRUE | Gnutella |
| **Movies** | >100,000 | TRUE | TRUE | Server |
| **Corporate** | 100 – 50000 | TRUE | FALSE | Pastry |

This process can also be performed dynamically; for instance, if the user decides to cease watching the lecture service and switch to the movie service, the application will submit new behavioural requirements to the context engine. The context engine then locates a more appropriate search mechanism using the meta-values provided by the different overlay configuration scripts available. This process yields the *Server* script which results in the Gnutella functionality being shutdown and detached from the application and replaced with the Server search mechanism. In future, whenever the application utilises the ISearch abstraction it will therefore be actually utilising a client-server search rather than Gnutella. This is performed transparently, however, to ensure consistency the application can stop any undesired reconfigurations e.g. if certain search information is not replicated on the multiple networks.

This experiment has highlighted how architectural adaptation can support applications with non-fixed behavioural requirements. Specifically, it has been shown that an application can be conveniently deployed for use in a number of different application scenarios without intensive application coding. Instead, through abstracted reconfiguration the context engine can adapt the overlay (and therefore the application) without modifications to application code.

## 5.2 Resource Overhead

Due to the necessity to manipulate software components during the adaptation process, an added overhead is introduced. This section briefly discusses the resource overheads involved. All tests are performed on a 2.1GHz Intel Core 2 Duo processor; 4 GB RAM; Sun JVM 1.6.0.5.

### 5.2.1 Processing Overhead
We first measure the processing costs of utilising the framework; Table 2 shows the maximum processing throughput of overlays built in the framework. This has been measured by benchmarking the maximum number of component invocations possible. For comparability, the same process is carried out with Java interfaces.

It can be seen that the framework has a noticeable decrease in throughput. This creates a trade-off between flexibility and overhead with the framework sacrificing processing capacity to support runtime abstraction and reconfiguration. It should be noted, however, that the ability to utilise lightweight configurations (e.g. Experiment B) can improve the overlay processing overhead for low-capacity peers.

**Table 2.** Throughput of Component Interactions

| Type | (Invocations/Second) |
|---|---|
| Native Java | $15.863570 \times 10^6$ (16 million) |
| Framework | $3.222367 \times 10^6$ (3 million) |

### 5.2.2 Memory Overhead

To validate that the framework does not create unacceptable memory consumption, Table 3 shows the dynamic footprints of a subset of the framework's overlay implementations; these include the JVM. These implementations have been developed using a range of component patterns and offer different levels of complexity. They all, however, show acceptable memory footprints when compared to existing Java implementations (e.g. FreePastry's [10] footprint is 12,232KB).

**Table 3.** Memory Footprint of Overlays

|  | Pastry [21] | Chord [22] | SCAMP [11] | TBCP [17] |
|---|---|---|---|---|
| Footprint (KB) | 9,656 | 11,932 | 13,708 | 15,144 |

### 5.2.3 Reconfiguration Time

To show the cost of architectural reconfiguration, Table 4 shows the time taken to execute reconfiguration in the middleware. Experiments A is shown as it offers very fine-grained adaptation whilst Experiment B involves a much heavier reconfiguration. Importantly, the application logic has been removed to ensure that the measurements aren't affected by overlay specific concerns.

**Table 4.** Reconfiguration Time

|  | Bootstrap (μSecs) | Adaptation (μSecs) |
|---|---|---|
| Experiment A | 12831 | 592 |
| Experiment B | 284 | 1617 |

Experiment A has a high configuration time during bootstrapping. This is because it has to install the full overlay. This can be contrasted with its adaptation process that requires only 5% of the time. This is because the framework's fine-grain component pattern allows the adaptation to take place by replacing only two small components. In contrast, Experiment B has a low configuration time during bootstrapping. This is because it exploits the lightweight pastry_client configuration. Its adaptation process, however, it significantly more complex as it requires the installation of the routing aspects of the Pastry overlay. Importantly, the adaptation process is shown not to require extended periods of reconfiguration.

# 6 Conclusion and Future Work

This paper has investigated the potential of exploiting architectural reconfiguration for the adaptation of peer-to-peer systems. To this end, an overlay middleware has been designed that exploits the reflective component-based implementation of overlays. Through generic, reusable patterns it becomes possible to host applications over specially configured overlays dynamically selected at runtime. This enables broad functional requirements to be satisfied by the framework through the instantiation of multiple concurrent overlays behind various standardised abstractions. An important feature of this procedure is the framework's ability to consider behavioural requirements during the selection of effective overlay configurations. This allows the application to transparently operate over the most effective overlay for its (dynamically changing) requirements. To supplement this, the framework also supports the explicit scripting of adaptive algorithms for any componentised aspect of the system, allowing externalised policies to be dynamically added during runtime.

A number of interesting areas of future work exist. We consider it important to establish such an engineering approach to overlay development. Therefore further investigation into generic patterns that can match the requirements of diverse overlays is necessary. This should not be restricted to adaptive considerations but also provide support for non-functional concerns such as QoS, fault-tolerance, resilience and error management. Also, large-scale investigations must be performed to observe the effects that local and community adaptation has on the system as a whole. Alongside this, important areas also include security and runtime configuration checking.

## Acknowledgements

This work is supported by the European Network of Excellence CONTENT (FP6-IST-038423)

## References

1. Bianchi, S., Serbu, S., Felber, P., Kropf, P.: Adaptive Load Balancing for DHT Lookups. In: Proc. Intl. Conference on Computer Communications and Networks, Arlington, Virginia (2006)
2. BitTorrent Specification,
   http://www.bittorrent.org/beps/bep_0003.html
3. Blair, G.S., Coulson, G., Andersen, A., Blair, L., Clarke, M., Costa, F., Duran-Limon, H., Fitzpatrick, T., Johnston, L., Moreira, R., Parlavantzas, N., Saikoski, K.: The Design and Implementation of Open ORB V2. In: IEEE Distributed Systems Online (2001)
4. Brampton, A., MacQuire, A., Rai, I.A., Race, N.J., Mathy, L.: Stealth Distributed Hash Table: A Robust and Flexible Super-Peered DHT. In: Proc. ACM CoNext, Lisbon, Portugal (2006)
5. Bruneton, E., Coupaye, T., Leclerc, M., Quema, V., Stefani, J.-B.: An Open Component Model and its Support in Java. In: Proc. Intl. Symposium on Component-Based Software Engineering Edinburgh, Scotland (2004)

6. Chawathe, Y., Ratnasamy, S., Breslau, L., Lanham, N., Shenker, S.: Making Gnutella-like P2P Systems Scalable. In: Proc. SIGCOMM, Germany (2003)

7. Coulson, G.: A Configurable Multimedia Middleware Platform. IEEE Multimedia Magazine 6(1), 62–76 (1999)

8. Coulson, G., Blair, G., Grace, P., Joolia, A., Lee, K., Ueyama, J., Sivaharan, T.: A Generic Component Model for Building Systems Software. ACM Transactions on Computer Systems 27(1), 1–42 (2008)

9. Dabek, F., Zhao, B., Druschel, P., Stoica, I.: Towards a common API for structured peer-to-peer overlays. In: Proc. IPTPS, Berkeley, CA (2003)

10. FreePastry, http://freepastry.org/

11. Ganesh, A., Kermarrec, A., Massoulie, L.: SCAMP: Peer-to-peer lightweight membership service for large-scale group communication. In: Crowcroft, J., Hofmann, M. (eds.) NGC 2001. LNCS, vol. 2233, p. 44. Springer, Heidelberg (2001)

12. Grace, P., Coulson, G., Blair, G., Mathy, L., Yeung, W., Cai, W., Duce, D., Cooper, C.: GridKit: Pluggable Overlay Networks for Grid Computing. In: Proc. Intl. Symposium on Distributed Objects and Applications, Larnaca, Cyprus (2004)

13. Gu, X., Nahrstedt, K., Yu, B.: SpiderNet: An Integrated Peer-to-Peer Service Composition Framework. In: Proc. 13th IEEE International Symposium on High Performance Distributed Computing, Honolulu, HA (2004)

14. Hughes, D.: AdaPtP - a Framework for Building Adaptable Peer-to-Peer Systems. PhD Thesis, Lancaster University (2007)

15. Hughes, D., Coulson, G., Warren, I.: A Framework for Developing Reflective and Dynamic Peer-to-Peer Networks (RaDP2P). In: Proc. 4th IEEE International Conference on Peer-to-Peer Computing, Zurich, Switzerland (2004)

16. Kon, F., Costa, F., Blair, G., Campbell, R.H.: The Case for Reflective Middleware. Commun. ACM 45(6), 33–38 (2002)

17. Mathy, L., Canonico, R., Hutchinson, D.: An Overlay Tree Building Control Protocol. In: Proc. Intl. Workshop on Group Communications, London, UK (2001)

18. Maymounkov, P., Mazières, D.: A Peer-to-Peer Information System Based on the XOR Metric. In: Druschel, P., Kaashoek, M.F., Rowstron, A. (eds.) IPTPS 2002. LNCS, vol. 2429, p. 53. Springer, Heidelberg (2002)

19. Oreizy, P., Medvidovic, N., Taylor, R.N.: Architecture-based runtime software evolution. In: Proc. Intl. Conference on Software Engineering Kyoto, Japan (1998)

20. Portmann, M., Ardon, S., Senac, P.: Seneviratne, PROST: A Programmable Structured Peer-to-Peer Overlay Network. In: Proc. Intl. Conference on Peer-To-Peer Computing, Zurich, Switzerland (2004)

21. Rowstron, A., Druschel, P.: Pastry: Scalable, Distributed Object Location and Routing for Large-scale Peer-to-Peer Systems. In: Guerraoui, R. (ed.) Middleware 2001. LNCS, vol. 2218, p. 329. Springer, Heidelberg (2001)

22. Stoica, I., Morris, R., Karger, R.D., Kaashoek, M., Balakarishnan, H.: Chord: A Scalable Peer-to-Peer Lookup Service for Internet Applications. In: Proc. of ACM SIGCOMM, San Diego (2001)

23. Tyson, G.: Component Based Overlay Development in Gridkit. M.Sc Thesis, Lancaster University, http://www.comp.lancs.ac.uk/~tysong/

24. Tyson, G., Mauthe, A., Plagemann, T., El-khatib, Y.: Juno: Reconfigurable Middleware for Heterogeneous Content Networking. In: Proc. 5th Intl. Workshop on Next Generation Networking Middleware (NGNM), Samos Islands, Greece (2008)

25. Zhang, X., Liu, J., Li, B., Yum, T.S.P.: CoolStreaming: A Data-driven Overlay Network for Live Media Streaming. In: Proc. IEEE Infocom, Miami, FL (2005)

# WiSeKit: A Distributed Middleware to Support Application-Level Adaptation in Sensor Networks

Amirhosein Taherkordi[1], Quan Le-Trung[1], Romain Rouvoy[1,2], and Frank Eliassen[1]

[1] University of Oslo, Department of Informatics
P.O. Box 1080 Blindern, N-0314 Oslo
{amirhost,quanle,rouvoy,frank}@ifi.uio.no
[2] ADAM Project-Team, INRIA-USTL-CNRS,
Parc Scientifique de la Haute Borne,
40 avenue Halley, Bt. A, Park Plaza,
F-59650 Villeneuve d'Ascq
romain.rouvoy@lifl.fr

**Abstract.** Applications for *Wireless Sensor Networks* (WSNs) are being spread to areas in which the contextual parameters modeling the environment are changing over the application lifespan. Whereas *software adaptation* has been identified as an effective approach for addressing context-aware applications, the existing work on WSNs fails to support context-awareness and mostly focuses on developing techniques to reprogram the whole sensor node rather than reconfiguring a particular portion of the sensor application software. Therefore, enabling adaptivity in the higher layers of a WSN architecture such as the middleware and application layers, beside the consideration in the lower layers, becomes of high importance. In this paper, we propose a distributed component-based middleware approach, named WiSeKit, to enable adaptation and reconfiguration of WSN applications. In particular, this proposal aims at providing an abstraction to facilitate development of adaptive WSN applications. As resource availability is the main concern of WSNs, the preliminary evaluation shows that our middleware approach promises a lightweight, fine-grained and communication-efficient model of application adaptation with a very limited memory and energy overhead.

**Keywords:** wireless sensor networks, distributed middleware, adaptation, reconfiguration.

## 1 Introduction

The challenges for application development on WSNs are becoming as prominent as the issues concerning sensor hardware, network architecture, and system software. It is because the new emerging applications for WSNs do not limit themselves to a single function called *"sense and send"* with trivial local data

T. Senivongse and R. Oliveira (Eds.): DAIS 2009, LNCS 5523, pp. 44–58, 2009.

processing tasks [1,2]. Applications for WSNs are gradually moving towards *pervasive computing environments*, where sensor nodes have tight interactions with actuators, deal with the dynamic requirements and unpredictable future events, and behave based on the context information surrounding them [3].

In such an environment, in addition to the basic tasks, an application needs to adapt its behavior to cope with changing environmental conditions, and different capabilities of each individual sensor node in the network. As different nodes are expected to run different tasks, software with dynamic adaptable functionalities becomes an essential need. Moreover, for applications deployed to a high number of nodes in inaccessible places, individual software updating becomes an impractical and inefficient solution.

As the common types of sensor nodes are still suffering from resource scarceness, researchers have not been willing to consider the application code on sensor node as adaptive software. This is because, on one hand, the typical adaptation frameworks mostly come with a high level of complexity in the reasoning process and reconfiguration mechanism. On the other hand, most of the software development paradigms for WSN application are not able to support reconfigurability due to the lack of modularity, such as in the case of script programming. Moreover, the lack of operating system level support for dynamic reconfiguration is the other critical challenge in the way of achieving application-level adaptivity in WSNs. Recently, operating systems, such as Contiki [4], have considered this issue by supporting dynamic binding and loading of software components.

A few works have been reported in the literature that address adaptation for embedded and sensor systems. In [6,7,8], the main contribution is to provide adaptivity at the middleware-level (not application-level) in order to make the network-level services reconfigurable and replaceable. In [9], a small runtime support is proposed over Contiki to facilitate dynamic reconfiguration of software components. Although it promises to achieve application-level reconfigurability, the level of abstraction is low and it does not propose a general framework supporting all essential aspects of application adaptation. In fact, it plays the role of component reconfiguration service in a typical adaptation framework.

The performance of the adaptation middleware depends on two major factors. The first is the *reconfigurability degree* of software modules. In a highly reconfigurable model, the update is limited to the part of the code that really needs to be updated instead of updating the whole software image. We term this feature *fine-grained reconfiguration*. The second is the mechanism by which a module is reconfigured. In this paper, we concentrate on the latter, whereas the former has been discussed in [5] by proposing a new component model, called *ReWiSe*, for lightweight software reconfiguration in WSNs.

In this paper, we present a novel distributed middleware approach, named WiSeKit, for addressing the dynamicity of WSN applications. WiSeKit provides an abstract layer accelerating development of adaptive WSN applications. Using this middleware, the developer focuses only on application-level requirements for adaptivity, while the underlying middleware services expose off-the-shelf APIs to formalize the process of adaptive WSN application development and hide the complexity of the technical aspects of adaptation. The adaptation decision logic of WiSeKit is also inspired from the hierarchical architecture of typical WSNs in order to achieve the adaptation goals in a light-weight and efficient manner.

The rest of this paper is organized as follows. In Section 2, we demonstrate a motivating application scenario. The basic design concepts of our middleware proposal are described in Section 3. In Section 4, the WiSeKit middleware is proposed with a preliminary evaluation presented in Section 5. Related work is presented in Section 6. Finally, Section 7 concludes the paper and gives an outlook on future research.

## 2    Motivating Application Scenario

In this section we present an application scenario in the area of *home monitoring* to further motivate our work. Most of the earlier efforts in this field employed a high-cost wired platform for making the home a smart environment [10,11]. Future home monitoring applications are characterized as being filled with different sensor types to observe various types of ambient context elements such as temperature, smoke, and occupancy. Such information can be used to reason about the situation and interestingly react to the context through actuators [3].

Figure 1 illustrates a hypothetical *context-aware home*. Each room is equipped with the relevant sensor nodes according to its attributes and uses. For instance, in the living room three "occupancy" sensors are used to detect the movement, one sensor senses the temperature, and one smoking sensor for detecting the fire in the room. Although each sensor is configured according to the preliminary requirements specified by the end-user, there may happen some predictable or unpredictable scenarios needing behavioral changes in sensor nodes. Basically, these scenarios can be considered from two different aspects: *i)* application-level, and *ii)* sensor-level. The former refers to the contextual changes related to the application itself, *e.g.*, according the end-user requirements for the living room, if one of the occupancy nodes detects a movement in the room, the temperature nodes should stop sensing and sending tasks. The latter further concerns with the capabilities and limitations of a particular sensor node, *e.g.*, if the residual energy of temperature sensor is lower than a pre-defined threshold, the aggregated data should be delivered instead of sending all individual sensor readings.

Besides the above concerns, the recent requests for *remote home monitoring*, which enables the owner to check periodically home state via a web interface, are being extended by the request of *remote home controlling*. This need also brings some other new challenges in terms of dynamicity and makes the issue of adaptivity more significant.

Considering statically all above concerns becomes quite impossible when you have many of these scenarios that should be supported simultaneously by the application on a resource-limited node. Moreover, at the same time you need to maintain the relation between the context elements and reason timely on a change. Obviously, supporting all these requirements during application run-time needs an abstract middleware approach to address the dynamicity and adaptivity challenges w.r.t. the unique characteristics of WSNs.

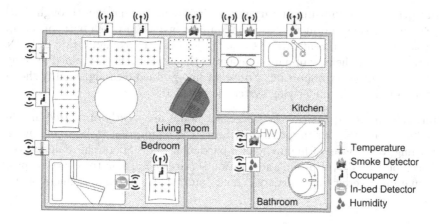

**Fig. 1.** Description of the home monitoring system

# 3   Basic Design Concepts

In this section, we describe the basic design concepts of WiSeKit middleware.

**Adaptation Time.** Basically, adaptation can be performed in two manners: *statically* and *dynamically*. Static adaptation relates to the redesign and reconfiguration of application architectures and components before deployment of the application. Dynamic adaptation is performed at application run-time due to the changing needs, resource and context conditions. We adopt dynamic adaptation in our proposal because most WSN applications are expected to work seamlessly for a long time and mostly deployed in inaccessible places.

**Adaptation Scope.** Two popular adaptation mechanisms are introduced in the literature [12], [13]: *parameter adaptation* and *component adaptation*. Parameter adaptation supports fine tuning of applications through the modification of application variables and deployment parameters, while component adaptation allows the modification of service implementation (replacement of component), adding new components, and removing running components. We explain later in this paper why and how our middleware supports both of these mechanisms.

**Adaptation Policy.** In general, there are three different approaches for identifying a policy: situation-action rules [13,14], goal-oriented [15] and utility-based [16]. The two latter techniques represent high level forms of policies, while the former specifies exactly what to do in given situations. As the adaptation policies of most WSN applications can be described easily through a set of conditional statements, WiSeKit follows the situation-action rules approach. Situations in our proposal are provided from the framework we proposed in [17]. This framework proposes a *context processing model* to collect data from different sources (environment, application, sensor resources, and user) and process them for the use of adaptation reasoning service.

**Fine-grained Reconfiguration.** Adaptation reasoning specifies through which mechanism (either parameter-based or component-based) which parts of the application should be reconfigured. As the major cost of reconfiguration in WSNs is in transferring the new update code across the network, fined-grained reconfiguration becomes very important. Note that fine-grained reconfigurability should be supported by the underlying system software.

**Hierarchical Adaptation.** As the sensor nodes are mostly organized in a hierarchical way [18], our proposal distributes the adaptation tasks among nodes according to the level of hierarchy of a particular node. Hierarchical adaptation is based on the idea of placing adaptation services according to: *i)* the scope of information covered by a particular node, and *ii)* the resource richness of that node.

## 4   WiSeKit Adaptation Middleware

WiSeKit aims to provide a set of APIs at the middleware level of WSNs in order to make an abstraction layer that formalizes and simplifies the development of adaptive WSN applications. In general, WiSeKit is characterized by the following features:

- *Local-adaptivity*: an application running on the sensor nodes has the possibility of identifying its adaptation policies. The APIs exposed at the middleware layer are able to read the policy object and maintain the application components' configuration according to the context information gathered periodically from both sensor node and application.
- *Intermediate-observation*: using WiSeKit, we can specify adaptation requirements for a region of the network, *e.g.*, a floor or a room in a building. At this level, we can specify high-level adaptation policies through WiSeKit APIs provided at more powerful nodes such as cluster head or sink node.
- *Remote-observation*: the end-user or the agent checking the application status locally through sink interface or remotely via a web interface might need to specify his/her own requirements regarding adaptation.
- *Component-based reconfiguration*: updates in WiSeKit can take place both at component attribute level and at component level. WiSeKit expects application developers implement predefined interfaces for components which are subject to reconfiguration. We present later in this section the signature of such interfaces and the mechanisms for reconfiguration.
- *Distribution*: The heterogeneity of WSNs in terms of the node's resource capabilities and functionalities necessitates support for distribution at the middleware layer in order to achieve the above goals and also optimize network resources usage. WiSeKit is within all nodes types built up over a set of *Core Services* which provides an infrastructure for distribution.

Figure 2 illustrates the complete logical architecture of the WiSeKit middleware distributed over the different node types. It shows how the adaptation services are located in different node types and mapped to a typical WSN architecture. At the left side of the figure, sensor node features a set of services for realizing *Local-adaptivity* and *Component-based reconfiguration*. Next to the sensor nodes, the cluster head has the responsibility of *Intermediate-observation* to observe data and analyze it in terms of adaptation required within the scope of a cluster. Finally, at the right side of Figure 2, WiSeKit in the sink node is able to retain the "whole" WSN application in a high degree of adaptivity via *Intermediate-observation* and *Remote-observation*. Therefore, the end user of the application can specify his/her own adaptation needs through the APIs provided within the sink node. Middleware services in different nodes interact through core services customized for each type of node. The details of WiSeKit services within each type of node are explained in the rest of this section.

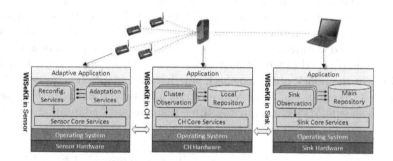

**Fig. 2.** WiSeKit in the hierarchical WSN architecture

## 4.1 Sensor Side

To address the middleware requirements of adaptive applications, we need first to explore the desired structure of an application deployed over the sensor nodes, then the adaptation middleware services will be discovered accordingly. Figure 3 illustrates a sample configuration of application components for a home monitoring application. There are three main aspects that should be considered for application development.

Firstly, the components which are subject to reconfiguration should implement the relevant interfaces. In general, four types of reconfigurations are likely to happen during the application runtime, including: *i)* replacing a component with a new one, *ii)* adding a new component, *iii)* component removal, and *iv)* changing the values of component member variables. For each type of reconfiguration the relevant interface(s) should be implemented. We explain later in this section the name and specification of those interfaces.

Secondly, as shown in the figure, the deployable package should include a predefined *policy file* describing situation-actions rules. It is one of the main sources of *local* adaptation decision. The local decision is limited to changing the values of component member variables, while the decision of full component image replacement is made by the cluster head. It is because the decisions for replacing or

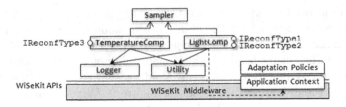

**Fig. 3.** A sample component configuration for an adaptive home application

adding components fall in the category of heavyweight reconfiguration requests. Such a decision should be assigned to a node being aware of what happens in the scope of a cluster. Moreover, sometimes we need to send a component image to a set of sensor nodes having similar attributes or responsibilities.

Finally, *Application Context* is a meta-data reporting application-related contextual information. Application components can update it when a contextual event is detected through APIs provided by WiSeKit. The content of application context is used together with sensor context information against the situations described in the policy object to check whether any adaption is needed.

Figure 4 describes the architecture of our adaptation middleware for sensor nodes. As shown, WiSeKit addresses three main areas of adaptation concern.

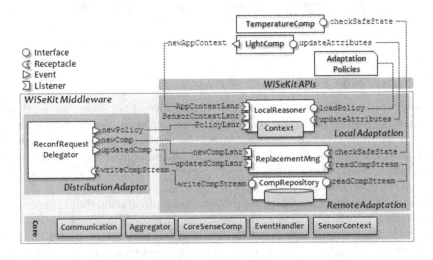

**Fig. 4.** WiSeKit services in the sensor node

*Local Adaptation* is in charge of carrying out local parameter adaptation requests. LocalReasoner, as the main service receives both the adaptation policies of the application and context information, then it checks periodically the situations within policy file against application context and sensor context for adaptation reasoning. Upon satisfying a situation, the corresponding action, changing the values(s) of component attribute(s), is performed via calling the updateAttributes interface of the component and passing the new values.

*Remote Adaptation* is concerned with adapting the whole component. In fact, the corresponding cluster node performs the reasoning task and notifies the sensor node the result containing which component should be wholly reconfigured. The key service in this part is ReplacementMng. Upon receiving either newComp or updatedComp event, it reads the component image from CompRepository, loads the new component and finally removes the image stored by CompRepository from the repository.

After loading the component image, the current component is periodically checked to identify whether it is in a *safe state of reconfiguration* or not. The safe state is defined as a situation in which all instances of a component are temporarily idle or not processing any request. There are several safe state checking mechanisms in the literature [19], [20]. In some solutions, safe state recognition is the responsibility of the underlying reconfiguration service, whereas in the other mechanisms this checking is assigned to the component itself. We adopt the second method because of its low overhead. Therefore, WiSeKit expects from each reconfigurable component to implement the checkSafeState interface.

*Distribution Adaptor* provides a distribution platform for adaptation decision and accomplishment. Specifically, it is proposed to address three issues: *i)* the possibility of updating adaptation policies during application lifespan, *ii)* receiving the result of high-level adaptation decision from cluster head, *i.e.*, the image of a component, and *iii)* providing an abstraction for distributed interactions between WiSeKit services. ReconfRequestDelegator reads the data received through the Communication service, checks whether it encompasses any event such as new policy, new component, or updated component, and finally unmarshals the content and generates the corresponding event object.

The bottom part of middleware is decorated with the *core* to provide an infrastructure for distribution as well as the utility and common services. The Communication service has the responsibility of establishing connection to the other nodes in the hierarchical structure. This service not only sends the data, but also receives the reconfiguration information (component image or policy). Aggregator is a service for performing aggregation of data received from CoreSenseComp. EventHandler handles events generated by the services within the middleware. The context information related to the sensor hardware and system software is reported by SensorContext service as an newSensorContext event.

## 4.2   Cluster Head Side

Based on *hierarchical adaptation*, when the context information of a sensor node is not sufficient to make an adaptation decision, the cluster head attempts to decide on an adaptation based on the data received from sensor nodes in its own cluster. Similarly, if the current information in the cluster head is not enough for the adaptation reasoning, the final decision is left to the sink node, *e.g.*, in our motivation scenario, if the occupancy sensors detect a movement in the living room, the cluster head notifies the temperature sensors to reduce the sampling rate. Figure 5 illustrates both the structure of WSN application and the WiSeKit architecture over the cluster head. The WiSeKit services within the cluster head make the high-level adaptation decisions through processing *application context model* and *cluster-level adaptation policies.*

The context model defines the possible contextual situations by describing the relations between the application data gathered by sensor nodes [17]. For example, "room occupied" is a situation that can be deduced from checking the data values of both occupancy sensors and light sensors in a room. The cluster-level adaptation policies are described in the same way as for sensor nodes (situation-action). However, in this case, the situations are those defined in the context model. The action also include loading a new policy or a new component in some selected nodes.

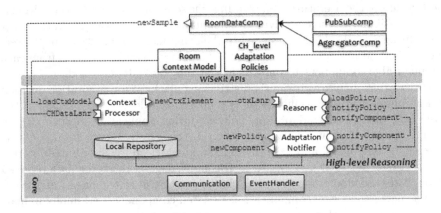

**Fig. 5.** WiSeKit in the cluster head

As depicted in Figure 5, WiSeKit aims at addressing the high-level reasoning issues within the cluster head. To this end, the middleware services expect from the application to provide: *i)* the context model, and *ii)* the adaptation policies. In this way, WiSeKit processes at first the context model along with the data received from sensor nodes in order to find out the current context situation(s) of environment, then the Reasoner service checks whether any adaption is needed. In fact, this service analyzes the adaptation policies based on the current context information, thereby it decides on update notifications, *i.e.*, either new policy or new component. If Reasoner makes the decision of a component update, AdptationNotifier loads the binary object of new component from the *Local Repository* and multicasts it along with the required meta-information to the nodes in its vicinity. AdaptationNotifier is also responsible for forwarding the adaptation requests of the sink node to the cluster members. We assume that the local repository of cluster head contains all versions of a component that might be needed during the application lifespan.

## 4.3   Sink Side

WiSeKit in the sink node is designed in the same way as it is proposed for the cluster head. The main differences between the sink node and the cluster head in the context of our middleware are in two aspects. Firstly, the scope of network covered by the sink node is the whole sensor network, while the cluster head has only access to the information retrieved within a cluster. Therefore, the global adaptation, the highest level of adaptation decision, takes place only in the sink node, where it has access to the status of all clusters. Secondly, the sink node is able to receive end-user preferences regarding to the adaptation requirements.

The component repository within the sink node contains all versions of all components. As the sink node is a powerful node with sufficient resources for processing tasks and storing application components, WiSeKit in the sink node has the ability of reasoning on the sophisticated adaptations and providing different versions of a component according to the adaptation needs.

The communication service within the core of sink provides the following functionalities: *i)* global context information exchange between the sink and the cluster heads, *ii)* code distribution, and *iii)* internetworking between WSNs and external networks, *e.g.*, the Internet. While the context information can be piggybacked into either the code distribution or routing protocols to reduce the signaling overhead, the internetworking provides more flexible facilities to manage and control WSNs remotely.

## 5   Preliminary Evaluation

As our adaptation middleware is customized for each type of node, the evaluation should take into account many performance figures. At first, we need to evaluate each type of node separately, then the effectiveness of WiSeKit should be assessed for all nodes together. As considering the evaluation for all nodes is a huge work, this paper focuses only on middleware performance in the sensor node as the critical part of our proposal, while evaluating the whole adaptation middleware is a part of our future work.

The efficiency of our approach for sensor node can be considered from the following performance figures:

- The *memory overhead* of middleware run-time, with respect to both program and data memory. The former can be evaluated by measuring the size of binary images after compilation. The latter includes the data structures used by the programs.
- The *energy usage* during adaptation, which refers to the energy overhead of running an adaptation task.
- The *communication overhead* between sensor nodes and cluster head in the presence of middleware for a typical adaptive application.

We chose the Instant Contiki simulator [22] to measure the overhead of memory. The prototype implementation shows the memory footprint for reconfiguration program and its data is no more than 3 Kbytes in total. As most of sensor nodes are equipped with more than 48 Kbytes of program flash (TelosB node), WiSeKit does not impose a high overhead in terms of memory. It should be noted that this cost is paid once and for all, regardless of the amount of memory is needed for the application components. There is also an application level memory overhead for the description of adaptation policies and implementing the reconfiguration interfaces (checkSafeState, updateAttributes, etc.). This cost depends directly on the degree of application adaptivity. Moreover, the amount of memory used by CompRepository varies with respect to the number of new components downloaded simultaneously in the sensor node. As WiSeKit removes the image of a component from repository when loading it to the memory, this overhead is kept at a very low level in the order of zero.

For measuring energy consumption, we assume that our hypothetical WSN application is similar to the configuration depicted in Figure 6 and Sampler is the replacement candidate. The main reconfiguration tasks include: *i)* checking the old Sampler to ensure that it is not in interaction with the other components before starting reconfiguration, *ii)* saving the state of old Sampler, *iii)* creating the new one and transferring the last state to it.

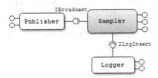

**Fig. 6.** Sample configuration

Each loadable module in Contiki is in *Compact Executable and Linkable Format* (CELF) containing code, data, and reference to other functions and variable of system. When a CELF file is loaded to a node, the dynamic linker in core resolves all external and internal references, and then writes code to ROM and the data to RAM [21]. For our sample configuration, the Sampler_CELF file (764 bytes) must be transferred to the node, and all mentioned tasks for dynamic loading must be done for the Sampler program (its code size is 348 bytes). As the energy consumption depends on the size of new update, the model of energy consumption will be [21]:

$$E = S_{New\_CELF} \times (P_p + P_s + P_l) + S_{New\_Sampler} \times P_f + E_{safeStateCheck}$$

Where $S_{New\_CELF}$ is the size of new CELF file and $P_p$, $P_s$, $P_l$ and $P_f$ are scale factors for network protocol, storing binary, linking and loading, respectively. $S_{New\_Sampler}$ is the code size of new Sampler, and $E_{safeStateCheck}$ is the energy cost of performing reconfiguration. Concretely, we obtain the following energy consumption for the considered adaptation scenario:

$$E = 764 \times (P_p + P_s + P_l) + 348 \times P_f + E_{safeStateCheck}$$

In this equation, we take into account the overhead of checking safe state (dependencies to the other two components). We believe that this value is very low compared to the first part, which is the reconfiguration cost imposed by Contiki.

To measure the communication overhead, we assume a scenario in the living room of home application in which the "occupancy" of context changes occasionally. According to the monitoring rules of home, when the room is empty the temperature sensors should report the temperature of room every 10 minutes. Once the room is occupied the temperature sensors should stop sensing until the room becomes empty again.

According to this scenario, when the room is occupied, ContextProcessor within the cluster head observes the new context and Reasoner notifies the relevant sensor nodes to stop sampling. WiSeKit does not impose any communication cost for context detection because it piggybacks the current value of a node's attributes at middleware layer of cluster head. Therefore, the communication cost is limited to sending policy objects to stop/restart sampling task.

Three parameters should be taken into account to measure the overhead of communication: $i)$ sampling rate $(r)$, $ii)$ context consistency duration $(c)$, and $iii)$ number of context changes during a particular period of time $(k)$. For the hypothesis scenario, if a room is occupied for two hours during one day, we have: $r = 10$ min, $c = 120$ min, and $k = 1$. In this case, the temperature sensors do not send the data for two hours, thus the number of communication for one day (24 hours) is:

$$
\begin{aligned}
N_{total} &= N_{forWholeDay} - N_{occupiedTime} + N_{WiSeKitOverhead} \\
&= (24 \times 60)/r - c/r + k \times N_{policySending} \\
&= 144 - 12 + 2 = 134
\end{aligned}
$$

Therefore for this case the number of saved communications is 10. Generally, we can evaluate that the saved number of communications is:

$$
\begin{cases}
N_{saved} = c/r \times k - 2 \times k \\
1 \leqslant k \leqslant 24/y
\end{cases}
$$

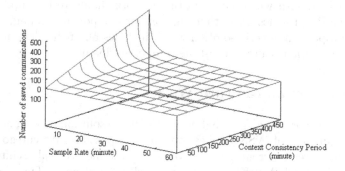

**Fig. 7.** Number of saved communications for a sample home monitoring scenario

Figure 7 shows the saved number of communication. As the consistency period of new context is increased and sampling rate is decreased, more number of communications will be saved. This is because the middleware prevents a sensor node to send data during the period of new context activation.

## 6   Related Work

The first prominent work reported to address reconfigurability for resource-constrained systems is [7]. In this paper, Costa et al. propose a middleware framework for embedded systems. Their approach focuses on a kernel providing primary services needed in a typical resource-limited node. Specifically, their work supports customizable component-based middleware services that can be tailored for particular embedded systems. In other words, this approach enables reconfigurability at the middleware level, while our proposal tries to give this ability to the application services through underlying middleware services.

Efforts for achieving adaptivity in WSNs have continued by Horr et al [6]. They proposed DAVIM, an adaptable middleware enabling dynamic service management and application isolation. Particularly, their main focus in this work is on the composition of reusable services in order to meet the requirements of simultaneously running applications. In fact, they consider the adaptivity from the view of dynamic integration of services, whereas our work tries to make the services adaptable.

A fractal composition-based approach for constructing and dynamically reconfiguring WSN applications is introduced in [23]. The approach uses $\pi$-calculus semantics to unify the models of interaction for both software and hardware components. The novel feature of that approach is its support for a uniform model of interaction between all components, namely communication via typed channels. Although the reconfiguration model in [23] is promising, it fails to explain under which conditions a reconfiguration should take place.

The most relevant work in the context of reconfiguration for WSN has been reported recently under the name of FiGaRo framework [9]. The main contribution of FiGaRo is to present an approach for *what and where* should be reconfigured. The former one is related to runtime component replacement, and latter is concern with which nodes in the network should receive update code. In fact, FiGaRo provides a run-time support for component loading, while our approach proposes a generic solution which includes all of-the-shelf adaptation services besides the feature of run-time component loading.

## 7   Conclusion and Future Work

In this paper, we proposed WiSeKit as a middleware solution making adaptation and reconfiguration of WSN application software possible. We categorized our proposal into three different layers according to the hierarchical architecture of WSN and presented WiSeKit features for each type of node. The hierarchical adaptation decision of WiSeKit conforms the hierarchical architecture of WSNs so that based on the resource availability in a node as well as the portion of the network covered by a node, adaptation and reconfiguration are performed.

This paper focused only on adaptation for the portion of application running on sensor nodes, while the part of application deployed on cluster head and sink may need to be adapted as well. This issue will be addressed in our future work. The work reported in this paper is a part of our comprehensive solution for self management in WSNs. Integrating this work with the other work reported in [5], [17] is another future direction. Developing a complete home monitoring application based on the proposed middleware is also included in the plan for future work.

**Acknowledgments.** This work was partly funded by the Research Council of Norway through the project SWISNET, grant number 176151.

# References

1. Puccinelli, D., Haenggi, M.: Wireless Sensor Networks: Applications and Challenges of Ubiquitous Sensing. IEEE Circuits and Systems 5(3) (2005)
2. Costa, P., et al.: The RUNES middleware for networked embedded systems and its application in a disaster management scenario. In: Proc. of PERCOM (2007)
3. Akyildiz, I.F., Kasimoglu, I.H.: Wireless Sensor and Actor Networks: Research challenges. Ad Hoc Networks Journal 2(4), 351–367 (2004)
4. Dunkels, A., Grnvall, B., Voigt, T.: Contiki-A Lightweight and Flexible Operating System for Tiny Networked Sensors. In: Proc. of EmNetS-I (2004)
5. Taherkordi, A., Eliassen, F., Rouvoy, R., e-Trung, Q.: ReWiSe: A New Component Model for Lightweight Software Reconfiguration in Wireless Sensor Networks. In: Meersman, R., Tari, Z., Herrero, P. (eds.) OTM 2008 Workshops. LNCS, vol. 5333, pp. 415–425. Springer, Heidelberg (2008)
6. Horré, W., Michiels, S., Joosen, W., Verbaeten, P.: DAVIM: Adaptable Middleware for Sensor Networks. IEEE Distributed Systems Online 9(1) (2008)
7. Costa, P., et al.: A Reconfigurable Component-based Middleware for Networked Embedded Systems. Journal of Wireless Information Networks 14(2) (2007)
8. Grace, P., Coulson, G., Blair, G., Porter, B., Hughes, D.: Dynamic reconfiguration in sensor middleware. In: Proc. of the 1st ACM MidSens, Australia (2006)
9. Mottola, L., Picco, G., Sheikh, A.: FiGaRo: Fine-Grained Software Reconfiguration for Wireless Sensor Networks. In: Verdone, R. (ed.) EWSN 2008. LNCS, vol. 4913, pp. 286–304. Springer, Heidelberg (2008)
10. Huebscher, M.C., McCann, J.A.: Adaptive middleware for context-aware applications in smart homes. In: Proc. of the MPAC, Canada, pp. 111–116 (2004)
11. Mozer, M.: Lessons from an Adaptive Home. In: Smart Environments: Technology, Protocols, and Applications, pp. 273–298. Wiley, Chichester (2004)
12. Poladian, V., Sousa, J.P., Garlan, D., Shaw, M.: Dynamic Configuration of Resource-Aware Services. In: ICSE, pp. 604–613. IEEE Computer Society, Los Alamitos (2004)
13. Garlan, D., et al.: Rainbow: Architecture-based self-adaptation with reusable infrastructure. Computer 37(10), 46–54 (2004)
14. Lutfiyya, H., et al.: Issues in Managing Soft QoS Requirements in Distributed Systems Using a Policy-Based Framework. In: Sloman, M., Lobo, J., Lupu, E.C. (eds.) POLICY 2001. LNCS, vol. 1995, p. 185. Springer, Heidelberg (2001)

15. Kephart, J.O., Chess, D.M.: The vision of autonomic computing. IEEE Computer 36(1), 41–52 (2003)
16. Kephart, J.O., Das, R.: Achieving Self-Management via Utility Functions. IEEE Internet Computing 11(1), 40–48 (2007)
17. Taherkordi, A., Rouvoy, R., Le-Trung, Q., Eliassen, F.: A Self-Adaptive Context Processing Framework for Wireless Sensor Networks. In: Proc. of the 3rd ACM MidSens in conjunction with Middleware 2009, Belgium, pp. 7–12 (2008)
18. Le-Trung, Q., Engelstad, P., Taherkordi, A., Pham, N.H., Skeie, T.: Information Storage, Reduction, and Dissemination in Sensor Networks: A Survey, In: Proc. of the IEEE IRSN Workshop, Las Vegas, US (2009)
19. Paula, J., et al.: Transparent dynamic reconfiguration for CORBA. In: Proc. of the 3rd International Symposium on Distributed Objects and Applications (2001)
20. Zhang, J., Cheng, B., Yang, Z., McKinley, P.: Enabling safe dynamic component-based software adaptation. In: de Lemos, R., Gacek, C., Romanovsky, A. (eds.) Architecting Dependable Systems III. LNCS, vol. 3549, pp. 194–211. Springer, Heidelberg (2005)
21. Dunkels, A., Finne, N., Eriksson, J., Voigt, T.: Run-Time Dynamic Linking for Reprogramming Wireless Sensor Networks. In: Proc. of ACM SenSys (2006)
22. http://www.sics.se/contiki/
23. Balasubramaniam, D., Dearle, A., Morrison, R.: A Composition-based Approach to the Construction and Dynamic Reconfiguration of Wireless Sensor Network Applications. In: Pautasso, C., Tanter, É. (eds.) SC 2008. LNCS, vol. 4954, pp. 206–214. Springer, Heidelberg (2008)

# Automated Assessment of Aggregate Query Imprecision in Dynamic Environments

Vasanth Rajamani[1], Christine Julien[1], and Jamie Payton[2]

[1] Department of Electrical and Computer Engineering
The University of Texas at Austin
{vasanthrajamani,c.julien}@mail.utexas.edu
[2] Department of Computer Science
University of North Carolina, Charlotte
payton@uncc.edu

**Abstract.** Queries are widely used for acquiring data distributed in opportunistically formed mobile networks. However, when queries are executed in such dynamic settings, the returned result may not be consistent, i.e., it may not accurately reflect the state of the environment. It can thus be difficult to reason about the meaning of a query's result. Reasoning about imperfections in the result becomes even more complex when in-network aggregation is employed, since only a single aggregate value is returned. We define the semantics of aggregate queries in terms of a qualitative description of consistency and a quantitative measure of imprecision. We provide a protocol that performs in-network aggregation while simultaneously generating quality assessments for the query result. The protocol enables intuitive interpretations of the semantics associated with an aggregate query's execution in a dynamic environment.

## 1 Introduction

The proliferation of laptops, sensors, and wireless devices has increased the number of data providers embedded in our environment. The ability to obtain data and expose meaningful information to applications in dynamic networks remains a major challenge. Queries are a popular abstraction for making information-rich environments more accessible by masking complex network details. An important class of queries are *aggregate* queries, which are particularly popular in dynamic networks because they enable *in-network aggregation* [1–3]—the observation that computation is significantly cheaper than communication in terms of resource consumption. Individual hosts, then, should aggregate as much raw data as possible to reduce the communication overhead of queries.

Though queries can simplify application development, the unpredictable connectivity changes in mobile ad hoc networks make it difficult to ensure that a query's result is *consistent*, i.e., the result completely and accurately reflects the state of the environment during query execution. Consider an application in the construction domain for intelligent asset management. A site supervisor needs to monitor the amount of some material present on the site (whether stationary

T. Senivongse and R. Oliveira (Eds.): DAIS 2009, LNCS 5523, pp. 59–72, 2009.
© IFIP International Federation for Information Processing 2009

or mobile, e.g., in a delivery truck) to determine when to order more. Each pallet is tagged with a device that represents the count (or weight) of the material present. The supervisor may issue a simple aggregate query that returns the sum of this material across the site. While the query is executing, pallets move around the site, which may cause a pallet's value to be counted more than once or not at all. In addition, the failure of any device results in the loss of all the values that were aggregated at that device. This results in an inconsistency between the reported total and the actual total of the material on the site. Traditionally, delivering query results with strong consistency semantics is achieved through distributed locking protocols, which are ill-suited for use in dynamic networks. Most existing solutions, therefore, rely on "best-effort" queries, which make no guarantees about the quality of the result. Consequently, the query result represents the ground truth to an arbitrary degree, making it difficult for applications to know how to use the results. Thus, a fundamental requirement for applications employing aggregate queries is the ability to interpret the imperfections associated with retrieving data from dynamic networks.

To measure query imperfection, we define semantics for a basic set of aggregate queries and demonstrate a query processing protocol that can automatically attach an intuitive indicator of the semantics achieved to the query result. We define query semantics qualitatively in terms of consistency and quantitatively in terms of numeric imprecision in the query result. Specifically, we make the following contributions. First, we define a conceptual model for estimating numerical bounds that define a query's imprecision and demonstrate how we can express the semantics of aggregate queries (Sections 2 and 3). Second, we develop a protocol that computes aggregate queries while assessing their semantics; this assessment is attached to the result to support reasoning about the returned value (Section 4). Third, we have prototyped and evaluated a reference implementation (Section 5).

## 2  Background : Modeling Query Execution

Our previous work [4] defined a query processing model to express mobility as state transitions and a set of consistency semantics for simple queries. We review this model and use it to define the semantics of aggregate queries.

In our model of a mobile network, a host is a tuple $(\iota, \nu, \lambda)$, where $\iota$ is a unique identifier, $\nu$ is a data value, and $\lambda$ is its location. The global abstract state of the network, a *configuration*, is a set of host tuples. An *effective configuration* $(E)$ is the projection of the configuration with respect to the hosts *reachable* from a specific host $\bar{h}$. Reachability is often defined in terms of network connectivity, captured by a relation that conveys the existence of a (possibly multi-hop) path between hosts. We use a binary logical connectivity relation $\mathcal{K}$ to express the existence of a direct link between two hosts. Reachability is defined as the reflexive transitive closure $\mathcal{K}^*$. An evolving network is a state transition system with a state space defined by the set of possible configurations, and transitions defined as configuration changes. Sources of configuration change include: 1) *variable* *assignment*, in which a host changes its data value, and 2) *neighbor change*, in which a host's changing location impacts the network connectivity.

Consider the configurations in Fig. 1. A query begins with its issue (the *query initiation bound*, $C_0$) and ends when the result is delivered (the *query termination bound*, $C_n$). Since there is processing delay when issuing a query to and returning results from the network, a query's *active configurations* are those within $\langle C_0, C_1, \ldots C_n \rangle$ during which the query interacted with the network. Every value contributing to a query's result must be

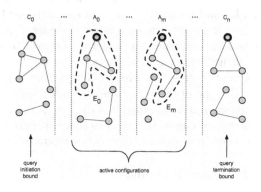

**Fig. 1.** Effective Active Configurations

present in some active configuration. Moreover, only reachable hosts can contribute to a query's result. The relevant configurations, then, are the *effective active configurations*, $\langle E_0, E_1, \ldots, E_m \rangle$, containing hosts reachable from the query issuer.

A query is a function from a sequence of effective active configurations to a set of host tuples that constitute the result. This model lends itself to a straightforward expression of a query's result as a configuration, simplifying the expression of the consistency of those results. While our original model considers the impact of environmental conditions on the achievable consistency of simple discrete queries, it does not capture how in-network aggregation impacts query results. In the next section, we explore consistency semantics for queries processed using in-network aggregation and offer an approach to present aggregate query results that intuitively convey their associated consistency semantics.

## 3   Integrating Aggregation and Consistency

We introduce a model for aggregate queries that applies an in-network aggregation operator and returns a bounded aggregate value. The bounds convey the degree to which the query result reflects the state of the environment during query execution. The bounded aggregate is the triple $[L, A, U]$: $L$ is a lower bound, $U$ is an upper bound, and $A$ is the aggregate value computed over the results available throughout query execution, i.e., $A$ is computed over $\bigcap_{i=0}^{m} E_i$.

### 3.1   Consistency Classes: Comparability

In our previous work for discrete queries, we defined a set of semantics that lie between the common atomic (i.e., exact) and weak (i.e., best effort) semantics [4]. Our consistency semantics can be divided into two classes: *comparable* and *non-comparable*. In the first, stronger class, all the elements of the computed aggregate are guaranteed to have existed at the same time, i.e., all of the aggregated results existed in the same configuration. In the weaker class, all of the aggregated values existed at some time during the query execution, but nothing can be said about the temporal relationships between the aggregated items.

In our construction example, consider a query for the truck with the fewest pallets. If material is transferred between trucks during query execution, the result may not report the truck with the fewest pallets because the query may aggregate values that are not comparable, e.g., the value of one truck before the transfer and of the newly loaded truck after the transfer. Conversely, if there was no configuration change, it is clear that the answer returned is correct. Adding this semantic information gives new clarity to the query result. In our evaluation, we revisit how consistency classes relate to the semantics of aggregation.

## 3.2   Numeric Bounds

We relax our definition of a query result ($\rho$) to allow for computation of imprecision bounds. A query result has two components: $\langle \mathcal{A}, Excess \rangle$, where $\mathcal{A}$ is the aggregate result, and $Excess$ is a set containing tuples of the form: $\langle a/d, h \rangle$, where the first component is either $a$ or $d$, indicating that the tuple represents an addition or a departure, and the second component $h$ is a host tuple. In the aggregation examples below, we do not use the $a$ and $d$ designations explicitly. However, these labels are necessary for computing the comparability class of a query result (discussed in Section 5). Each element in $Excess$ was present in at least one of the query's effective active configurations but missing from another:

$$e \in Excess \Rightarrow \langle \exists i,j : 0 \leq i,j \leq m \wedge i \neq j :: e.h \in E_i \wedge e.h \notin E_j \rangle^1$$

If a host's value or location changed multiple times during execution, there may be multiple tuples in $Excess$ for the same host. This must be handled with care for *duplicate-sensitive* aggregation operators [2] like sum and average.

## 3.3   Determining the Semantics of Aggregate Queries

A query result comprises a conservative estimate of the aggregate ($\mathcal{A}$) and a measure of its imprecision. Each aggregation type includes a different method for using the $Excess$ set to calculate bounds; we look at several types of aggregation and show how bounds are calculated to define the triple $[L, A, U]$.

**Set Union Aggregation.** Set union aggregation can be expressed as an aggregation operation where $\mathcal{A}$ contains the stable subset of query results, i.e., results from hosts that experienced no changes during the query's execution:

$$\mathcal{A} = \langle set \ h : \langle \forall i : 0 \leq i \leq m :: h \in E_i \rangle :: h \rangle$$

*Excess* contains values either added or removed (or both) during execution:

---

[1] In the three-part notation: $\langle op \ quantified\_variables \ : \ range \ :: \ expression \rangle$, the variables from *quantified_variables* take on all possible values permitted by *range*. Each instantiation of the variables is substituted in *expression*, producing a multiset of values to which op is applied, yielding the value of the three-part expression.

$$S_{\text{excess}} = \langle \text{set } e : e \in \textit{Excess} :: e.h \rangle$$

A set union query returns $[-, \mathcal{A}, \mathcal{A} \cup S_{excess}]$, where $-$ indicates an absent lower bound. When no changes occurred, *Excess* is empty, and the upper bound is the same as the estimate. For example, $\mathcal{A}$ consists of the values for pallets of material whose data value or connectivity did not change during execution. The upper bound will contain data values for pallets of materials that may have been delivered or consumed during the query.

**Minimum/Maximum Aggregation.** In this simple form of aggregation, $\mathcal{A}$ contains the minimum (or maximum) value from in-network aggregation. As an example, a minimum aggregation can tell the site supervisor what area of the site may lack a particular material:

$$\mathcal{A} = \langle \text{MIN } h \in E_i : \langle \forall i : 0 \le i \le m :: h \in E_i \rangle :: h.\nu \rangle$$

To compute bounds on the minimum, we need only to inspect *Excess*. If any result in this set is less than $\mathcal{A}$, it is the lower bound:

$$\text{MIN}_{excess} = \langle \text{MIN } e : e \in \textit{Excess} :: (e.h).\nu \rangle$$

A minimum aggregate query returns $[min(\text{MIN}_{excess}, \mathcal{A}), \mathcal{A}, -]$. When *Excess* is empty or contains no value less than $\mathcal{A}$, this query returns $[-, \mathcal{A}, -]$.

**Counting Aggregation.** The counting aggregate is the first of our aggregates that is *duplicate sensitive*, and so it should attempt to avoid counting the same host more than once. When the query returns, $\mathcal{A}$ contains the number of items that were present in every configuration.

$$\mathcal{A} = \langle +h : \langle \forall i : 0 \le i \le m :: h \in E_i \rangle :: 1 \rangle$$

We use *Excess* to place an upper bound on the number of items that *could* have been present using the host's ID to prevent double counting.

$$C_{excess} = \langle +i : \langle \exists e :: e \in \textit{Excess} \wedge (e.h).\iota = i \rangle :: 1 \rangle$$

The result returned to the querier is $[-, \mathcal{A}, \mathcal{A} + C_{excess}]$. The site supervisor can use the conservative estimate $\mathcal{A}$ if he is interested in the number of pallets of material guaranteed to be on site. Alternatively, he can use the upper bound if he is concerned about avoiding left-over material.

**Summation Aggregation.** An aggregate summation should represent the sum over all hosts receiving the query:

$$\mathcal{A} = \langle +h : \langle \forall i : 0 \le i \le m :: h \in E_i \rangle :: h.\nu \rangle$$

In this case, the upper and lower bounds are calculated based on the worst possible scenario. We create all of the permutations of *Excess*, combine their sums with $\mathcal{A}$, and take the minimum (if less than $\mathcal{A}$) as the lower bound and the maximum (if greater than $\mathcal{A}$) as the upper bound. In calculating these permutations, we must also suppress duplicates. We first define a set of sets, $\mathcal{P}$, a duplicate sensitive power set of *Excess*. $\mathcal{P}$ contains all possible sets $p$ that satisfy:

$$|p| \ne 0 \wedge \langle \forall h : h \in p :: \langle \exists e : e \in \textit{Excess} :: e.h = h \rangle \rangle \wedge$$
$$\langle \forall h_1, h_2 : h_1 \in p \wedge h_2 \in p :: h_1.\iota \ne h_2.\iota \rangle$$

$p$ is a legal permutation if $p$ is not empty, every element in $p$ corresponds to an element in *Excess*, and no two elements in $p$ are from the same host. $U_{SUM}$ is:

$$U_{SUM} = max(\langle \max p :: p \in \mathcal{P} :: \langle +h : h \in p :: h.\nu \rangle + \mathcal{A} \rangle, \mathcal{A})$$

$L_{SUM}$ is defined similarly using min. A summation query returns $[L_{SUM}, \mathcal{A}, U_{SUM}]$.

**Average Aggregation.** Average aggregation is similar to summation. However, to recalculate averages for computing bounds, we must also keep track of how many results contribute to the aggregate average. So in this case, $\mathcal{A}$ is a tuple: $\mathcal{A} = \langle \mathcal{A}', C \rangle$, where $C$ is a count of contributors to $\mathcal{A}'$:

$$\mathcal{A}' = \langle \text{avg } h : \langle \forall i : 0 \leq i \leq m :: h \in E_i \rangle :: h.\nu \rangle$$

We use the elements of the *Excess* set to calculate all of the potential average values after removing duplicates, using $\mathcal{P}$ as above. $U_{AVG}$ is:

$$U_{AVG} = max \left( \left\langle \max N : N \in \mathcal{P} :: \frac{\langle +p : p \in N :: p.\nu \rangle + \mathcal{A}'}{C + |N|} \right\rangle, \mathcal{A} \right)$$

$L_{AVG}$ is defined similarly using min. Assuming $L_{AVG} < \mathcal{A}'$ and $U_{AVG} > \mathcal{A}'$, an aggregate average query returns $[L_{AVG}, \mathcal{A}', U_{AVG}]$. In our construction site example, if the amounts of available material on pallets varies during query execution, the site supervisor can use the range provided by the upper and lower bounds to determine how much confidence to place in the query response.

# 4     Assessing Aggregation Imprecision

The previous section discussed how to determine the semantics of an aggregate query with global knowledge using our model. We next present a practical query execution protocol that performs in-network aggregation and calculates error bounds on the aggregate result using nodes' local perspectives on the world.

## 4.1     Protocol Overview

Query protocols that lock data values to ensure strongly consistent results are impractical in dynamic networks. Our protocol provides different semantics under different conditions, while dynamically assessing the result's imprecision. Our self-assessing protocol makes an initial examination of data values accessed during aggregate computation and maintains state about the values during query processing to determine the consistency class and compute the result's bounds.

We employ two controlled floods—*Pre-Query* and *Aggregation Assessment*. The Pre-Query establishes the query participants. Additionally, it computes and caches partial aggregates at each participant. The Aggregation Assessment performs the in-network aggregation and provides a conservative aggregate result. Establishing participants in the first phase provides a reference that we use to observe changes that impact the query execution semantics, and the cached partial aggregates help provide error bounds on the returned aggregate.

As shown in Fig. 2, each phase consists of two *waves*: one to disseminate a request; one to return the response. Each node waits for its children to respond before responding itself. Participating hosts monitor changes that can impact the query's imprecision; these include changes in data values or connectivity that occur behind the second wave of the Pre-Query and in front of the second wave of the

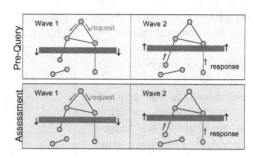

**Fig. 2.** Protocol Phases and Waves

Aggregation Assessment. If no changes occur, the query has comparable consistency and requires no bounds since it is exact.If the changes include only departing participants, the aggregate is computed from results that existed at the same time, and the query has comparable consistency. The bounds include the values of the departed nodes. Finally, if the query encountered both departing and arriving participants, the aggregate is computed from results that did not necessarily coexist, resulting in non-comparable consistency, and the bounds account for both departed and added values.

Flooding an entire network can be expensive, so we constrain the flood using the query's logical connectivity relation $\mathcal{K}$; this is similar to other constrained flooding approaches [5, 6].

## 4.2    Self-assessing Aggregation

We next detail our protocol. Fig. 3 shows the state for a single query. We use I/O Automata [7] to show the behaviors of a host, A. Each *action* has an effect guarded by a precondition and executes in a single atomic step. Actions without preconditions are

| | |
|---|---|
| *id* | – A's unique host identifier |
| *neighbors* | – A's logically connected neighbors (given $\mathcal{K}$) |
| *membership* | – boolean, indicates A is in the query |
| *monitoring* | – boolean, indicates A is preparing result |
| *parent* | – A's parent in the tree |
| *replies-waiting* | – neighbors still to respond |
| *participants* | – A's participating descendants |
| *op* | – query's aggregation operator |
| *data-val* | – A's local data |
| *estimated-val* | – estimate of applying *op* on A's subtree |
| *actual-set* | – data values of A and A's neighbors |
| *actual-val* | – conservative aggregate value computed |
| *count* | – number of nodes in subtree rooted at A |
| *child-yield(x)* | – contributions of child x to the aggregate |

**Fig. 3.** State Variables for Protocol for Node A

*input actions* triggered by another host. We abuse notation slightly by using, for example, "send *ParticipationRequest(r)* to *Neighbors*" to indicate a sequence of actions that triggers *ParticipationRequestReceived* on each neighbor.

**Pre-query Phase.** The Pre-Query establishes a core set of participants used to determine how well the query's result compares to the "ground truth."

The query issuer initiates the phase by sending a *ParticipationRequest* message. Fig. 4 depicts a host's behavior upon receiving such a request. Generally, each host forwards the request to its neighbors, waiting for their responses before replying.[2] This wave continues until a participation request reaches a host at the network boundary (defined by $\mathcal{K}$). A boundary host caches its current data value as an estimated aggregate result. All nodes also compute the number of

$$
\begin{aligned}
&ParticipationRequestReceived_A(r) \\
&\quad \text{Effect:} \\
&\qquad \textbf{if } \neg membership \textbf{ then} \\
&\qquad\quad membership := true \\
&\qquad\quad parent := r.sender \\
&\qquad\quad op := r.op \\
&\qquad\quad \textbf{if } (neighbors - r.sender) \neq \emptyset \textbf{ then} \\
&\qquad\qquad \textbf{for each } B \in (neighbors - r.sender) \\
&\qquad\qquad\quad \text{send } ParticipationRequest(r) \text{ to } B \\
&\qquad\qquad replies\text{-}waiting := neighbors - r.sender \\
&\qquad\quad \textbf{else} \\
&\qquad\qquad estimated\text{-}val := data\text{-}val \\
&\qquad\qquad count := 1 \\
&\qquad\qquad \text{send } ParticipationReply \text{ to } parent \\
&\qquad \textbf{else} \\
&\qquad\quad \text{send } CancelParticipationRequest \text{ to } r.sender
\end{aligned}
$$

**Fig. 4.** *ParticipationRequestReceived* Action

nodes currently in their subtree; for a boundary node, this *count* is one. The boundary node then initiates the second wave of the Pre-Query by packaging the estimated aggregate and the counter into a *ParticipationReply* message that it sends to its parent.

When a host receives a *ParticipationReply* (Fig. 5), the reporting child is considered to be committed to the query. Any future changes impact the quality of the returned aggregate result. On receiving this message, a host locally stores the child's estimated aggregate and count values. In Fig. 5, *op(child-yield(\*))* refers to performing operation *op* on the entire child-

$$
\begin{aligned}
&ParticipationReplyReceived_A(r) \\
&\quad \text{Effect:} \\
&\qquad replies\text{-}waiting := replies\text{-}waiting - r.sender \\
&\qquad participants := participants \cup \{r.participants\} \\
&\qquad child\text{-}yield(r.id) := (r.estimated\text{-}val, r.count) \\
&\qquad \textbf{if } replies\text{-}waiting = \emptyset \textbf{ then} \\
&\qquad\quad child\text{-}yield(id) := (data\text{-}val, 1) \\
&\qquad\quad (estimated\text{-}val, count) := op(child\text{-}yield(*)) \\
&\qquad\quad \textbf{if } r.requester \neq id \\
&\qquad\qquad \text{send } ParticipationReply \text{ to } parent \\
&\qquad\quad \textbf{else} \\
&\qquad\qquad \text{send } Query \text{ to } neighbors
\end{aligned}
$$

**Fig. 5.** The *ParticipationReplyReceived* Action

list contained in *child-yield*. After all its children have reported, it computes the partial aggregate for its subtree (*estimated-val*), and forwards it to its parent.

The Pre-Query ends when the querier has collected *ParticipationReply* messages from all of its children. The estimates of aggregates established in

---

[2] If a node receives more than one participation request for a query (e.g., along different communication paths), the node cancels the duplicate and notifies the sender, removing the node from the sender's subtree. This action is omitted for brevity.

Pre-Query allow each node to capture a local "snapshot" of the environment and the cached values aid in calculating the aggregate query result's imprecision later.

**Aggregation Assessment Phase.** Once the Pre-Query completes, the query issuer initiates Aggregation Assessment. As before, a parent waits for responses from all of its children before sending its own reply, and boundary hosts initiate the second wave. Only results from nodes present in both phases and without any value change contribute to the final aggregate. This value for each subtree is stored in *actual-val* at the root of each subtree and propagated to the query issuer. The *actual-val* (i.e., $\mathcal{A}$ in our framework) returned to the user reflects a conservative aggregation, as defined by the consistency class. Once the query issuer has received *QueryReply* messages from all of its children, it prepares the result. The protocol dynamically assesses and tags a result with bounds indicating the query's imprecision and the achieved consistency class.

**Handling Dynamics.**
If a host detects that one of its children departs after the participants are established but before the node has replied in the Aggregation Assessment, then the *actual-val* returned will not be computed using all values that existed during query execution. Consider a minimum aggregate. If a node with the smallest value departs the network during the query, the computed aggregate will not reflect the smallest value that existed in the network. We must therefore include the departed value in the query result's bounds. To do so, the parent calculates its estimated value for the departed

```
NeighborAdded_A(B)
  Precondition:
      connected(A, B) ∧ B ∉ neighbors
  Effect:
      neighbors := neighbors ∪ {B}
      if membership then
          if ¬monitoring ∧ (replies-waiting ≠ ∅) then
              send ParticipationRequest to B
              replies-waiting := replies-waiting ∪{B}
          else
              send EstimateRequest to B

NeighborDeparted_A(B)
  Precondition:
      ¬connected(A, B) ∧ B ∈ neighbors
  Effect:
      neighbors := neighbors − {B}
      if membership then
          if B = parent then
              [reset state]
          else if ¬monitoring ∧ (replies-waiting ≠ ∅) then
              replies-waiting := replies-waiting −{B}
          else if ¬monitoring then
              participants := participants − {B}
              send EstimateReply(B) to parent
          else
              replies-waiting := replies-waiting−{B}
              send EstimateReply(B) to parent
```

**Fig. 6.** Actions for Neighbor Changes

node's subtree using the value stored in *child-yield* and sends this value to the root in an *EstimateReply* message. Similarly, an inconsistency arising due to a node adding itself to the network should be reflected in the aggregate's bounds. When a node detects such an addition, it sends a new *EstimateRequest* message to the added node, which creates and sends an *EstimateReply* containing its data value and unique node identifier. We model a data value change as a node departure followed a node addition. Since the *EstimateReply* includes the unique node identifier, we can perform post-processing at the query issuer to account for duplicate values when necessary. These actions are shown in Fig. 6.

Fig. 7 illustrates network dynamics for an average query. In the first three scenarios, the nodes are in the Aggregation Assessment phase but have not yet sent replies. The first graph shows the query's participants. In the second graph, a node with a value of 20 departs. The neighboring node detects the departure and uses locally cached values to compute and send an *EstimateReply*. In the third graph, a node with a value of 0 departs. The final graph depicts the final computation. The values present and unchanged are used to perform in-network aggregation, which results in the average $\mathcal{A} = 10$.

Bounds on the aggregate result are computed using the *EstimateReply* messages (arrows in Fig. 7) which carry the "excess" values to the querying host. In this example, we calculate all potential average values after removing duplicate contributions. The lowest possible average includes the node with value 0 that departed, yielding an average of 8.89. The highest possible average is 11.11; this comes from the configuration that included the departed node with value 20 but not the departed node with value 0. Therefore, the numerical result for this query would be [8.89, 10, 11.11]. In addition, because the query issuer has recorded *EstimateReply* messages that indicate node departures but no additions, the query achieved *comparable* consistency. Thus, the bounds were computed using comparable values, i.e., values that existed at the same time.

In general, the query result includes the aggregate result, bounds on the result, and an assessment of the result's consistency semantics. Application developers can use the protocol in different network settings and receive different query replies and their associated semantics and bounds. This enables users to intuitively reason about the uncertainty associated with query responses.

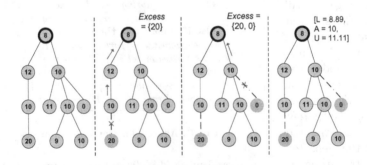

**Fig. 7.** Example Average Query

# 5  Evaluation

We have prototyped our protocol using the OMNeT++ simulator and its mobility framework [8, 9]. Our protocol executes a query, establishes its consistency, and provides bounds on the response.[3] We executed our protocol in a 1000m x 900m rectangular area with 50 nodes (a network of moderate density and good connectivity). The nodes move according to the random mobility model, in which each node is initially placed randomly in the space, chooses a random destination, and moves in the direction of the destination at a given speed. Once a node reaches the destination, it repeats the process. We used the 802.11 MAC protocol. When possible, 95% confidence intervals are shown on the graphs.

## 5.1  Using Aggregate Imprecision: An Application Scenario

We first demonstrate how an application might apply our protocol using a construction asset management example. In our scenario, materials are delivered to the site over a period of time and then consumed. Devices attached to the palettes of material measure the amount of available material, and the palettes may move around the site as

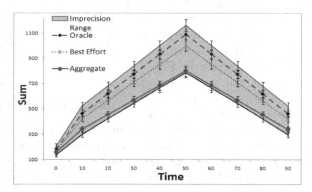

**Fig. 8.** An Application Example

they are positioned for use. Initial data values are generated using a Gaussian distribution ($\mu = 0$, $\sigma = 20$); a value increases in steps of 10 for 50 seconds (representing material delivery) then reduces to its original value in steps of 10. We model a dynamic scenario where all devices are mobile and move at 20 m/s. A node selected to be the query issuer requests the sum of the amount of material across the site every 10 seconds. Fig. 8 plots three lines: our protocol's conservative estimate of the aggregate value ($\mathcal{A}$); the *actual* sum of the material amounts (the "oracle"); and the summation value that would be calculated by an existing state-of-the-art best-effort querying technique (e.g., [2]). The shaded region contains values between our upper and lower bounds, and it represents the imprecision range associated with our result.

The plot confirms that best effort solutions often differ (sometimes significantly) from the truth. Our approach provides both a stated consistency semantic (here, the results are *non-comparable*) as well as imprecision bounds. While our aggregate result is conservative and may differ from the oracle, the range gives an indication of the space of all possible answers. The behavior exhibited here is true for all other operators; these graphs are omitted for brevity. The

---

[3] The source code and settings used are available at
http://mpc.ece.utexas.edu/AggregationConsistency/index.html

upper and lower bounds typically encapsulated the oracle value. In relatively static networks, the aggregate value ($\mathcal{A}$) returned is close to the oracle, and the distance between the upper and lower bounds is small. In highly dynamic networks, the aggregate value tends to be closer to the lower bound, and the imprecision range is wider. An exception is in very dense networks, where the oracle tends to be higher than our upper bound due to the significant numbers of packets dropped because of contention in the wireless medium.

## 5.2   Impact of Mobility

We now show how our imprecision measures change with changing network conditions. We evaluated all five of our aggregation operators but use the average operator to elucidate the impact of mobility. The shaded region in Fig. 9 represents the percentage of query responses that were *comparable* as node speed in

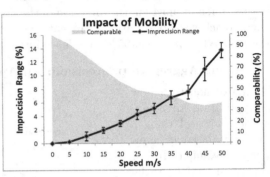

**Fig. 9.** Imprecision Change with Dynamics

creased. When the network is static, all the query results are *comparable* because the configuration remains the same during query execution. However, as mobility increases, the results are increasingly *non-comparable*. Fig. 9 also shows the impact of mobility on aggregate imprecision. The line shows the size of the imprecision range obtained by executing our protocol[4]. As mobility increases, the imprecision range widens. Using a best effort protocol can produce responses that vary significantly from the ground truth; the difference between the oracle and best effort responses varied from 0 to 20%. The imprecision range is lower than Fig. 8 because mobility alone (not data changes) contributes to the uncertainty here. This shows that, in a highly dynamic environment, the query responses of current protocols can be a poor reflection of the ground truth. By explicitly exposing the degree of uncertainty, we allow applications to reason about query results.

## 5.3   Protocol Performance

We measured our protocol's performance in terms of overhead (the number of bytes transmitted to evaluate a query) and latency (the time to process a query). Our protocol effectively runs the best effort protocol twice, so the overhead is about double that of the best effort protocol. In addition, our overhead increases slightly with mobility due to sending additional information to calculate the bounds. (This graph is omitted for brevity.) Fig. 10 shows that our protocol does not incur significant delays. Although our protocol is clearly more expensive than current best-effort techniques, it provides significantly more information to enable applications to effectively reason about results of aggregate queries in dynamic environments.

---

[4] The line in Fig. 9 plots the difference between the upper and lower bounds normalized by the answer returned by a best effort protocol.

# 6    Related Work

Consistency has been expressed in terms of precise metrics defining numerical error, order error, and services [10]. The authors explore the design space between strong consistency and no consistency for data access in replicated file systems. In contrast, we focus on aggregation of (non-replicated) data items and provide an accuracy range for a given query result. Similarly, *completeness* de-

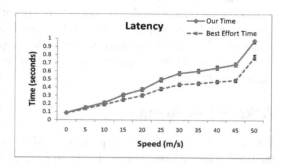

**Fig. 10.** Protocol Overhead

scribes the probability that a node's data will be included in a query result [11]. This has been applied only to a distributed shared memory system with no concern for mobility.

Recent work has explored the impact of in-network aggregation on consistency, defining the "single site validity" principle, in which a query result appears to be equivalent to an atomic execution from the query issuer's perspective [12]; essentially, a result is valid if every host that was connected to the querier during the querying interval contributed. In a complementary manner, we categorize contributions from nodes depending on the type of environmental change which allows us to provide a range of semantics. More recent work exposes inconsistency in query results through network imprecision [13]. This work, like ours, provides a network monitoring approach that reports the network imprecision with the query result. Information indicating network imprecision includes the number of reachable nodes and the number of potentially over-counted nodes. Both these approaches are designed for static networks. Since the impact of dynamics is significant, these architectures are not feasible in dynamic pervasive computing networks. In addition, we combine a measure of consistency with a measure of imprecision providing a more complete way to convey query semantics.

Researchers in sensor networks have explored a model-driven approach to query processing [14, 15]. Each node constructs a local model of the data in the network and estimates the error in the model. If the estimated error is acceptable, a node conserves energy by querying the local model. Another popular approach provides approximate answers that trade accuracy for energy efficiency [16]. We calculate the error on demand at query time since pro-actively maintaining local models can be expensive in mobile environments.

# 7    Conclusions

In this paper, we presented an approach to defining semantics for aggregate queries issued in dynamic pervasive computing networks. Our approach combines a qualitative measure of consistency and a quantitative measure of imprecision to provide a more intuitive way of communicating the meaning and quality of a query's aggregate result. To make this approach more accessible to developers of query-based applications, we developed an automated process for query execution that simultaneously assesses the aggregate query's semantics while performing in-network aggregation, and returns the assessment along with the aggregate result.

## Acknowledgements

This research was funded, in part, by NSF Grants # CNS- 0620245 and OCI-0636299. The authors express thanks to EDGE. The conclusions herein are those of the authors and do not necessarily reflect the views of the sponsoring agencies.

## References

1. Krishnamachari, B., Estrin, D., Wicker, S.B.: The impact of data aggregation in wireless sensor networks. In: Proc. of ICDCS, pp. 575–578 (2002)
2. Madden, S., Franklin, M.J., Hellerstein, J.M., Hong, W.: TAG: A tiny aggregation service for ad-hoc sensor networks. ACM SIGOPS 36(SI), 131–146 (2002)
3. Manjhi, A., Nath, S., Gibbons, P.: Tributaries and deltas: Efficient and robust aggregation in sensor network streams. In: Proc. of SIGMOD, pp. 287–298 (2005)
4. Payton, J., Julien, C., Roman, G.C.: Automatic consistency assessment for query results in dynamic environments. In: Proc. of ESEC/FSE, pp. 245–254 (2007)
5. Kabaday, S., Julien, C.: A local data abstraction and communication paradign for pervasive computing. In: Proc. of PerCom, pp. 57–66 (2007)
6. Roman, G.C., Julien, C., Huang, Q.: Network abstractions for context-aware mobile computing. In: Proc. of ICSE, pp. 363–373 (2002)
7. Lynch, N., Tuttle, M.: An introduction to I/O automata. CWI-Quarterly 2(3), 219–246 (1989)
8. Loebbers, M., Willkomm, D., Koepke, A.: The Mobility Framework for OMNeT++ Web Page, http://mobility-fw.sourceforge.net
9. Vargas, A.: OMNeT++ Web Page, http://www.omnetpp.org
10. Yu, H., Vahdat, A.: Design and evaluation of a conit-based continuous consistency model for replicated services. ACM Trans. on Computer Systems 20(3), 239–282 (2002)
11. Singla, A., Ramachandran, U., Hodgins, J.: Temporal notions of synchronization and consistency in Beehive. In: Proc. of SPAA, pp. 211–220 (1997)
12. Bawa, M., Gionis, A., Garcia-Molina, H., Motwani, R.: The price of validity in dynamic networks. In: Proc. of ACM SIGMOD, pp. 515–526 (June 2004)
13. Jain, N., Kit, D., Mahajan, D., Yalagandula, P., Dahlin, M., Zhang, Y.: Network imprecision: A new consistency metric for scalable monitoring. In: Proc. of OSDI, pp. 87–102 (2008)
14. Deshpande, A., Guestrin, C., Madden, S., Hellerstein, J., Hong, W.: Model-driven data acquisition in sensor networks. In: Proc. of VLDB (2004)
15. Muttreja, A., Raghunathan, A., Ravi, S., Jha, N.: Active learning drive data acquisition for sensor networks. In: Proc. of ISCC (2006)
16. Considine, J., Li, F., Kollios, G., Byers, J.: Approximate aggregation techniques for sensor databases. In: Proc. of ICDE, pp. 449–460 (2004)

# Fault-Tolerant Aggregation by Flow Updating

Paulo Jesus, Carlos Baquero, and Paulo Sérgio Almeida

University of Minho (CCTC-DI)
Campus de Gualtar, 4710-057 Braga, Portugal
{pcoj,cbm,psa}@di.uminho.pt

**Abstract.** Data aggregation plays an important role in the design of scalable systems, allowing the determination of meaningful system-wide properties to direct the execution of distributed applications. In the particular case of wireless sensor networks, data collection is often only practicable if aggregation is performed. Several aggregation algorithms have been proposed in the last few years, exhibiting different properties in terms of accuracy, speed and communication tradeoffs. Nonetheless, existing approaches are found lacking in terms of fault tolerance. In this paper, we introduce a novel fault-tolerant averaging based data aggregation algorithm. It tolerates substantial message loss (link failures), while competing algorithms in the same class can be affected by a single lost message. The algorithm is based on manipulating flows (in the graph theoretical sense), that are updated using idempotent messages, providing it with unique robustness capabilities. Furthermore, evaluation results obtained by comparing it with other averaging approaches have revealed that it outperforms them in terms of time and message complexity.

## 1 Introduction

Traditional solutions based on centralized and tightly architected computation infrastructures are being challenged by new designs that amass the resources in highly distributed computing systems. Notable examples are found in large scale peer-to-peer systems, now in common use, and in the algorithms that will support the deployment of vast sensor networks.

In these settings, aggregation of data across large numbers of nodes plays a basal role in the design of scalable solutions [1]. Distributed aggregation along active nodes allows the efficient determination of meaningful global system properties, that can direct the actions of self-adaptive distributed algorithms.

Examples can be found when using estimates of the network size to direct the dimensioning of distributed hash table structures [2], when setting a quorum for voting algorithms [3], when estimates of the average system load are needed to direct local load-balancing decisions, or when an estimate of the total disk space in the network is required in a P2P sharing system.

Several aggregation algorithms have been introduced in the recent years, tackling the problem for different settings, and yielding different characteristics in terms of accuracy, time and communication tradeoffs. Traditional approaches

T. Senivongse and R. Oliveira (Eds.): DAIS 2009, LNCS 5523, pp. 73–86, 2009.
© IFIP International Federation for Information Processing 2009

relay on the existence of a specific aggregation structure (e.g. tree) [4,5,6], executing the aggregation process along a predefined routing topology. Another common class of distributed aggregation algorithms is based on averaging techniques [7,8,9,10]; Here, the values of a variable across all nodes are averaged iteratively. This kind of approaches are independent from the routing topology, often using a gossip-based communication scheme between peers.

*Averaging* techniques allow the derivation of different aggregation functions besides average (like counts, sums, and ranks), according to the combinations of input values. In particular, if the input value is set to 1 in a single node and to 0 in all remaining nodes, it is possible to derive an estimate of the network size, by averaging until a given level of convergence is reached, and later inspecting the inverse of the resulting value [8]. Other types of aggregation algorithms are also known, based on the application of *probabilistic* methods. This is the case of Extrema Propagation [11] and COMP [12], which reduce the computation of an aggregation function to the determination of the maximum/minimum of a collection of random numbers. These probabilistic techniques tend to emphasize speed, being less accurate than averaging techniques.

Specific aggregations, such as counting the number of nodes, are amenable to specialized probabilistic algorithms that can operate using properties of random walks, sample and re-sample techniques and other statistic tools [13,14,15].

Up to now, it has not been proposed any aggregation technique which is simultaneously accurate and tolerates faults (e.g. message loss) efficiently. In this paper, we introduce a novel averaging based aggregation technique: *Flow Updating*. This new algorithm tolerates quite easily high levels of message loss; a feature that was lacking in previous approaches, where message loss often implies "mass" loss in the amount subject to averaging. Moreover, even in lossless scenarios, our new technique achieves an improved convergence speed compared to previous approaches. We compare the new algorithm with two other established averaging algorithms (Push-Sum Protocol [7] and DRG [9]) in a common simulation environment and contrast the results.

The rest of this paper is organized as follows. The closest related work, in terms of averaging aggregation algorithms, is discussed in Section 2. *Flow Updating* will be described in Section 3. The evaluation of the proposed approach will be presented in Section 4, comparing it to other averaging algorithms, and discussing the obtained results. Finally, conclusions and future work directions will be drawn in Section 5.

## 2   Related Work

Unlike classical tree-based approaches (e.g. TAG [4]), some approaches that are independent from the routing strategy used to communicate have been proposed in the recent years. Commonly, these distributed aggregation algorithms are based on *averaging* techniques. Nodes start with a given real value, $x_i$, and an anti-entropy protocol is used to iteratively average the values between pairs of nodes. Eventually all values will converge to the same amount.

This kind of approaches tend to be very accurate, producing the correct result or converging to it along time. Compared with tree-based schemes, these algorithms remove the dependency from a specific routing topology, introducing more flexibility, and allowing the iterative calculation of the aggregation result at all network nodes (instead of a single node). Follows, a brief description of some of those algorithms.

## 2.1 Push-Sum Protocol

The push-sum protocol [7] is a gossip-based aggregation algorithm, which essentially consists of an iterative pairwise distribution of aggregated values throughout the network. At each round $t$, each node $i$ maintains and propagates information of a pair of values $(s_{t,i}, w_{t,i})$, where $s_{t,i}$ represents the sum of the exchanged aggregates, and $w_{t,i}$ denotes the weight associated to this sum at the given time $t$ and node $i$. In order to compute distinct aggregation functions, from the initial input value $x_i$ of node $i$, one resorts to distinct initializations to the pair of values, $(s_{0,i}, w_{0,i})$ in each $i$. E.g. AVERAGE: $s_{0,i} = x_i$ and $w_{0,i} = 1$ for all nodes; SUM: $s_{0,i} = x_i$ for all nodes, only one node sets $w_{0,i} = 1$ and the remaining assume $w_{0,i} = 0$; COUNT: $s_{0,i} = 1$ for all nodes, only one with $w_{0,i} = 1$ and the others with $w_{0,i} = 0$.

The protocol works has follows: at each round, each node sends a pair of values corresponding to half of their current values $(s_{t,i}, w_{t,i})$ to a target node chosen uniformly at random, and to itself. The local values are updated with the correspondent sum of all the data received in the previous round. At each time $t$, the aggregation result can be estimated at each node by $s_{t,i}/w_{t,i}$. The accuracy of the produced estimate will tend to increase along each round, converging to the correct value.

As referred by the authors, the correctness of this algorithm relies on a fundamental property defined as the *mass conservation*: the global sum of all network estimates is always constant along time. When no messages are in transit, the value $\sum_i \frac{s_{t,i}}{w_{t,i}}$ is the same for any round $t$. The convergence to the true result will depend on the conservation of this property. Considering the crucial importance of this property, the authors assume the existence of a fault detection mechanism, that allows nodes to detect when a message did not reach its destination. In this situation, the "mass" is restored by sending the undelivered message to the node itself.

We should point out that, contrary to *indulgent* distributed algorithms in which an incorrect output from the failure detector (FD) merely postpones termination, assuming the use of a FD is problematic for realistic implementations, as FD inaccuracy means violating mass conservation.

## 2.2 Push-Pull Gossiping

A push-pull gossiping approach, similar to the previous one, is proposed in [16,8]. This protocol benefits from the better convergence of push-pull interactions, as opposed to push only. Periodically, each node sends its current aggregated value to a random neighbor and waits for the response with the aggregate value of the target. The aggregation function is further applied to both values (sent and received), in order to determine the new estimation and update the local aggregate. Each time a node receives an aggregate from a neighbor, it sends back its current value, and afterwards computes the new aggregate, using the received and sent value as inputs.

Unlike push-sum, the protocol does not use weight variables, imposing greater atomicity requirements on the interaction between node pairs.

### 2.3   DRG (Distributed Random Grouping)

A different approach based on a distributed random grouping (DRG) was proposed in [9]. DRG was designed to take advantage of the broadcast nature of wireless transmission, in which all nodes within radio range will be prone to hear a transmission. This algorithm defines three different working modes for each node: *leader*, *member*, and *idle* mode.

According to the defined modes, one could divide the execution of the algorithm in three main steps. First, each node in idle mode independently decides to become a group leader (according to a predefined probability), and consequently broadcasts a Group Call Message (GCM) to all its neighbors, subsequently waiting for members. Second, all nodes in idle mode respond to the first received GCM with a Joining Acknowledgment (JACK) tagged with their aggregated value, updating their state mode accordingly to become members of that group. Finally, after gathering the group members values from all received JACKs, the leader computes the group aggregate and broadcast a Group Assignment Message (GAM) with the result, returning to idle mode afterwards. Each group member waits for the leader GAM, not responding to any other request until then, to update its local state (setting its local value with the received group aggregate and returning to idle mode).

The execution of this scheme along time creates distributed random groups that coordinate in-group aggregation. Since groups overlap over time, the estimation will convergence at all nodes to the desired network wide global aggregate. The performance of this algorithm is highly influenced by its capacity to create aggregation groups (quantity and size of groups), which is defined by the predefined probability of a node becoming leader.

This algorithm is vulnerable to message loss between coordinators and neighbors, partial fixes to avoid the possibility of nodes waiting forever may incur in violating mass conservation.

### 2.4   Further Considerations

Averaging aggregation algorithms depend on the mass conservation principle to converge to a correct result. Consequently, the robustness of these algorithms is strongly related to their ability to preserve the global mass of the system. The loss of a partial aggregate (mass) may result in the subtraction of the lost value from the global mass, and convergence to an incorrect value.

A few approaches have recently introduced some practical concerns about aggregation robustness. This is the case of G-GAP [10], that tackles the mass conservation problem, extending the push-synopses protocol [7] in order to provide accurate estimates in the presence of node failures. Despite their effort, G-GAP only supports discontinuous failures of adjacent nodes within a short time period.

In this paper, we introduce an aggregation algorithm that fully overcomes the mass conservation issue under link failures. Apart from its robustness properties, our technique also exhibits good performance. We compare it, in failure-free scenarios, with a representative set of the existing averaging approaches, namely the push-sum protocol [7] and DRG [9].

Push-pull gossiping [16,8] is not considered in the comparison, since simulations exhibited a violation of mass conservation. We found out that this is due to message interleaving resulting from the natural concurrency in the distributed system model we adopted. This means it does not work, even under no failures, in a realistic model. Fixes can be devised, towards making a pair of push and pull messages to behave as if they are atomic (as implied by the papers presenting the mechanism). However, it means some substantial changes (including preventing deadlock), and we would not be making a comparison with the original algorithm. Even so, we found out the corrected algorithm to be even slower and it does make an unfair comparison.

# 3    Flow Updating

## 3.1    System Model

We model a distributed system as a connected undirected graph $G(\mathcal{V}, \mathcal{E})$, in which the set of vertices $\mathcal{V}$ represent the network computation nodes, and the set of edges $\mathcal{E}$ correspond to bidirectional communication links. We consider only a fixed topology. We define $\mathcal{D}_i$ as the set of adjacent nodes of $i$ in the communication graph, and denote its size as $|\mathcal{D}_i|$ which corresponds to the node *degree*. The existence of global unique identifiers to distinguish nodes is not considered, nor required. We only assume that each node is able to distinguish its neighbors.

We consider the execution of the aggregation algorithms in a synchronous model (as in Chapter 2 of [17]). Each round, executed in lockstep, is composed of two steps: message generation, where each node uses its local state to compute and send messages to its neighbors; and state transition, where each node uses its local state and the received messages to compute the new state.

We use this model in order to provide a fair comparison of the simulated algorithms. For example, each iteration in DRG, consisting of three phases with different kinds of messages sent in each one, will be three rounds.

We do not consider node failures, only link failures, in the algorithm and its evaluation. However, in Section 4.3 we briefly discuss why the *Flow Updating* algorithm is suitable to be adapted to cope with node failures and be used in asynchronous systems.

## 3.2   Key Idea

*Flow Updating* is a novel averaging based aggregation algorithm, which enables the computation of aggregation functions (e.g. AVERAGE, COUNT or SUM) over a distributed system. It works independently from the network communication topology, and it is robust against message loss, a common fault in relevant application scenarios, such as Wireless Sensor Networks (WSN).

This algorithm departs from current approaches, that send "mass" in messages (with message loss implying mass loss) and keep the current mass value in a variable. The key idea is to use the *flow* concept from graph theory (which serves as an abstraction for many things like water flow or electric current; see Chapter 6 of [18]), and instead of storing in each node the current average in a variable, compute it from the initial value and the contribution of the flows along edges to the neighbors:

$$a_i = v_i - \sum_{j \in \mathcal{D}_i} f_{ij}. \tag{1}$$

This can be read as: the current average in a node is the initial input value less the flows from the node to each neighbor. Here we are not concerned with classic network flow concepts like capacity or trying to maximize flows; we focus on exploring the symmetry property of the flow along an edge:

$$f_{ij} = -f_{ji}. \tag{2}$$

This says that the flow from node $i$ to node $j$ is the symmetrical of the flow from node $j$ to node $i$ (see Figure 1(a)). The essence of the algorithm is: each node $i$ stores the flow $f_{ij}$ to each neighbor $j$; node $i$ sends flow $f_{ij}$ to $j$ in a message; a node $j$ receiving $f_{ij}$ updates its variable $f_{ji}$ with $-f_{ij}$. Messages simply update flows, being idempotent; the value in a subsequent message overwrites the previous one, it does not add to the previous value.

If the symmetry property of flows holds, the sum of the averages for all nodes (the global mass) will remain constant:

$$\sum_{i \in V} a_i = \sum_{i \in V} (v_i - \sum_{j \in \mathcal{D}_i} f_{ij}) = \sum_{i \in V} v_i. \tag{3}$$

The intuition is that if a message is lost the symmetry is temporarily broken, but as long as a successful messages arrives, it re-establishes the symmetry (see Figure 1(b) and 1(c)). What really happens, due to interleaving, is that the symmetry may never hold but $f_{ij}$ converges to $-f_{ji}$, and the global mass converges to the sum of the input values of all nodes.

## 3.3   Algorithm

Algorithm 1 shows *Flow Updating*, according to the defined system model (Section 3.1). In this algorithm, the local state of each node $i$ will keep a variable $v_i$ with the local input value, the individual flows $f_{ij}$ toward its neighbors, and

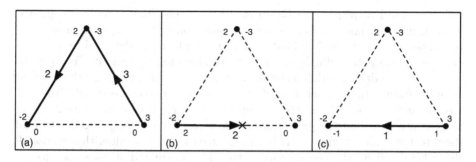

**Fig. 1.** Key concept of *Flow Updating*, illustrated by arbitrary flow exchanges between 3 nodes, considering a temporary link failure in (b)

the estimated aggregates $e_{ij}$ of the neighborhood. Initially, at each node $i$ the neighbors flows and estimates are set to zero ($f_{ij} = 0$ and $e_{ij} = 0$ for all $j \in \mathcal{D}_i$), and $v_i$ to the local input value to aggregate.

---

**state variables:**
  $f_{ij}, \forall j \in \mathcal{D}_i$, flows, initially $f_{ij} = 0$
  $e_{ij}, \forall j \in \mathcal{D}_i$, estimates, initially $e_{ij} = 0$
  $v_i$, input value

**message-generation function:**
  $\text{msg}(i, j) = (f_{ij}, e_{ij}), \forall j \in \mathcal{D}_i$

**state-transition function:**
  **forall** $(f_{ji}, e_{ji})$ **received do**
    $f_{ij} \leftarrow -f_{ji}$
    $e_{ij} \leftarrow e_{ji}$
  $e_i \leftarrow \dfrac{\left(v_i - \sum_{j \in \mathcal{D}_i} f_{ij}\right) + \sum_{j \in \mathcal{D}_i} e_{ij}}{|\mathcal{D}_i| + 1}$
  **forall** $j \in \mathcal{D}_i$ **do**
    $f_{ij} \leftarrow f_{ij} + (e_i - e_{ij})$
    $e_{ij} \leftarrow e_i$

---

**Algorithm 1.** *Flow Updating* algorithm (at each node $i$)

In the message generation step a pair of values (flow and estimate) is created for each neighbor $j$, to be sent by $i$. An individual flow value $f_{ij}$ is assigned and send to each neighbor, while the same estimate $e_i$ is send by $i$ to all its neighbors (both calculated and locally stored at the end of the previous round).

In the state transition step, each node starts by setting the local values associated to the sender of each received message with the ones (estimate and symmetric flow) within the message pair addressed to him. Notice that, different estimates (and corresponding flows) may be received from different neighbors. Thereafter, each node computes a new prediction of the aggregation value $e_i$ by averaging the received estimates and the one locally calculated by (1), and updates its state accordingly, in order to produce the new result. To do so, to the flow $f_{ij}$ is added the difference between the new estimate $e_i$ and the received estimate from $j$; the estimates $e_{ij}$ of all neighbors $j$ are set directly with the new foreseen estimate $e_i$. The newly computed state will be used in the next round to generate and send the proper data values to all neighbors, in order to lead them to the same estimate. The iterative execution of this algorithm across all the network allows the convergence of the value estimated at each node to the correct global average of the input values.

---

**state variables:**
>   $f_{ij}, \forall j \in \mathcal{D}_i$, flows, initially $f_{ij} = 0$
>   $e_{ij}, \forall j \in \mathcal{D}_i$, estimates, initially $e_{ij} = 0$
>   $v_i$, input value
>   $k$, chosen neighbor

**message-generation function:**
>   $\mathrm{msg}(i, k) = (f_{ik}, e_{ik})$

**state-transition function:**
>   **forall** $(f_{ji}, e_{ji})$ **received do**
>>      $f_{ij} \leftarrow -f_{ji}$
>>      $e_{ij} \leftarrow e_{ji}$
>
>   $e_i \leftarrow \dfrac{\left(v_i - \sum_{j \in \mathcal{D}_i} f_{ij}\right) + \sum_{j \in \mathcal{D}_i} e_{ij}}{|\mathcal{D}_i| + 1}$
>   $k \leftarrow chooseNeighbor(\mathcal{D}_i);$
>   $f_{ik} \leftarrow f_{ik} + (e_i - e_{ik})$
>   $e_{ik} \leftarrow e_i$

---

**Algorithm 2.** Unicast version of *Flow Updating* (at each node $i$)

Notice that, in practice, when broadcast is supported by the physical communication medium, all the messages generated at each round by a node can be sent in a single transmission to all neighbors. If broadcast is not physically supported, the messages are individually transmitted to each adjacent node. According to this, and in order to supply an impartial evaluation of this algorithm, when compared with others that do not take advantage of message broadcast (e.g. push-sum protocol), we defined an unicast version of *Flow Updating*. The differences of this variation of the algorithm are depicted by Algorithm 2, mainly consisting in the addition of a function $chooseNeighbor(\mathcal{D}_i)$ to choose a specific target $k$ from the set of neighbors of node $i$. In the state transition process, only the flow and estimate corresponding to the chosen node $k$ will be updated, instead of all neighbor nodes. Afterwards, in the next round, a single message will be generated and sent to the previously chosen node $k$.

Several heuristics can be used to implement the function $chooseNeighbor(\mathcal{D}_i)$. For instance, the node can be simply picked up uniformly at random from the set of neighbors $\mathcal{D}_i$, or it can be chosen in accordance to a specific criteria, taking advantage of the neighbors data locally available. In particular, in the evaluated unicast version of the algorithm, we consider a criteria in which the neighbor possessing the estimate with the greater discrepancy relatively to the averaged estimate $e_i$ will be selected in each round.

Considering the system settings in which the algorithm is executed, the choice of the correct heuristic to select the target neighbor in each round may improve the overall performance of the aggregation process. Some simulations comparing both of the the referred heuristics have evidenced an improved performance of the unicast version of the algorithm using the latter criteria, instead of using a naif random choice. This optimization study is out of the scope of this paper.

## 4   Evaluation

### 4.1   Simulation Setup

We prepared a simulation environment compliant with the system model enunciated in Section 3.1, in order to allow comparisons between Flow Updating and two established approaches: the push-sum protocol [7] and DRG [9]. We evaluated all the aggregation algorithms under strictly identical simulation settings (same network topologies and initial distribution of input values), aiming for an impartial and fair comparison between them. Two different network topologies were taken into account for simulation purposes: *random* and *2D/mesh*. The random network fits the Erdős–Rényi model [19] and consists on a connected network in which all nodes are randomly linked to each other (according to a predefined average connection degree). The 2D/mesh network defines a connected network in which the communication links are established according to geographical proximity, modeling an approximation to the connectivity in WSN. Nodes are spread uniformly at random and links are set within a given fixed radius. Independently from the topology, along the algorithms execution the network remains static (no link changes, and no nodes arriving or leaving).

In order to evaluate the robustness of *Flow Updating*, we consider that each message sent in each round can be lost according to a predefined probability.

The same aggregation function is computed by all algorithms: COUNT, which can be used to determine the network size of the system. Shown results correspond to the average value obtained from 50 repetitions of the execution of the same algorithm under identical simulation settings, using different generated networks with the same characteristics in each repetition. Two main metrics are used to evaluate each aggregation algorithm: speed and overhead. The first criteria defines how fast, in number of rounds, a given accuracy is reached. Accuracy is expressed by the normalized RMSE (Root Mean Square Error) of the estimate when contrasted to the target value. The second criteria is defined in terms of the number of messages required to compute the aggregation result with the desired accuracy. This message overhead can be interpreted as an approximation to energy expenditure in WSN, since message transmission is often the dominating factor in those settings.

## 4.2   Results

The first scenario corresponds to a random network with 1000 nodes ($n = 1000$) and an average connection degree $d$ approximately equal to $\log n$ ($= 3$). The same network size ($n = 1000$) and degree ($d \approx \log n$) are considered in the second scenario, but a different network topology is used: 2D/mesh. We choose to use a degree of value $\log n$, since it is the degree value that nodes must have in order to keep the network connected with constant probability, considering that all nodes fail with a probability of 0.5 [20]. Notice that all specific parameters of the analyzed algorithms (e.g. the probability to become leader in DRG) have been tuned to provide them with the best performance in each scenario.

For a matter of convenience, to reduce the space consumed by graphics, we depict unicast and broadcast algorithms in the same figure. Nevertheless, in order to perform a correct analysis of the obtained results, approaches using different communication assumptions should be observed separately. Concretely, the push-sum protocol should be contrasted with the unicast version of *Flow Updating*, and DRG with the broadcast version. The simulation results obtained for the outlined network topologies (random and 2D/mesh) are respectively depicted by Figure 2 and Figure 3.

In the random network scenario, the two versions of *Flow Updating* clearly outperform both competitors, both in terms of convergence speed Figure 2(a) (from 4 to more than 10 times faster), and resource consumption (sending considerably less messages) Figure 2(b).

As expected, the 2D/mesh topology penalizes the convergence rate in all algorithms. Again, both *Flow Updating* variations (unicast and broadcast) reach better results than the ones obtained by the other aggregation algorithms (Figure 3). The broadcast version of *Flow Updating* shows the best overall results both in speed and overhead.

We now concentrate on the behavior of *Flow Updating* under message loss, since under this failure pattern the other algorithms (without extensions) do not converge to the correct value. Here we compare three levels of message loss affecting transmitted messages, 0% (no loss), 20% and 40%. This values are compared in a random network running the unicast version and in a 2D/mesh network using the broadcast version of the algorithm. These combinations should reflect the more commonly available communication capabilities in each topology. Although not shown in the figures, we confirmed that the broadcast version is always better than the unicast, so that when possible broadcast should be preferred.

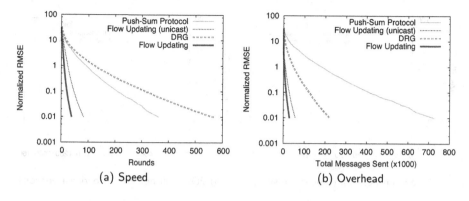

**Fig. 2.** Random networks, $n = 1000$, and $d \approx 3$ ($\log n$)

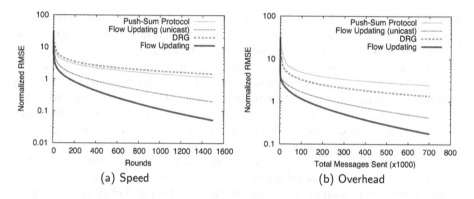

**Fig. 3.** 2D/mesh networks, $n = 1000$, and $d \approx 3$ ($\log n$)

Figure 4 shows a degradation of the performance of the algorithm proportional to each fault rate. The results show that message loss does not prevent convergence of the estimate, it only increases the time and messages needed to reach it.

It is curious to observe that even under the occurrence of high amounts of message loss *Flow Updating* can still outperform the classical algorithms operating under no message loss. Notice that, comparing the results of Figure 2(a) against Figure 4(a) for the random network scenario, and the results of Figure 3(a) versus Figure 4(b) for the 2D/mesh network, even considering a substantial amount of faults (40%) on both versions of *Flow Updating*, they outperform the other approaches without faults.

### 4.3   Discussion

The obtained results reveal a significantly greater performance of *Flow Updating* on all evaluated scenarios, both in terms of speed and overhead, when compared

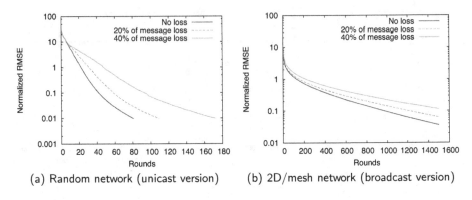

(a) Random network (unicast version)    (b) 2D/mesh network (broadcast version)

**Fig. 4.** *Flow Updating* fault tolerance – $n = 1000$, and $d \approx 3$ $(\log n)$

to well-known approaches. Most important, *Flow Updating* is naturally robust against message loss, due to its flow exchange scheme that keeps the aggregation inputs unchanged along the execution of the algorithm.

Fault tolerance has not been a key concern in the design of aggregation by averaging. Typically, existing approaches require the use of additional mechanisms in order to tolerate faults. For instance, G-GAP [10] extended the push-sum protocol by explicitly acknowledging mass and computing recovery shares, in order to support discontinuous failures of adjacent nodes within a short time period. As we pointed out, failure detection is trickier in this setting, since wrong assessments will lead to deviations in the total mass and ruin convergence. Additionally, the use of acknowledgment messages and timeouts leads to extra consumption of resources and time, adding to the overall overhead of the underlying algorithm even if no faults occur. In contrast, *Flow Updating* is per se tolerant to message loss faults, and its performance is only affected when faults do occur.

In presenting and evaluating *Flow Updating* we have focused on message loss (transient link failures). However, the basic algorithm can be trivially extended to cope with both permanent link failures and node failures. In fact, even though it can be impossible in a distributed system to distinguish between these types of failure, *Flow Updating* can tolerate both without having to make a distinction. The principle is quite simple: if a link/neighbor is suspected to have permanently failed (e.g. because no message arrived for some rounds), the entries (flow and estimate) regarding that neighbor are removed from the state. For all purposes the flow will converge as if that link or node did not exist. If the suspicion turns out to be wrong because a message arrives, the state can be simply augmented using the message content. Even if the network becomes partitioned, each partition will be aggregated independently (in the case of counting, only the partition having the 1 initial value will be counted).

A similar strategy could also be applied, in order to cope with dynamic changes of the network structure, adding or removing the local neighbors information whenever a node is arriving or leaving the neighborhood. Even in this case, the flow values should adjust and all the estimates should converge to a correct value, continuously adapting to reach the network equilibrium. The tolerance exhibited by *Flow Updating* when working in adverse scenarios prone to considerable amounts of message loss, suggest that the algorithm can be successfully used in practice on asynchronous and dynamic systems. We leave the analysis and study of *Flow Updating* in this kind of setting for future work.

## 5   Conclusion

The main contribution of this paper consists on the introduction of a new distributed data aggregation approach: *Flow Updating*. An empirical analysis of the proposed algorithm is provided, comparing it with existing approaches under identical simulation settings. *Flow Updating* was shown to be robust against message loss, overcoming the problem of "mass" loss verified on existing averaging algorithms, and can be easily extended to tolerate permanent link failures or node failures. Moreover, the results obtained reveal that our algorithm performs better than its peers, requiring less time and communication resources.

*Flow Updating* allows the accurate computation of aggregates at all nodes, converging to the exact result along time. The algorithm execution is independent from the network routing topology. The "flow" exchange scheme implemented by this algorithm enables the execution of idempotent update operations, which is the key to its unique robustness capabilities.

Averaging based aggregation is of special relevance when seeking high accuracy estimates of a given global property in a distributed system. The proposed approach can be used on overlay networks with unicast, and is particularly efficient when broadcast capabilities are present. The broadcast version of the algorithm can bring a robust implementation of aggregation by averaging to wireless sensor networks, where a high level of message loss can be expected.

## References

1. Van Renesse, R.: The importance of aggregation. In: Schiper, A., Shvartsman, M.M.A.A., Weatherspoon, H., Zhao, B.Y. (eds.) Future Directions in Distributed Computing. LNCS, vol. 2584, pp. 87–92. Springer, Heidelberg (2003)
2. Stoica, I., Morris, R., Karger, D., Kaashoek, M., Balakrishnan, H.: Chord: A scalable peer-to-peer lookup service for internet applications. In: SIGCOMM 2001: Proceedings of the 2001 conference on Applications, technologies, architectures, and protocols for computer communications, pp. 149–160 (August 2001)
3. Abraham, I., Malkhi, D.: Probabilistic quorums for dynamic systems. Distributed Computing 18(2), 113–124 (2005)
4. Madden, S., Franklin, M., Hellerstein, J., Hong, W.: TAG: a Tiny AGgregation service for ad-hoc sensor networks. ACM SIGOPS Operating Systems Review 36(SI), 131–146 (2002)
5. Li, J., Sollins, K., Lim, D.: Implementing aggregation and broadcast over distributed hash tables. ACM SIGCOMM Computer Communication Review 35(1), 81–92 (2005)

6. Birk, Y., Keidar, I., Liss, L., Schuster, A., Wolff, R.: Veracity radius: capturing the locality of distributed computations. In: PODC 2006: Proceedings of the twenty-fifth annual ACM symposium on Principles of distributed computing (July 2006)

7. Kempe, D., Dobra, A., Gehrke, J.: Gossip-based computation of aggregate information. In: Proceedings. 44th Annual IEEE Symposium on Foundations of Computer Science, pp. 482–491 (2003)

8. Jelasity, M., Montresor, A., Babaoglu, O.: Gossip-based aggregation in large dynamic networks. In: ACM Transactions on Computer Systems, TOCS (2005)

9. Chen, J.-Y., Pandurangan, G., Xu, D.: Robust computation of aggregates in wireless sensor networks: Distributed randomized algorithms and analysis. IEEE Transactions on Parallel and Distributed Systems 17(9), 987–1000 (2006)

10. Wuhib, F., Dam, M., Stadler, R., Clemm, A.: Robust monitoring of network-wide aggregates through gossiping. In: 10th IFIP/IEEE International Symposium on Integrated Network Management, pp. 226–235 (2007)

11. Baquero, C., Almeida, P.S., Menezes, R.: Fast estimation of aggregates in unstructured networks. In: International Conference on Autonomic and Autonomous Systems (ICAS), Valencia, Spain. IEEE Computer Society, Los Alamitos (2009)

12. Mosk-Aoyama, D., Shah, D.: Computing separable functions via gossip. In: PODC 2006: Proceedings of the twenty-fifth annual ACM symposium on Principles of Distributed Computing, pp. 113–122 (2006)

13. Kostoulas, D., Psaltoulis, D., Gupta, I., Birman, K., Demers, A.: Decentralized schemes for size estimation in large and dynamic groups. In: Fourth IEEE International Symposium on Network Computing and Applications, pp. 41–48 (2005)

14. Massoulié, L., Merrer, E., Kermarrec, A.-M., Ganesh, A.: Peer counting and sampling in overlay networks: random walk methods. In: PODC 2006: Proceedings of the twenty-fifth annual ACM symposium on Principles of Distributed Computing (July 2006)

15. Ganesh, A., Kermarrec, A., Le Merrer, E., Massoulié, L.: Peer counting and sampling in overlay networks based on random walks. Distributed Computing 20(4), 267–278 (2007)

16. Jelasity, M., Montresor, A.: Epidemic-style proactive aggregation in large overlay networks. In: 24th International Conference on Distributed Computing Systems (2004)

17. Lynch, N.A.: Distributed Algorithms. Morgan Kaufmann Publishers Inc., San Francisco (1996)

18. Diestel, R.: Graph Theory, 3rd edn. Graduate Texts in Mathematics, vol. 173. Springer, Heidelberg (2005)

19. Erdős, P., Rényi, A.: On the evolution of random graphs. Publications of the Mathematical Institute of the Hungarian Academy of Sciences 5, 17–61 (1960)

20. Kaashoek, M.F., Karger, D.R.: Koorde: A simple degree-optimal distributed hash table. In: Kaashoek, M.F., Stoica, I. (eds.) IPTPS 2003. LNCS, vol. 2735, pp. 98–107. Springer, Heidelberg (2003)

# Foraging for Better Deployment of Replicated Service Components

Máté J. Csorba[1], Hein Meling[2], Poul E. Heegaard[1], and Peter Herrmann[1]

[1] Department of Telematics,
Norwegian University of Science and Technology, N-7491 Trondheim, Norway
{Mate.Csorba,Poul.Heegaard,Peter.Herrmann}@item.ntnu.no
[2] Department of Electrical Engineering and Computer Science,
University of Stavanger, N-4036 Stavanger, Norway
hein.meling@uis.no

**Abstract.** Our work focuses on distributed software services and their requirements in terms of system performance and dependability. We target the problem
of finding optimal deployment mappings involving multiple services, i.e. mapping service components in the software architecture to the underlying platforms
for best possible execution. We capture important non-functional requirements
of distributed services, regarding performance and dependability. These models
are then used to construct appropriate cost functions that will guide our heuristic
optimization method to provide better deployment mappings for service components. This paper mainly focuses on dependability. In particular, a logic enabling
replication management and deployment for increased dependability is presented.
To demonstrate the feasibility of our approach, we model a scenario with 15 services each with different redundancy levels deployed over a 10-node network.
We show by simulation how the deployment logic proposed is capable to satisfy
replica deployment requirements.

## 1 Introduction

Distributed applications and services are increasingly being hosted by infrastructure
providers over virtualized architectures, enabling on-demand resource scaling, such as
in the Amazon EC2 platform [1]. An important concern in such platforms is the problem of *finding optimal deployment mappings* involving multiple services spread across
multiple sites. During service execution a plethora of parameters influence the optimal
deployment mapping, and more so in a distributed environment where concurrent services influence each other as well. Furthermore, some applications have non-functional
requirements related to dependability, such as fault tolerance and high availability. Up-
holding such requirements demands replication protocols to ensure consistency, but
also adds additional complexity to the optimization problem. Ideally, the deployment
mappings should minimize the resource consumption, yet provide enough resources to
satisfy the dependability requirements of services.

This paper presents a novel modeling and optimization methodology for deployment
of replicated service components. We model services in a platform independent manner

T. Senivongse and R. Oliveira (Eds.): DAIS 2009, LNCS 5523, pp. 87–101, 2009.

using the SPACE [3] methodology. As previously shown by Fernandez-Baca [4], the general module allocation problem is NP-complete except for certain communication configurations, thus heuristics are required to obtain solutions efficiently. Based on our service models, we apply an heuristic optimization method called the Cross-Entropy Ant System (CEAS) [5], which is able to take multiple parameters into account when making a decision on the deployment mapping. The approach also enables us to perform optimizations in a decentralized manner, where replicated services can be deployed from anywhere within the system, avoiding the need for a centralized control for maintaining information about services and their deployment.

There are a number of reasons to develop replicated services, including fault tolerance, high availability and load balancing. This work focuses on fault tolerance and availability, and in this context, the objective is to improve the availability characteristics of the service by appropriate allocation of service replicas to nodes, such that the impact of replica failures and network failures is reduced. And at the same time minimizing the resource consumption.

Generally, to support replicated services the underlying architecture needs to provide *replication protocols* to ensure consistency between replicas, e.g., active or passive replication protocols [16,2]. Such protocols have different implicit communication and computation costs and can be taken into account in our model. In addition, a *replication management* infrastructure, e.g. [11,10,9], is necessary to support deployment of replicas and managing reconfigurations when failures occur. One example is the distributed autonomous replication management framework (DARM) [9]. DARM focuses on the deployment and operational aspects of the system, where the gain in terms of improved dependability is likely to be the greatest. DARM is equipped with mechanisms for localizing failures and system reconfiguration. Reconfiguration is handled without any human intervention, and according to application-specific dependability requirements. The benefits of DARM are twofold: (i) the cost of deploying and managing highly available applications can be significantly reduced, and (ii) its dependability characteristics can be improved as shown in [6]. The approach presented in this paper can be combined with frameworks such as DARM in order to improve the deployment mapping operation; such an implementation has been left as future work.

There are at least three cases where finding suitable deployment mappings are of significance to replication management: (i) initial deployment of replicas according to some policy; (ii) reconfiguration of deployed replicas that have failed or become unavailable due to a network partition according to some maintenance policy; (iii) migration of replicas to re-balance the system load. The deployment mapping policy used in this paper, is formulated as a cost function to the optimization problem, essentially stating that replicas should be placed on nodes and domains (sites) so as to improve the dependability of the service being deployed.

The paper is organized as follows. The next section presents how replicas are modeled in the SPACE modeling framework. Sec. 3 introduces CEAS and provides a description of the deployment algorithm. Subsequently, we formulate the optimization problem and present cost functions used to solve it. Simulation results using our logic are presented in Sec. 5. Finally, in Sec. 6 we conclude and touch upon future work.

## 2    Replica Services in SPACE

To account for dependability requirements while deploying replicated service components, collaboration-oriented models can be used. To this end, the SPACE [3] methodology provides a modeling technique for automated engineering of distributed applications. In contrast to other UML-based methods, it enables the composition of system descriptions from collaboration-oriented sub-models that does not specify the behavior of a single physical component, but rather describes the sub-functionality encompassing various system entities. Such sub-models are typically easier to reuse than component-oriented building blocks, since different systems in a particular do-main often have similar sub-functions, which can be coupled in various ways. Each sub-function can then easily be specified as a collaborative building block once, and thus the creation of a new system can be reduced to the design of a new combination of these pre-defined blocks.

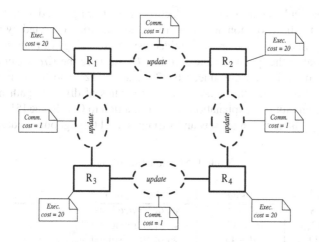

**Fig. 1.** Example service, $S1$ with 4 replicas and corresponding costs

In SPACE, the topology of a system is modeled with UML collaborations, while be-havior is described using UML activities. SPACE is accompanied by the Arctis [7] tool, which enables composition of models, various model checker-based correctness proofs and automated transformation to executable Java code.

In this paper, only UML collaborations are used. Fig. 1 depicts a simple example model. It describes the pair-wise replication of data between the physical components $R_1$ to $R_4$. The updating function is modeled by four collaboration uses called *update*, each specifying the alignment of data between the two linked components. Although SPACE offers specification of multiple instances of a collaboration [8], for clarity only four instances of *update* are used here. SPACE models can be embellished with ad-ditional non-functional requirements that can be exploited by our deployment logic, i.e., the execution costs assigned to components or costs that are specific to each col-laboration between replicas. Within a given service specification, some (or all) of the service components might require replication to improve their dependability. We propose to model and specify component replication using the same methodology applied for designing the services themselves. In other words, we specify a set of replicas related to a specific component separately, i.e. as a collaboration of replicas of a single component.

To test our deployment logic, we assume an active replication approach, where each replica of the service performs according to the client requests. Thus, replicas have the same execution cost. Each replica is also assigned a communication (collaboration) cost to account for the cost of ensuring consistency (state updates) between replicas. The example scenario illustrated in Fig. 1 is used as a basis for the simulations presented in Sec. 5.

## 3   Replica Deployment Using the Cross Entropy Ant System

To find suitable replica placements a collection of ant-like agents, denoted *ants*, search iteratively for the best solution according to a cost function, restricted by the problem constraints. To find a solution ants are guided using the analogy of *pheromones*, which are proportional to the quality of the solution. CEAS uses the *Cross Entropy method* for stochastic optimization introduced by Rubinstein [12], and has demonstrated its capabilities and relevance through a variety of studies of different path management strategies. For an intuitive explanation and introduction to CEAS, see [5].

Table 1 gives the notation for sets and variables used throughout our description.

**Table 1.** Notational shorthand

| Shorthand | Usage | Description |
|---|---|---|
| $\mathbf{S}$ | $S_k \in \mathbf{S}$ | set of service instances |
| $\mathbf{C}_k$ | $c_i \in \mathbf{C}_k$ | set of all replicas in $S_k$ |
| $\mathbf{D}$ | $d \in \mathbf{D}$ | set of all existing domains |
| $\mathbf{N}$ | $n \in \mathbf{N}$ | set of all existing nodes |
| $|\mathbf{C}_k|$ | $|\mathbf{C}_k|$ | number of replicas to be deployed |
| $D_r$ | $d \in D_r$ | list of domains used in deployment of $S_k$ |
| $N_r$ | $n \in N_r$ | list of nodes used in deployment of $S_k$ |
| $NL_r$ | $nl_{n,r} \in NL_r$ | load-level samples for $S_k$ |
| $M_r$ | $m_{n,r} \in M_r$ | mapping list for $S_k$ |
| $H_r$ | $n \in H_r$ | hop-list for $S_k$ |

In this paper, we apply CEAS to obtain the best mapping of a set of replicas onto a set of nodes, $M : \mathbf{C} \rightarrow \mathbf{N}$. The pheromone values used by the ants, denoted $\tau_{mn,r}$, correspond to a set of replicas, $m$ mapped to node $n$ at iteration $r$. Ants use a random proportional rule for selecting the individual mappings.

$$p_{mn,r} = \frac{\tau_{mn,r}}{\sum_{l \in M_{n,r}} \tau_{ln,r}} \qquad (1)$$

The pheromone values $\tau_{mn,r}$ in (1) are updated continuously by the ants as follows:

$$\tau_{mn,r} = \sum_{k=1}^{r} I(l \in M_{n,r})\beta^{\sum_{j=k+1}^{r} I(j \in M_k)} H(F(M_k), \gamma_r) \tag{2}$$

where $I(x) = 1$ if $x$ is true, 0 otherwise. See [5] for further details.

A parameter $\gamma_r$ denoted the *temperature*, controls the update of the pheromone values and is chosen to minimize the performance function

$$H(F(M_r), \gamma_r) = e^{-F(M_r)/\gamma_r} \tag{3}$$

which is applied to all $r$ samples.

To enable a distributed optimization process the cost of a mapping, $F(M_r)$ is calculated *immediately* after each sample i.e., when all replicas are mapped, and an autoregressive performance function, $h_r(\gamma_r)$ is applied, Eq. 4.

$$h_r(\gamma_r) \approx \frac{1 - \beta}{1 - \beta^r} \sum_{i=1}^{r} \beta^{r-i} H(F(M_r), \gamma_r) \tag{4}$$

where $\beta \in \langle 0, 1 \rangle$ is a *memory factor* weighting (geometrically) the output of the performance function. This mechanism smooths variations in the cost function, hence rapid changes in the deployment mapping and undesirable fluctuations can be avoided. The temperature, $\gamma_r$ is determined by minimizing it subject to $h(\gamma) \geq \rho$, thus

$$\gamma_r = \{\gamma \mid \frac{1 - \beta}{1 - \beta^r} \sum_{i=1}^{r} \beta^{r-i} H(F(M_i), \gamma) = \rho\} \tag{5}$$

where $\rho$ is a parameter (denoted *search focus*) close to 0 (typically 0.05 or less).

Eq. (5) is a transcendental function that is storage and processing intensive since all observations up to the current sample, i.e., the entire mapping cost history $F(M_r), \forall r$ should be stored, and weights for all observations would have to be recalculated, thus putting an impractical burden on the on-line operation of the logic. Accordingly, we assume that, given a $\beta$ close to 1, changes in $\gamma_r$ are typically small from one iteration to the next, enabling a first order Taylor expansion of (5), and a second order Taylor expansion of (2), see [5] for more details. More importantly, we are able to obtain an optimal deployment mapping with high confidence, since CEAS can be considered as a subclass of Ant Colony Optimization (ACO) algorithms [13], which have been proven to be able to find the optimum at least once with probability close to one. Once the optimum has been found, convergence is secured in a finite number of iterations.

We now present the steps executed by the deployment logic to obtain a mapping of replicas. Behavior of the logic is separated into Algorithm 1, which describes the simple functionality of a *Nest*, i.e. basic additional intelligence in one of the nodes, and Algorithm 2, which describes the behavior of the ants that are subsequently emitted from the *Nest*. The role of a *Nest* can be played by an arbitrary node. The steps are executed independently by ants of each species, where a species is directly involved in the deployment of a specific service. Each ant initiated from the nest node of a species is assigned a set of replicas, **C**; in this case the replica instances to deploy. The ant then

---

**Algorithm 1.** Code for $Nest_k$

---

1: Initialization:
2:     $r \leftarrow 0$                                          *{Number of iterations}*
3:     $\gamma_r \leftarrow 0$                                    *{Temperature}*

4: **while** $r < R$                                      *{Stopping criteria}*
5:     $antAlgo(r, \gamma_r)$                            *{Emit new ant}*
6:     $r \leftarrow r + 1$

---

starts a random-walk in the network, selecting the next hop at random. Behavior at a node depends on if the ant is an *explorer* or a *normal* ant. *Normal* ants select a subset of **C** for mapping to the current node according to the pheromone database and store this selection in the mapping list, $M_r$. An *explorer* ant, however does the selection without using the pheromone values in a completely random manner.

The benefits of applying *explorer* ants are twofold, first they initially explore the solution space and second, they are used for faster discovery of changes in the network during optimization. In both cases, *explorers* do not use the pheromone tables, instead they build up an initial database. Besides, they are used to detect alternative solutions while the system undergoes short- or long-term changes. The amount of *explorer* vs. *normal* ants is a configurable ratio parameter to the logic. Initial exploration is essentially a random sampling of the problem space and the number of iterations depends on the problem size. However, the end of this phase can be detected by monitoring the pheromone database size. Optimizing the deployment mappings based on the available cost functions should be performed using a distributed method, avoiding a centralized structure. To do so, each node provides a processing power reservation mechanism. Ant species use this mechanism to indicate their resource usage in every node they utilize for their replicas. Processing power reservation can be updated by a given percentage of ants, which is again a parameter to the logic, i.e., only a certain fraction (e.g. 10%) of iterations result in re-allocation at the nodes, see Lines 18 − 21 in Algorithm 2. Outdated allocations get invalidated in the nodes to preserve consistency. In addition, the allocation mechanism can serve as a means of interaction between the species. Thus, the current sum of allocations in a node can be sampled providing a general overview for the ants. These load-level samples are denoted $NL_r$. The decreased ratio of reservations by the ants (e.g. only 10% of them) contributes to obtaining a smoother series of $NL_r$ samples. The actual implementation of sampling is left to the middleware.

The *forward search* phase of an ant is over when all component replicas are mapped and the resulting mapping is stored in $M_r$. The algorithm proceeds with evaluating the resulting mapping using the appropriate cost function $F_i()$. After evaluating the cost of the mapping, the ant *backtracks* to its nest using the hop-list, $H_r$. During *backtracking*, pheromone values distributed across the network of nodes are updated according to Eq. (2). After the ant finds its way back to the nest node or times out a new ant can be initiated and emitted. The same behavior can be used for all ants, even though they are of different species.

The main purpose of the pheromone database is its usage in Algorithm 2, Line 13. In every iteration, an ant will form $|N_r|$ discrete subsets of **C** as it visits $n \subseteq N_r$ nodes.

**Algorithm 2.** Ant code for deployment mapping of component replicas $\mathbf{C} \in S_k \subset \mathbf{S}$ from $Nest_k$

```
 1: Initialization:
 2:     H_r ← ∅                                          {Hop-list; insertion-ordered set}
 3:     M_r ← ∅                                          {Deployment mapping set}
 4:     D_r ← ∅                                          {Set of utilized domains}
 5:     NL_r ← ∅                                         {Set of load samples}

 6: function antAlgo(r, k)
 7:     γ_r ← Nest_k.getTemperature()                   {Read the current temperature}
 8:     while C ≠ ∅                                      {More replicas to deploy}
 9:         n ← selectNextNode()                        {Select first node}
10:         if explorer ant
11:             m_{n,r} ← random(⊆ C)        {Explorer ant; randomly select a set of replicas}
12:         else
13:             m_{n,r} ← rndProp(⊆ C)       {Normal ant; select replicas according to Eq. (1)}
14:         if {m_{n,r}} ≠ ∅, n ∈ d_k            {At least one replica mapped to this domain}
15:             D_r ← D_r ∪ d_k                          {Update the set of domains utilized}
16:             M_r ← M_r ∪ {m_{n,r}}                    {Update the ant's deployment mapping set}
17:             C ← C − {m_{n,r}}                        {Update the set of replicas to be deployed}
18:             if r mod 10 = 0                          {Only every 10th ant modifies allocations}
19:                 foreach c_i ∈ m_{n,r}
20:                     sumpp ← sumpp + f_{c_i}          {Sum the exec. costs imposed by S_k}
21:                     n.reallocProcLoad(S_k, sumpp)    {(re-)allocate processing power needed by S_k}
22:                     nl_{n,r} ← n.getEstProcLoad()    {Get the estimated processing load at node n}
23:                     NL_r ← NL_r ∪ {nl_{n,r}}         {Add to the list of samples}

24:         cost ← F(M_r, D_r, NL_r)                     {Parameters depending on the cost function}
25:         γ_r ← updateTemp(cost)      {Given cost, recalculate temperature according to Eq. (5)}
26:         foreach n ∈ H_r.reverse()                    {Backtrack along the hop-list}
27:             n.updatePheromone(m_{n,r}, γ_r)          {Update pheromone value at n, Eq. (2)}
28:     Nest_k.setTemperature(γ_r)                       {Update γ_r at Nest_k}

29: function selectNextNode()                           {SELECT UNIQUE RANDOM NODE}
30:     R ← N − currentNode                             {Set of candidate nodes for ant traversal}
31:     n ← random(R)                                   {Select candidate node at random}
32:     H_r ← H_r ∪ {n}                                 {Add node to the hop-list}
33:     return n
```

In order to be able to describe replica mappings to nodes, values of the pheromone database have to be aligned with replica sets. Accordingly, the pheromone database is built by assigning a flag to every replica available for deployment in a service, $\forall c_i \in \mathbf{C}$, with the exception of replicas that are bound to specific nodes explicitly by requirements and thus, they cannot be moved.

The pheromone database will contain $2^{|C|}$ elements, equal to the number of possible combinations for a set $c_i$ at a node, which is specific for each service. This determines a physical requirement for the execution platform that supports our logic, namely to be able to accommodate $2^{|C|}$ floating point numbers for each of the services in every node. If the pheromone database in a node is normalized between $\{0 \dots 1\}$ it can be observed as a probability distribution of replica sets mapped to that node. In a converged state the optimal solution(s) will emerge with probability one.

## 4   Construction of the Cost Function

When applying the optimization method presented in Sec. 3 it is essential to formulate a proper cost function aimed at guiding the optimization process towards an *appropriate solution*. An *appropriate solution* is a solution to the deployment mapping problem satisfying the system requirements, $F_{req}$ derived from the service specification, while accounting for the costs of the mapping, $F_i()$. Trying to find a global optimal solution does not make much sense in the systems considered here, as the solution would most likely be suboptimal by the time, the optimal mapping could be applied. However, the algorithm can continue optimization even after a feasible mapping is found, that can trigger (re-)deployment of replicas. By optimal mapping we mean mappings with the lowest possible cost, while for a feasible mapping $F_i() < F_{req}$ is enough. Note that the formulation of the deployment problem below is independent of the methods we apply to obtain a solution.

$$\boxed{\begin{aligned} &\min F_i() \quad \{< F_{req}\} \\ &\text{subject to } \varPhi \end{aligned}}$$

In each iteration of our deployment logic, the cost function is evaluated for every suggested mapping, $m_{n,r}$, (cf. Algorithm 2, Line 24). Properties of this function impact the quality of the solutions obtained as well as the convergence time, or in other words, the number of iterations required to reach a stable solution. In order to develop a logic that can aid replica deployment and increase dependability by influencing the mapping of software architecture the cost function has to be carefully selected. However, what is the proper function to use depends on the requirements and goals of the service. Here, we target efficient placement of component replicas in an active replication scheme aimed at improving the dependability.

We define the mapping functions $f_k$ and $g_{k,d}$ as follows.

**Definition 1.**   *Let $f_k \colon r_k \to d$ be the mapping of replica $r_k$ to domain $d \in \mathbf{D}$*

**Definition 2.**   *Let $g_{k,d} \colon r_k \to n_d$ be the mapping of replica $r_k$ to node $n_d \in \mathbf{N}$ in domain $d \in \mathbf{D}$*

We then define two distinct rules that the deployment logic targets. The first one states that replicas shall be distributed across as many domains as possible for increased dependability, i.e. two replicas of the same service shall not be placed in the same domain preferably, or if there are more replicas than domains available there shall be at least one replica in all domains ($\phi_1$).

**Rule 1.**    $\phi_1 : f_k \neq f_l \iff k \neq l \wedge |S_k| < |\mathbf{D}|$

Whereas the other rule declares that two replicas of the same service should not be co-located on the same node ($\phi_2$).

**Rule 2.**    $\phi_2 : g_{k,d} \neq g_{l,d} \iff k \neq l, \forall d$

Deployment mappings of component replicas can be evaluated by the deployment cost function $F_i()$. Accordingly, we formulate the replica deployment problem as the task of minimizing $F_i()$ subject to $\Phi = \phi_1 \wedge \phi_2$.

The problem of producing deployment mappings that conform to the rules introduced above is approached step-wise by introducing different types of cost functions. We start by considering $\phi_1$ only and use information collected by the ant species during *forward search* by counting the number of domains that have been used to map replicas at an iteration, this variable will be denoted $D_r$. Using $D_r$ we will experiment with a reciprocal (6) and a linear function (7) too. The latter case uses the number of replicas, $|\mathbf{C}|$, a constant derived from the service model and thus known to each species.

$$F_1(D_r) = \frac{1}{|D_r|} \tag{6}$$

$$F_2(D_r, \mathbf{C}) = |\mathbf{C}| - |D_r| + 1 \tag{7}$$

Similarly, we include $\phi_2$ into the cost function by a reciprocal and a linear function and combine it with (6) and (7) as follows.

$$F_3(D_r, N_r) = \frac{1}{|D_r|} \cdot \frac{1}{|N_r|} \tag{8}$$

$$F_4(D_r, N_r, \mathbf{C}) = (|\mathbf{C}| - |D_r| + 1) \cdot (|\mathbf{C}| - |N_r| + 1) \tag{9}$$

$$F_5(D_r, N_r, \mathbf{C}) = \frac{1}{|D_r|} \cdot (|\mathbf{C}| - |N_r| + 1) \tag{10}$$

$$F_6(D_r, N_r, \mathbf{C}) = (|\mathbf{C}| - |D_r| + 1) \cdot \frac{1}{|N_r|} \tag{11}$$

In (8)-(11) we utilize a variable, $N_r$, which denotes the number of nodes that have been used by a specific species for deploying replicas at iteration $r$, this is also reported by each ant during the *forward search* phase. We evaluate all four possible combinations of the reciprocal and linear functions targeting $\phi_1$ and $\phi_2$.

The last combination of cost functions, in (12), is a combination of the simple reciprocal function in (6) targeting $\phi_1$ combined with a more complex function used successfully in service component deployment [14].

$$F_7(D_r, M_r, NL_r) = \frac{1}{|D_r|} \cdot F_{lb}(M_r, NL_r) \tag{12}$$

$F_{lb}$ uses two parameters that are updated in every iteration, the replica mapping set $M_r$ and the load-level samples taken in the nodes visited by the ant ($n_j \in H_r$), denoted $NL_r$. This function accounts for the execution and communication costs derived from the service specification as introduced in Sec. 2. Correspondingly, the function consists of two main parts, node ($NC$) and collaboration related costs ($LC$).

$$F_{lb}(M_r, NL_r) = [ \sum_{\forall n_j \in H_r} NC(n_j)] \cdot (1 + x \cdot LC) \tag{13}$$

where $x$ is a parameter used to balance the effect of the $LC$ term, as needed. The component $LC$ is strictly local to each species and incorporates the collaboration costs

$$LC(M_r) = \sum_{j=1}^{K} I_j \, f_{k_j}; \text{ where } I_j = \begin{cases} 1, \text{ if } Collab_k \text{ external} \\ 0, \text{ if } Collab_k \text{ internal to a node} \end{cases} \tag{14}$$

Thus, the term $LC$ will take into account communication costs ($f_{k_j}$) assigned to those collaborations that happen between different nodes only, in other words aiming at minimizing remote communication.

Costs related to execution of replicas, i.e., node local costs are incorporated into the first term in (13). Node local costs aim at achieving load-balancing among the nodes hosting replicas. Importantly, in this term only the subset of nodes an ant has actually visited ($H_r$) is taken into account, not the total amount of nodes. The term that is calculated individually for each of the nodes in $H_r$ is shown in (15).

$$NC_{n_j}(NL_{n,r}) = [ \sum_{i=0}^{NL_{n,r}(n_j)} \frac{1}{\sum_{\forall n_j \in H_r} NL_{n,r} + 1 - i}]^y \tag{15}$$

The term $NC$ counteracts the other term in (13), $LC$, which puts weight on replica mappings that have as much as possible of the collaborations within the same node(s). $NC$ has an effect of distributing replicas, thus equalizing execution load among the available nodes to the highest extent possible. This way two counteracting requirement types are tackled in the same function. The exponent $y$ in (15) can shift the focus towards load-balancing against minimization of remote communication in collaborations. In the experiments in this paper we use $x = 10^{-5}$ and $y = 2$, which are adjusted to the cost values derived from the models, e.g. see the example service in Fig. 1.

Using $F_{lb}$ we are able to smoothen the output of the cost evaluation executed for each iteration of the deployment logic. Its purpose is to ease convergence of the logic by making the solution space more fine grained, i.e. simplifying differentiation between very similar deployment mappings with nearly the same cost value.

The next section presents simulation results evaluating all the cost functions presented here using an example setup.

## 5   Simulation Results

To evaluate our approach and the proposed cost functions, we developed a test scenario. The scenario consists of a network of 10 identical nodes clustered into 5 domains (cf. Fig. 2). The 5 domains have 3, 2, 1, 1, 3 nodes. Using this network of nodes, each ant species executing Algorithm 2 is assigned a replica service for deployment. A set of 15 actively replicated services with redundancy levels shown in Table 2 is used for the evaluation.

**Table 2.** Service instances in the example

| Service | $S_1$ | $S_2$ | $S_3$ | $S_4$ | $S_5$ | $S_6$ | $S_7$ | $S_8$ | $S_9$ | $S_{10}$ | $S_{11}$ | $S_{12}$ | $S_{13}$ | $S_{14}$ | $S_{15}$ |
|---|---|---|---|---|---|---|---|---|---|---|---|---|---|---|---|
| #replicas | 4 | 6 | 4 | 4 | 4 | 5 | 5 | 6 | 6 | 6 | 6 | 7 | 8 | 9 | 10 |

For example, see $S1$ in Fig. 1. Each replica within a service has identical execution cost, and all replicas have the same cost in all services. Similarly, the same is true for the communication costs, i.e. $f_{c_i} = 20, \forall i$ and $f_{k_j} = 1, \forall j$.

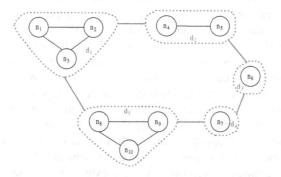

**Fig. 2.** Test network of hosts clustered into 5 domains

For the evaluation scenario with $S_1 \ldots S_{15}$, the deployment logic (Algorithm 2) is executed 50 times using the cost functions discussed in Sec. 4 and we compare their behavior. The deployment logic was described by a process-oriented simulation model implemented in Simula/DEMOS [15].

For the problem at hand, deploying replicas of each service yield $\mathbf{N}^{C_k}$ mapping combinations; deploying all 15 services simultaneously would account for an exhaustive search of $\mathbf{N}^{\Sigma\, C_k} = 10^{90}$ possible configurations. For the evaluation, the execution of Algorithm 2 was limited to $r_{max} = 30000$ iterations (significantly smaller than exhaustive search), unless convergence is obtained earlier. All 15 species, one for each service, were executed simultaneously. This is in accordance with our goal to find an appropriate solution within reasonable time, even though it may not be the optimal mapping. After each run, the obtained deployment mapping was checked against $\phi_1$ and $\phi_2$. Results for selected functions are presented in Table 3.

In case of $F_1(D_r)$, which is based on observing the number of domains ($D_r$) utilized for deployment mapping of replicas, $\phi_2$ (cf. Sec. 4) is not checked because the cost function does not consider this rule. From the 50 independent runs we see that in some cases $\phi_1$ is not satisfied; some of the 15 services fail to utilize as many domains as they could. That is due to the limited number of iterations we allowed for the species to

**Table 3.** Replication rules satisfied, 50 trials each

| Cost function | $\phi_1$ | $\phi_2$ | Comments |
|---|---|---|---|
| $F_1(D_r)$ | 88% | n/a | all due to no convergence |
| $F_5(D_r, N_r, \mathbf{C})$ | 100% | 96% | all due to no convergence |
| $F_7(D_r, M_r, NL_r)$ | 100% | 98% | all converged |

achieve convergence and because this cost function is very simple, i.e. lacking a more smooth, more fine grained evaluation of the deployment mappings for the ant species.

In the second branch of cost functions, Eq. (8)–(11), we apply two very simple functions together to take into account $\phi_1$ and $\phi_2$ at the same time. The experiments show that the combination of two functions of the same kind, i.e. two linear or two reciprocal functions, gives inferior results to applying a combination of one reciprocal and a linear. This might be caused by smoother cost output in case of the latter, which results in better convergence and better solution quality, i.e. a deployment mapping that satisfies the requirements with a higher probability. Nevertheless, there were 2 violations of $\phi_2$ within the 50 runs, that means that one replica was co-located with another in one of the services. This is possible for services that have a high number of replicas, e.g. 9 or 10, which easily occupy 5 domains, thus obtain the lowest cost possible considering the first part of the cost function resulting in a mapping that violates $\phi_2$ after convergence. These services, with these simple cost functions are able to decrease their mapping costs only marginally by spreading their replicas further among the available hosts, which results in sub-optimal solutions, thus violations of $\phi_1$ or $\phi_2$.

Now, if we look at the last combination of functions in Table 3, we can see how our load-balancing function performed with the extension of taking into account the number of domains utilized ($D_r$). From the 50 independent runs the deployment logic converged to a stable solution in all of the cases. $\phi_1$ was successfully taken into account by the first reciprocal term and resulted in no violations. In one case however, one of the services failed to satisfy $\phi_2$, i.e. a replica was co-located with another one. After a closer look we can see that this involved service $S_{15}$ comprising 10 replicas. The reason for this violation is that the load-balancing function, $F_{lb}(M_r, NL_r)$, has enforced a deployment mapping, which was better for global load-balancing in this particular case by taking into account this global goal to a greater extent and thus, violating the rule prohibiting co-location of replicas. However, as in $S_{15}$ the number of replicas is equal to the number of available nodes there is not much space left for the logic to place replicas so that load-balancing is also achieved, which is the main goal for this part of the cost function. Clearly, applying the cost function we propose implies taking a broader view on the deployment problem. The tradeoff might be that under certain circumstances the mapping of replicas might violate one of the rules formulated, but the gain is that we can obtain a globally better and more effective mapping, still using a fully distributed logic and doing so faster, i.e. within reasonable time.

To get a picture of how replicas are mapped to the underlying nodes clustered into domains one of the possible mappings is depicted in Fig. 3, in which each slice of the pie diagram corresponds to a specific service $S_k \subset \mathbf{S}$. As in this optimal mapping there is no co-location of replicas, a slice being shaded means that there is a single replica

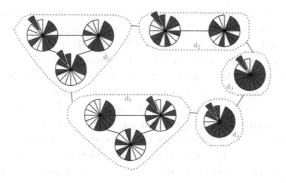

**Fig. 3.** Example mapping of replicas in $S_1 \ldots SS_{15}$, with $S_2$ exploded

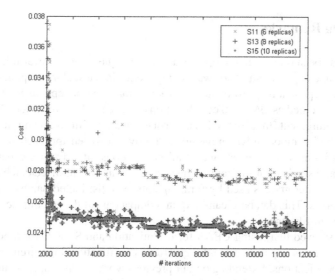

**Fig. 4.** Costs with 6, 8 and 10 replicas

placed on the particular node. It is easy to notice that the two domains consisting of a single node ($d_3$, $d_4$) are heavily packed with replicas due to the fact that there are many services, which can exploit 5 domains or more. This makes overall load-balancing among the available nodes more difficult.

Furthermore, to illustrate the behavior and convergence of our logic, in Fig. 4 we look at the cost output of some species that guides the mapping of replicas as a function of number of iterations.

The three services presented have 6 ($S_{11}$), 8 ($S_{13}$) and 10 ($S_{15}$) replicas to deploy. The first 2000 iterations, i.e. the *exploration phase* is not shown in the figure. After 2000 initial iterations optimization continues and the cost values decrease, thus indicating increasingly improved mapping of replica components. We stop the simulation where the costs do not improve anymore, in this particular case after approximately 10000 additional iterations. By checking $\phi_1$ and $\phi_2$ we can see that the mapping obtained in this run satisfies both. In case where the number of replicas is high, e.g. 10, values do not deteriorate too much from a consensus level between the parallel species (considering $N = 10$) as $\phi_1$ restricts the solution space. That means that for service $S_{15}$ all of the nodes have to host one replica according to the rule. Whereas services with less replicas to deploy have a significantly larger valid solution space, i.e. service $S_{11}$ and $S_{13}$ find, in some cases, a solution satisfying $\phi_1$ and $\phi_2$ but with a higher overall cost, thus we can see some deviations in the cost output in the figure before obtaining convergence. After consensus is reached among the species the actual deployment of component replicas can be triggered. Practically, when a species detects that the cost values obtained by its ants are stable over a period of time, replicas corresponding to this species can be (re-)deployed. The technical solution as well as the protocol of replica placement/re-deployment is, however, left to the middleware (e.g., DARM).

## 6  Closing Remarks

Our focus has been on a heuristic optimization technique aided by swarm intelligence that can manage deployment of software components, in particular component replicas for increased dependability. To obtain an efficient mapping of replicas we utilize service models specified as UML 2.0 collaborations. These models are enriched with non-functional requirements that are used in the cost evaluation of the mappings made by the deployment logic. Importantly, our method is a fully distributed approach, thus it is free of discrepancies most of the existing centralized solutions suffer from, e.g. performance bottlenecks and single points of failure. Instead of having a centralized database we use the analogy of pheromones used by foraging ants as a distributed database across the network of hosts. This database can be quite compact as all the intelligence is carried along by the ant-like agents.

We have showed that, using CEAS for optimization and SPACE for modeling, the deployment logic is capable of handling various non-functional requirements present in service specifications. Extending on our previous work, in this paper focus has been on how the logic can deal with basic dependability requirements concerning replication management. Eventually, our goal is to aid run-time (re-)deployment and replication of software components while considering the execution environment and satisfying the requirements of the service.

For future work we plan to introduce new types of species corresponding to user demands towards the services being deployed. However, this will introduce new challenges as it will increase the dimensions of the deployment problem significantly. More fine grained cost modeling, e.g. passive replication, with costs dependent on replica attributes will be part of future investigations. This will also involve more extensive simulations with new experimental settings. Larger network sizes will also be investigated together with their impact on convergence and scalability. Another interesting aspect we will experiment with is how splitting/merging of domains influences the output of our logic, besides assessing what level of node churn can be tolerated by our method. Generally, context-aware adaptation is considered one of the main tracks we follow in our future work.

# References

1. Amazon Elastic Compute Cloud, http://aws.amazon.com/ecs2
2. Budhiraja, N., Marzullo, K., Schneider, F.B., Toueg, S.: The Primary-Backup Approach. In: Mullender, S. (ed.) Distributed Systems, 2nd edn., ch. 8, pp. 199–216. Addison-Wesley, Reading (1994)
3. Kraemer, F.A., Herrmann, P.: Service Specification by Composition of Collaborations - An Example. In: Proc. IEEE/WIC/ACM Int'l Conference on Web Intelligence, Int'l Workshop on Service Composition (Sercomp 2006), Hong Kong, pp. 129–133. IEEE CS, Los Alamitos (2006)
4. Fernandez-Baca, D.: Allocating modules to processors in a distributed system. IEEE Transactions on Software Engineering 15(11) (1989)
5. Heegaard, P.E., Helvik, B.E., Wittner, O.J.: The Cross Entropy Ant System for Network Path Management. Telektronikk 104(01), 19–40 (2008)
6. Helvik, B.E., Meling, H., Montresor, A.: An Approach to Experimentally Obtain Service Dependability Characteristics of the Jgroup/ARM System. In: Dal Cin, M., Kaâniche, M., Pataricza, A. (eds.) EDCC 2005. LNCS, vol. 3463, pp. 179–198. Springer, Heidelberg (2005)
7. Kraemer, F.A., Bræk, R., Herrmann, P.: Compositional Service Engineering with Arctis. Telektronikk (to appear, 2009)
8. Kraemer, F.A., Bræk, R., Herrmann, P.: Synthesizing Components with Sessions from Collaboration-Oriented Service Specications. In: Gaudin, E., Najm, E., Reed, R. (eds.) SDL 2007. LNCS, vol. 4745, pp. 166–185. Springer, Heidelberg (2007)
9. Meling, H., Gilje, J.L.: A Distributed Approach to Autonomous Fault Treatment in Spread. In: Proc. 7th European Dependable Computing Conference. IEEE CS, Los Alamitos (2008)
10. Meling, H., Montresor, A., Helvik, B.E., Babaoglu, O.: Jgroup/ARM: a distributed object group platform with autonomous replication management. Software: Practice and Experience 38(9), 885–923 (2008)
11. OMG. Fault Tolerant CORBA Specification. OMG Document ptc/00-04-04 (April 2000)
12. Rubinstein, R.Y.: The Cross-Entropy Method for Combinatorial and Continuous Optimization. Methodology and Computing in Applied Probability (1999)
13. Dorigo, M., et al.: The Ant System: Optimization by a colony of cooperating agents. IEEE Transactions on Systems, Man, and Cybernetics Part B: Cybernetics 26(1) (1996)
14. Csorba, M.J., Heegaard, P.E., Herrmann, P.: Adaptable model-based component deployment guided by artificial ants. In: Proc. 2nd Int'l Conf. on Autonomic Computing and Communication Systems (Autonomics), ICST/ACM, Turin (September 2008)
15. Birtwistle, G.: Demos - a system for discrete event modelling on simula (1997)
16. Schneider, F.B.: Replicated Management using the State-Machine Approach. In: Mullender, S. (ed.) Distributed Systems, 2nd edn., ch. 7, pp. 169–198. Addison-Wesley, Reading (1994)

# A Generic Group Communication Approach for Hybrid Distributed Systems

Raimundo José de Araújo Macêdo[1] and Allan Edgard Silva Freitas[1,2]

[1] Distributed Systems Laboratory (LaSiD)
Computer Science Department
Federal University of Bahia
Campus de Ondina, Salvador, Bahia, Brazil
[2] Federal Institute of Bahia
Campus de Salvador, Salvador, Bahia, Brazil
macedo@ufba.br, allan@ifba.edu.br

**Abstract.** Group Communication is a powerful abstraction that is being widely used to manage consistency problems in a variety of distributed system models, ranging from synchronous, to time-free asynchronous model. Though similar in principles, distinct implementation mechanisms have been employed in the design of group communication for distinct system models. However, the hybrid nature of many modern distributed systems, with dynamic and varied QoS guarantees, has put forward the need for integrated models. Furthermore, adaptation with degraded service is a common requirement in such scenarios. This paper tackles this new challenge by introducing a generic group communication mechanism. Because of its integrated feature, our approach is capable of handling group communication for both synchronous and asynchronous distributed systems, dynamically adapting to the available QoS. For example, it can dynamically switch to the asynchronous version when the run-time system can no longer guarantee a timely operation. The properties and algorithms of the integrated approach are presented in this paper, as well as a performance evaluation through simulation, comparing this mechanism with some classical approaches.

## 1 Introduction

It is widely recognized that Group communication is a powerful abstraction to design fault-tolerant distributed applications, and the list of publications on the topic is vast [1,2,3,4,5]. Due to the uncertainties inherent to distributed systems, group communication protocols have to face situations where, for instance, a sender process fails when a multicast is underway or where messages arrive in an inconsistent order at different destination processes. Despite such uncertainties, group services should provide application processes with certain message delivery and consistent membership view guarantees. The provisioning of such guarantees depends, however, on the timeliness behavior observed in the underlying run-time and communication systems, ranging from synchronous, to time-free asynchronous systems.

T. Senivongse and R. Oliveira (Eds.): DAIS 2009, LNCS 5523, pp. 102–115, 2009.

In synchronous systems, message transmission and process execution delays are bounded. This model simplifies the treatment of failures because a process failing to send a message (or processing it) within the delay bound can be considered to have crashed. As a consequence, several problems related to fault-tolerant computing, such as membership, consensus, and atomic broadcast have been solved in such a model [6,7,8].

In an asynchronous system, on the other hand, there is no known bound for message transmission or processing times. This makes the system more portable and less sensitive to operational conditions (for example, long unpredictable transmission times will not affect safety properties of the system). However, problems such as distributed consensus [9][1] and (primary-partition) group membership cannot be solved in this model unless some additional assumptions are considered [3]. Fortunately, in practice, most systems (specially those built from off-the-shelf components) are neither fully synchronous, nor fully asynchronous. Most of the time they behave synchronously, but can have "unstable" periods during which they behave in an anarchic way. That is why many researches have successfully identified distinct stability conditions necessary to solve fundamental fault-tolerant problems [10,11], which allows the implementation of group services in these environments [4,5].

Other researches have considered hybrid systems composed by synchronous and asynchronous parts. This is the case of the TCB, which relies on a synchronous wormhole to implement fault tolerant services [12]. Another example is the so-called real-time dependable channels (RTD) that allow an application to customize a channel according to specific QoS requirements [13]. Resource reservation and admission control have been used in *QoS architectures* in order to allow processes to dynamically negotiate the quality of service of their communication channels, leading to settings with hybrid characteristics that can change over time [14]. In this context, we have addressed the problems of uniform consensus and perfect failure detection for hybrid and dynamic distributed systems [15,16].

A challenge not adequately addressed so far is how to design generic group communication mechanisms suitable to hybrid distributed systems with adaptive characteristics. As it has been pointed out in [2], though similar in principles, distinct strategies have been adopted, depending on the system environment (synchronous or asynchronous). Therefore, the design of integrated group communication schemes, which can work on dynamic hybrid models, remains a challenge. The present paper tackles this challenge by introducing a mechanism called the Timed Causal Blocks (*TimedCB*), which is an extension of the so-called Causal Blocks model used for asynchronous systems - a framework for developing group communication protocols and related services with a number of ordering and reliability properties (e.g. ordered message delivery in overlapping groups, flow control. etc.) [17,18,19]. Because it combines physical clock time and logical time in the same infrastructure, *TimedCB* represents an integrated framework capable of handling group communication for both

---

[1] consensus can be used as a building block to implement membership protocols [10].

synchronous and asynchronous distributed systems. This is especially relevant to achieve dynamic adaptation (one could switch to the asynchronous version when timely conditions can no longer be met) and fast message delivery (for instance, there is no need to wait for a timing condition when some logical time property is already satisfied within a time window - for example, for timely total ordered message delivery). The remainder of this paper is structured as follows. Section 2 presents the system model, assumptions, and message delivery and group view properties of the generic group approach. The development of *TimedCB* is then presented in section 3. A simulation environment and a performance evaluation of the proposed protocol in a synchronous environment is presented in section 4, and conclusions are drawn in section 5.

## 2    The Generic Group Approach

### 2.1    The System Model and Assumptions

A system consists of a finite set $\Pi$ of $n > 1$ processes, namely, $\Pi = \{p_1, p_2, ..., p_n\}$. Processes communicate and synchronize by sending and receiving multicast messages[2] through channels and every pair of processes $(p_i, p_j)$ is connected by a reliable bidirectional channel: they do not create, alter, or lose messages. In particular, if $p_i$ sends a message to $p_j$, then if $p_i$ is correct (i.e., it does not crash), eventually $p_j$ receives that message unless it fails. Transmitted messages are received in FIFO order. A process executes steps (a step is the reception of a message, the sending of a message, each with the corresponding local state change, or a simple local state change), and have access to local hardware clocks with drift rate bounded by $\rho$.

It is assumed that the underlying system is capable of providing timely and untimely QoS guarantees for both message transmission and process scheduling times. For a given timely channel it is known the maximum and minimum bounds for message transmission times, denoted $\Delta_{max}$ and $\Delta_{min}$, respectively. For timely processes, there is a known upper bound $\phi$ for the execution time of a step. For untimely processes and channels, there is no such a known time bound. We assume that $\Delta >> \phi$, so $\phi$ can be neglected when calculating end-to-end message latencies. It is assumed that the underlying system behavior can change over time, such that processes and channels may alternate their QoS - due to failures and/or QoS renegotiations. It is also assumed that the underlying system is equipped with a monitoring mechanism that provides processes with the information about the current QoS ensured for a given channel or process.

According to the QoS related to process executions, the system observed by a process $p_i$, leads to the identification of sub-sets of $\Pi$ that share a certain QoS (e.g., a set of processes and channels may form a synchronous component). In

---

[2] no particular implementation is assumed for message multicast. For example, it can either be implemented by a multi-send operation or by a network level broadcast facility.

particular, dynamic QoS modifications and process crashes lead to the observation of the sub-sets *live, uncertain,* and *down,* as defined in [15]. That is, if $p_j \in live_i$, $p_j$ is timely and $p_j$ is connected to (at least) another timely process $p_k$ (not necessarily k = i), by a bidirectional timely channel $(p_j, p_k)$. Otherwise, $p_j \in uncertain$. If processes that crash were in *live,* they are moved from *live* to *down.* [3]. These sets are dynamically updated by the above-mentioned monitoring mechanisms and processes can fail only by prematurely halting execution (i.e. crashing). Byzantines failures are not considered. Processes that do not crash are named correct processes.

## 2.2 Generic Group Properties

Processes form a unique group $g$, whose initial configuration is $g = \Pi$. Due to space limitations, multiple groups are not considered in this paper.

A process $p_i$ of a group $g$ installs views, named $v_i(g) \subseteq \Pi$. A view represents the set of group members that are mutually considered operational. This set can change dynamically on the occurrence of process crashes (suspicions) (or when processes leave or join $g$ - but these events are not considered in this paper). Every time a view change occurs, a new view is installed, and each one is associated with a number that increases monotonically. $v_i^k(g)$ denotes the view number k installed by $p_i$. Where suitable, the process identity of a view will be omitted (e.g., $v^k(g)$), or the group identity (e.g., $v_i^k$). A process $p_i$ multicast messages only to the processes of its current view.

In general, a group communication protocol must satisfy a number of safety and liveness properties, related to both the views installed by distinct processes and the set of messages delivered. Such properties vary from one implementation to another, following a given target computing environment [4,2]. The group communication suite presented in this paper aims at, among other applications, the implementation of the so-called active replication of servers. Therefore, the properties specified for the presented protocol must satisfy total order message delivery (respecting causality) and agreement on a linear group view history [20,21]. In the following the properties of our generic group communication protocol will be informally presented. A formal and complete description of the protocol properties can be found in [22].

To achieve message delivery liveness, the **validity** property assures that a correct process will deliver at $t + \Delta_1$ a message sent by it at time $t$. To achieve message delivery safety, the properties that must be satisfied are **agreement** (i.e. if a correct process delivers a message in a view, all correct ones must do the same), **uniform total order** and **causal order,** so the processes observe the same message delivery order, respecting potential causality [21]. To assure view delivery liveness, a **failure detection** property guarantees that if a process fails at a time $t$ in a view, all correct processes will detect it at time $t + \Delta_2$ and install a new view that excludes the failed process. For view delivery safety, correct processes must agree on a view, according to the **unique sequence**

---

[3] the way these sets are dynamically updated according to the available QoS will not be presented in this paper. Such descriptions can be found in [15].

of views property. Also, exclusions from a group must be justified by process crashes or suspicions. That is, if a process does not belong to a new view, then either it failed or it was suspected (exclusion justification). Finally, a process only installs a new view if it belongs to it (self-inclusion). The bounds $\Delta_1$ and $\Delta_2$ are known if the system is synchronous, and unknown, otherwise.

## 3   Development of the Generic Approach

The proposed approach is based on the so-called Causal Blocks model that is briefly presented below. A detailed discussion can be found in [17,18,19].

Each process $p_i$ maintains a logical clock called the Block Counter and denoted $BC_i$, and messages timestamped with Block Counters respect potential causality [21]. A $p_i$ constructs Causal Blocks to represent concurrent messages it sent/received with the same block-number. Construction of Causal Blocks leads to the notion of Block Matrix that can be viewed as a convenient way of representing sent and received messages with different block-numbers.

Figure 1 shows the Block Matrix of a 6-member process group. It represents all messages sent/received by the process which owns this particular matrix. The $BM$ matrix showed in figure 1, indicates, for example, that the block-numbers of the last messages received from processes $p_1$ and $p_2$, are 4 and 5, respectively.

|   | $P_1$ | $P_2$ | $P_3$ | $P_4$ | $P_5$ | $P_6$ |
|---|---|---|---|---|---|---|
| 1 | + |   |   | + |   |   |
| 2 |   | + |   |   | + | + |
| 3 | + |   | + | + |   |   |
| 4 | + |   |   |   | + |   |
| 5 |   | + |   |   |   |   |

**Fig. 1.** The Block Matrix of a 6-member Group Process

To enable a process to accurately determine that a given block contains all messages that can be represented in it, we use the notion of *block completion*. In the example shown in figure 1, block 2 ($BM[2]$) is complete because processes $p_2$, $p_5$, and $p_6$ have sent a message with block-number 2, and processes $p_1$, $p_3$, and $p_4$ have sent a message with block-number 3. Blocks get completed in the sequential order of their block numbers (thanks to the FIFO order channel delivery property).

A given causal block is guaranteed to complete only if processes in $g$ remain lively by sending messages so that block counter increases with time. To accomplish that, the Causal Blocks model provides each process with a simple mechanism, called the time-silence, which enables a process to remain lively during those periods when it is not generating computational messages. Briefly explaining, the time-silence mechanism of $p_i$ acts after a time period of inactivity ($ts$), sending a message to contribute to the completion of all incomplete blocks.

The above block completion definition has been used to implement asynchronous protocols in the Causal Blocks framework. We now introduce the notion of timely block completion, meaning the upper bound time by which a created causal block will be completed, when the system is synchronous [4].

**Lemma 1.** *The time bounds for a BM[m.b] to complete at a process $p_i$, as measured by its local clock is (a proof can be found in our technical report [22]) :*

- *TC1:* $(t_i + ts(m.b) + 2\Delta_{max})(1 + \rho)$, *if m was sent by $p_i$*
- *TC2:* $(t_i + ts(m.b) + 2\Delta_{max} - \Delta_{min})(1 + \rho)$, *if m was received by $p_i$*

### 3.1 The Generic Adaptive Protocol

A message $m$ sent to a group reaches all destinations if the sender process does not crash during transmission; in case of crash, some destination processes may not receive $m$. Hence, when a message is received by a destination process, it can not be immediately discarded as its retransmission may be required to satisfy the *agreement* property; instead, the received message must be stored until it is known that all processes have received it. Messages that have not been acknowledged by all member processes are called unstable messages (stable messages, otherwise)[5]. As soon as a message becomes stable, it is then discarded from the local storage. Unstable and/or not delivered messages are kept in the local storage.

In order to assure that group members deliver the same set of messages and in the same order (*agreement* and *total order*, respectively), the following constrictions must be satisfied, where $m.b$ is the block number of message $m$.

- *safe1*: a received $m$ is deliverable if *BM[m.b]* is complete;
- *safe2*: deliverable messages are delivered in the non-decreasing order of their block numbers; a fixed pre-determined delivery order is imposed on deliverable messages with the same block number.

Algorithm 1 describes the steps executed every time a new message is sent or received. After creating the related causal block (if it does not exist) and setting its completion timeout, the message is stored in a local buffer. After that, the *delivery* task (Algorithm 2) will be signaled in order to check for delivery conditions in all existing incomplete causal blocks (including the new one)[6]. However, a causal block will become complete as long as processes do not fail in sending messages. Suppose now that a process $p_k$ fails by stop functioning (crashing) and, as a consequence, a block completion timeout (*TC1* or *TC2*)

---

[4] actually, it is sufficient that all processes are timely and there exist a spanning tree of timely channels covering all processes. However, for simplifying our presentation this particular case is not considered.

[5] the interested reader should refer to [17,18] for the details on the detection of stable messages in the context of Causal Blocks.

[6] Observe that the reception or sending of a message may result in the completion of more than one causal block.

expires at $p_i$ for a $BM[m.b]$. In order to proceed with message delivery, a new membership for $g$ must be established that excludes $p_k$ (or any other processes that did not contribute for the completion of $BM[m.b]$). In order to guarantee that all group members engage in the same view installation procedure, a reliable multicast primitive, denoted $rmcast(Change ViewRequest, B)$, $B = m.b$, is employed to launch the change view procedure (Algorithm 3). The *agreement property* of the reliable multicast primitive guarantees that if any operational group member delivers the message *(Change ViewRequest, B)*, all the other operational members will do so. These requests are then processed by the changing view task (Algorithm 4), presented below.

Consider that $V_i^k(g)$ is the current view of $g$ when *TC1* or *TC2* expires for $BM[B]$. Let $F \in \Pi$ be the set of all $p_j$ that failed in sending a message with block-number $B$ or larger (as required by block completion). In other to establish a new view $v_i^{k+1}(g)$ that excludes the processes in $F$, the adaptive *consensus* presented in [15] is used (line 9 algorithm 4). Such a consensus algorithm makes progress despite distinct views of the QoS of the underlying system, adapting to the current QoS available (via the sets *live*, *uncertain*, and *down*). However, it is assumed that the system QoS can only degrade during the system execution[7], as required by the adaptive consensus. It is also assumed, as required by the adaptive consensus, the existence of a failure detector of class $\diamond S[10]$ (named FD, where $FD(p_i)$ = true if $p_i$ is suspected of crash), and that the majority of processes in the *uncertain* set does not fail. The membership protocol uses repeated (possibly concurrent, but completely independent) executions of consensus where a given execution of consensus is used to decide on identical views to be installed at all group members (thanks to the *uniform agreement* property of the consensus). All the messages related to a tentative view change and a given consensus execution are tagged with the block-number $B$ related to the timeout expiration. Hence, the *consensus* primitive for the completion of $BM[B]$ is denoted as $consensus(B, v_i)$, where $v_i$ is the consensus proposed value.

Before installing a new view, the same set of messages must be delivered at operational processes. This is because agreement must be reached not only on the new view $v_i^{k+1}$, but also on the set of messages delivered in view $v_i^k$ (*agreement* property). Thus, before a view installation, all processes will collect the unstable messages from all operational and non-suspected processes. The union of such unstable messages (lines 5-7 of algorithm 4) together with the identities of the processes that provided these sets (line 8) form the new proposed value for the consensus. Afterwards, messages from *allunstable* are stored in the local buffer of processes that decide the consensus (lines 9-10). As the decided view may not include a given $p_i$ (that fails in sending its unstable set), it might be terminated (line 12). Finally, a new view is only installed if some process has been removed from the current view (lines 13-14). Otherwise, the missing messages to complete BM[B] have been recovered and no view change is necessary.

---

[7] this assumption can actually be relaxed by adding to the consensus proposed value the new upgraded QoS - but this alternative will not be explored in this paper.

---

**Algorithm 1.** Executed by $p_i$ on a *send/receive* event of a message $m$

---

if BM[m.b] does not exist **then**
   create BM[m.b]
   if $p_i = m.sender$ **then**
     set timeout TC1 for BM[m.b]
   **else**
     set timeout TC2 for BM[m.b]
   **end if**
**end if**
store $m$ at a local buffer and *signal* delivery task (Algorithm 2)

---

**Algorithm 2.** Delivery Task

---

1: **if** any causal block gets completed **then**
2:    deliver messages according to *safe1* and *safe2*
3:    cancel timeouts of complete causal blocks
4: **end if**

---

**Algorithm 3.** Executed by $p_i$ on the expiration of a timeout for BM[B]

---

1: *rmcast(ChangeViewRequest,B)*

---

**Algorithm 4.** Executed by $p_i$ on the reception of a *(ChangeViewRequest,B)* message

---

1: **if** *(unstable,B)* was already been sent by $p_i$ **then**
2:    exit
3: **end if**
4: block ordinary delivery at *delivery task*
5: rmcast(unstable, B)
6: *wait until* ($\forall p_j \in v_i^k$: received (unstable,B) from $p_j$ or $p_j \in down_i$ or
    $FD_i(p_j) = true$) and for majority of *uncertain*: received (unstable,B) from $p_j$
7: *let allunstable$_i$* be the union of the *unstable* sets received from all $p_j$
8: *let $v_i^{k+1}$* be set of all $p_j$ from which (unstable,B) was received.
9: *consensus(B,($v_i^{k+1}$, allunstable$_i$))*
10: store messages from *allunstable* not yet received by $p_i$ and apply *safe1* and *safe2*
    only for the blocks that get completed with the messages from *allunstable$_i$*.
11: **if** $p_i \notin v_i^{k+1}$ **then**
12:    *terminate* $p_i$ (* $p_i$ was removed due to a false suspicion from a $p_j, i \neq j$ *)
13: **else if** $v_i^k \neq v_i^{k+1}$ **then**
14:    install the decided view $v_i^{k+1}$ at $p_i$
15: **end if**
16: *signal delivery task* (Algorithm 2) for resuming ordinary message delivery

---

## 3.2 Protocol Correctness

To be correct, the generic protocol must satisfy the properties previously described. In the following, we formalize and prove the *validity* property for message delivery. The proofs for the remaining properties are omitted due to space restrictions, but can be easily derived from the system assumptions, the properties of the causal block framework, and the adaptive consensus.

**Theorem 1.** *(Validity): If a correct $p_i$ sends a message $m$ in view $v_i^r(g)$ at real time $t$, than, provided that it continues to function as a member of $g$, it will deliver $m$ at time $t + \Delta_1$, $\Delta_1 > 0$, in some view $v_i^s(g)$, $s \geq r$.*

**Proof.** Assume that a correct $p_i$ has sent a message $m$ in view $v_i^k$. By the reliable channel assumption, $m$, timestamped with block number $m.b$, is always received at its destinations. Hence, lines 1-2 of Algorithm 1 guarantee that a causal block that contains $m$ is eventually created at all functioning processes, including $p_i$. If processes do not crash, the *time-silence* mechanism guarantees that created blocks eventually get completed and its messages, including $m$, delivered (Algorithm 2). Now, suppose that process crashes occur so that $BM[m.b]$ will not complete. But, in this latter case, a timeout for $BM[m.b]$ (lines 4 and 6 of algorithm 1) will eventually expire and a message for installing a new view will eventually be reliably multicast to all processes (Algorithm 3). The reliable multicast of Algorithm 3 guarantees that all processes will execute the changing view request related to block $m.b$ (Algorithm 4). As the proposed value used in the consensus is carefully constructed to contain all unstable messages from all the members of the proposed view (lines 5 to 8 of algorithm 4), then either messages to complete $BM[m.b]$ from all members in $v_i^k$ will be received, or a new view $v_i^{k+1}$ will be established that excludes processes those fail in sending a null (from time-silence) or application message for $BM[m.b]$. In both cases, BM[m.b] will eventually complete and $m$ delivered (thanks to the *termination* property of consensus that guarantees all correct $p_i$ eventually decide).

Theorem 1

## 4    Simulation and Evaluation

In order to simulate protocols for dynamic and hybrid distributed systems, it is required that all possible behaviors in such environments can be expressed, including distinct QoS for channels and processes, changes in topology, processes and channels. Because we have not found in the literature a simulation environment with the required characteristics, we had to develop a new one, which was done in Java. By using our simulator, named *HDDSS* (after "'hybrid and dynamic distributed system simulator"'), one can define a system that can be composed by a mix of different kinds of processes and channels, each of them implementing a distinct fault model, and allowing the change of component behavior dynamically. For instance, one could define a set of processes that communicate to each other by asynchronous channels, but forming a spanning tree of synchronous channels; still, this system could degrade its QoS, so the spanning tree eventually split, changing dynamically the system properties. In *HDDSS*, a fault model is defined according to a chosen probabilistic density function. Moreover, fault models and timeliness properties can be combined in the definition of the behavior of channels and processes. For instance, a given system can be made of a sub-set of correct processes, another sub-set of processes that fail by crashing with certain probability, and, yet, another sub-set of processes that fail by omission with another probability.

The same can be applied for channels. For instance, a channel can be reliable and characterized by a Poison density function for message delivery and another one can fail by omission but with deterministic message delivery delay. Furthermore, during the simulation, one can replace a channel between two processes by an instance of another channel class - switching dynamically its behavior.

*HDDSS* is equipped with a serial execution engine of discrete-events, where tasks can be scheduled by time or by events. The processes are Java threads that invoke methods of a package of the message-passing environment - so it could be easily replaced, for instance by Unix sockets, in a real execution.

An instance of the main class *Simulator* defines the sets of processes and channels. Processes and channels inherit from the classes *Agent* and *Channel*, respectively. Arbitrary topologies are defined at the beginning of the simulation, and can be changed during its evolution. Due to space restrictions, a more detailed description of the simulation environment is omitted in this paper.

We simulated our protocol with *HDDSS* and evaluated its performance in a fault-free synchronous system - this is done by comparison with the protocols proposed in [23,6], which altogether perform group communication by membership management and atomic broadcast in a synchronous distributed system. For the sake of simplicity, these protocols are referred here just by the name of the membership protocol, named Periodic Group Creator or *PGC*. Our adaptive generic protocol will be named *TimedCB*.

In *PGC*, each process periodically sends a membership checking message (period $\pi$). The related atomic broadcast algorithm is based on flooding and delivers messages using synchronized clocks, considering the network maximum delay, the number $k$ of retransmissions and a maximum difference $\epsilon$ between the synchronized clocks. In absence of application messages, the *TimedCB* uses the time-silence mechanism to guarantee block completion at each period $ts$. This allow us to monitor the membership in a similar way to *PGC*. So, in our experiments, we will consider scenarios where $ts = \pi$.

For this experiment, a node executes a processing step in at most 1 time unit and the system is made of deterministic communication channels with $\Delta_{MAX} = 14$ time units and $\Delta_{MIN} = 10$ time units - so the communication delay is much larger than the processing delay. The network topology is full-connected. We consider that *PGC* is initialized so that its flooding mechanism tolerates just one process failure in the sending path ($k = 1$). With this initialization, we obtain the minimum cost for the flooding mechanism. For comparison, the resiliency level is also adjusted to support two failures ($k = 2$). Also, the synchronization algorithm used in *PGC* is the simple algorithm presented in [24] modified to be aware of clock drifting, considering $\epsilon = 4$ time units. In *TimedCB*, no synchronization of clocks is needed.

The simulation factors considered are the number of network nodes (10, 30 or 50) and the periods $ts$ and $\pi$ (16, 24 or 32). In order to simulate the generation of application messages, each process is defined to send an application message at each advance of a time unit according to a Bernoulli probabilistic distribution function. To calculate averages, each experiment was replicated 5 times and had a time window of 500 time units. Varying the probability $P$ of generating a message in a time unit, we run two scenarios, named A and B. The first one is characterized by the probability $p = 0.1$, resulting in an average of 517, 1526 and 2516 application messages, when 10, 30 and 50 nodes were considered, respectively. In the scenario B, the sending load is characterized by $P = 0.02$ and the corresponding averages were 105, 314 and 517. Observe that in scenario A message transmission load is roughly 5 times larger than scenario B. So, with these scenarios we tried to simulate distinct message transmission loads (high and low, respectively).

An important evaluation metric is the proportion of protocol messages against the total messages transmitted - including the application messages. That is, the overhead of the protocol. The protocol messages for *TimedCB* are the ones generated by algorithms 3 and 4 and time-silence. For *PGC*, the protocol messages are those generated by the Atomic Broadcast and *PGC*'s view monitoring mechanisms. Another important metric is the delay for message delivery, here measured from the reception of the message at a local buffer up to the corresponding delivery to the application. Tables 1 and 2 refer to these metrics in *PGC* and *TimedCB*, respectively. The figures are the mean time (and corresponding standard deviation) for scenarios A and B.

Analyzing the results, it should be noticed that *TimedCB*, as expected, presents much less overhead than *PGC*: for instance, in scenario A (table 1), *TimedCB* overhead in the worst case (shorter checking period and greater number of nodes) is 26.82 %, against 62.81 % of *PGC* in same conditions (the best case for *PGC* is 36.72 %). One of the reasons is the fact that *PGC* requires the periodic transmission of protocol messages to monitor membership and *TimedCB* uses application messages to carry (when possible) protocol messages. It can also be observed that increasing the checking period of both protocols ($ts$ to *TimedCB* and $\pi$ to *PGC*), decreases, significantly, the respective overhead.

**Table 1.** Simulation results of scenario A

| Factors | | Delivery delay | | | Overhead (%) | |
|---|---|---|---|---|---|---|
| n | $\pi$ or $ts$ | PGC (k=1) | PGC (k=2) | TimedCB | PGC | TimedCB |
| 10 | 16 | $17.696 \pm 3.120$ | $31.482 \pm 4.828$ | $21.933 \pm 8.117$ | 46.54% | 21.79% |
| 10 | 24 | $17.523 \pm 3.494$ | $31.451 \pm 4.630$ | $25.731 \pm 9.238$ | 40.37% | 15.11% |
| 10 | 32 | $17.794 \pm 3.298$ | $31.369 \pm 4.462$ | $30.683 \pm 10.682$ | 36.72% | 11.62% |
| 30 | 16 | $17.630 \pm 3.996$ | $30.616 \pm 6.550$ | $19.853 \pm 6.444$ | 56.10% | 26.14% |
| 30 | 24 | $17.660 \pm 3.929$ | $30.632 \pm 6.744$ | $24.900 \pm 8.074$ | 51.95% | 18.92% |
| 30 | 32 | $17.706 \pm 3.694$ | $30.772 \pm 6.643$ | $32.405 \pm 9.150$ | 49.57% | 14.84% |
| 50 | 16 | $17.795 \pm 3.999$ | $30.392 \pm 7.478$ | $19.799 \pm 6.079$ | 62.81% | 26.82% |
| 50 | 24 | $17.849 \pm 3.787$ | $30.504 \pm 7.453$ | $25.845 \pm 7.710$ | 59.85% | 20.28% |
| 50 | 32 | $17.870 \pm 3.948$ | $30.594 \pm 7.086$ | $34.161 \pm 9.023$ | 58.18% | 15.66% |

**Table 2.** Simulation results of scenario B

| Factors | | Delivery delay | | | Overhead (%) | |
|---|---|---|---|---|---|---|
| n | $\pi$ or $ts$ | PGC (k=1) | PGC (k=2) | TimedCB | PGC | TimedCB |
| 10 | 16 | $16.659 \pm 5.477$ | $28.266 \pm 10.492$ | $20.865 \pm 9.819$ | 81.08% | 71.07% |
| 10 | 24 | $17.272 \pm 4.124$ | $28.052 \pm 10.208$ | $30.382 \pm 11.396$ | 76.92% | 61.68% |
| 10 | 32 | $17.405 \pm 4.517$ | $27.904 \pm 10.671$ | $38.960 \pm 13.270$ | 74.07% | 51.83% |
| 30 | 16 | $17.338 \pm 4.536$ | $30.328 \pm 7.118$ | $22.748 \pm 7.606$ | 86.13% | 71.74% |
| 30 | 24 | $17.112 \pm 4.507$ | $30.353 \pm 7.514$ | $30.757 \pm 9.669$ | 84.01% | 61.94% |
| 30 | 32 | $17.431 \pm 4.416$ | $30.420 \pm 6.924$ | $39.105 \pm 11.043$ | 82.69% | 53.76% |
| 50 | 16 | $17.301 \pm 4.707$ | $30.086 \pm 7.943$ | $24.307 \pm 6.584$ | 89.15% | 71.79% |
| 50 | 24 | $17.367 \pm 4.789$ | $30.024 \pm 8.243$ | $30.842 \pm 8.832$ | 87.88% | 62.78% |
| 50 | 32 | $17.313 \pm 4.650$ | $29.913 \pm 8.232$ | $40.182 \pm 9.727$ | 87.13% | 55.04% |

Also, it should be noticed that, even in lower load scenarios (like scenario B in table 2), where there are few application messages to be used, *TimedCB* takes advantage of them, presenting always lower overhead than *PGC*. On the other hand, observe that, because *PGC* relies on synchronized clocks, it achieves a more regular delivery delay than *TimedCB*.

We observe also that *TimedCB* delivery delay can be improved for either smaller checking periods or higher message transmission loads. Another advantage of the *TimedCB* is that, in absence of failures, no additional price will be paid. For more resilient atomic broadcasts of *PGC*, the related flooding mechanism will result in much larger delivery delays (for values of $k > 1$). For *TimedCB*, if failures are considered, the price is the same (the consensus price), no matter the number of tolerated failures (from 1 to $n - 1$).

## 5 Final Remarks

*TimedCB* has been introduced to handle group communication in hybrid systems. With *TimedCB*, the same algorithms and information structure can be instantiated in distinct system models (synchronous, asynchronous, or a hybrid system), which simplifies system design. When a pure synchronous system is considered, *TimedCB* can provide early delivery, since logical block completion can be achieved before the pessimistic bounds ($TC1$ or $TC2$) hold, and also the expiration of these bounds is an accurate indication of failures. When an asynchronous system is considered, these bounds trigger failure suspicions.

In the simulated experiments, if we consider the runs without failures and the synchronous scenario, *TimedCB* produces lower message transmission overhead when compared with classical approaches such as in [8], where messages are sent using an atomic broadcast primitive (which is equivalent to consensus as proved in [10]). In the approach presented in this paper, the cost of consensus is paid only when crashes occur. However, the execution of consensus impact the worst case time delay for message delivery. Thus, the advantages of our protocol will be more observed in scenarios less bounded to failures.

For the asynchronous case, asymmetric approaches [5] may be more efficient in terms of the number of messages transmitted. However, these will also need extra heartbeat messages to detect failures, whereas in *TimedCB*, failure detection and ordered message delivery are integrated. The presented approach can be particularly relevant for applications that require run-time adaptiveness characteristics, such as those running on networks where previously negotiated QoS cannot always be delivered between processes and in which the number of extra transmitted messages should be minimized during failure-free executions.

There are also hybrid, not necessarily dynamic, system settings and applications that can benefit from this new approach. Consider for instance, grid clusters interconnected via the Internet, and that tasks are distributed among distinct clusters (for instance, for parallel computations). Maintaining a mutually consistent view of the functioning processes distributed in distinct clusters is an important requirement, for instance, for re-executing failed tasks when the task coordinator is replicated for improving availability. Such a functionality can be achieved with the presented approach, where each grid cluster forms a synchronous partition. However, as connections among the clusters are realized via TCP/IP, the whole grid system is non-synchronous. We call such hybrid configuration *partitioned synchronous*, and elsewhere we presented an algorithm for the related perfect failure detector [16] - that can be used to manage the *down* set (algorithm 4).

At last, we have not assumed a specific implementation for the underlying QoS provision and monitoring systems. This can be carried out, for instance, by using hybrid real-time systems, where there are guaranteed deadlines for critical tasks and best-effort response times for aperiodic or non-critical tasks (for instance, by using aperiodic servers [25]). The same kind of solution can be used in the network level that must be a hybrid real-time network. Another possible approach is to use QoS architecture solutions [26], and we have developed a prototype implementation with this purpose [15].

# References

1. Birman, K.P.: The process group approach to reliable distributed computing. Communications of the ACM 36(12), 37–53 (1993)
2. Cristian, F.: Synchronous and asynchronous group communication. Communications of the ACM 39(4), 88–97 (1996)
3. Chandra, T.D., Hadzilacos, V., Toueg, S., Charron-Bost, B.: On the impossibility of group membership. In: Proc. of the 15th annual ACM Symposium on Principles of Distributed Computing, pp. 322–330. ACM Press, New York (1996)
4. Chockler, G.V., Keidar, I., Vitenberg, R.: Group communication specifications: a comprehensive study. ACM Computing Surveys 33(4), 427–469 (2001)
5. Défago, X., Schiper, A., Urbán, P.: Total order broadcast and multicast algorithms: Taxonomy and survey. ACM Computing Surveys 36(4), 372–421 (2004)
6. Cristian, F., Aghili, H., Strong, R., Volev, D.: Atomic Broadcast: from simple message diffusion to byzantine agreement. In: Proc. of the 25th International Symposium on Fault-Tolerant Computing. IEEE CS Press, Los Alamitos (1995)
7. Kopetz, H., Grunsteidl, G.: Ttp - a protocol for fault-tolerant real-time systems. IEEE Computer 27(1), 14–23 (1994)

8. Cristian, F.: Reaching agreement on processor-group membership in synchronous distributed systems. Distributed Computing (4), 175–187 (1991)
9. Fisher, M.J., Lynch, N., Paterson, M.S.: Impossibility of distributed consensus with one faulty process. Journal of the ACM 32(2), 374–382 (1985)
10. Chandra, T.D., Toueg, S.: Unreliable failure detectors for reliable distributed systems. Journal of the ACM 43(2), 225–267 (1996)
11. Dolev, D., Dwork, C., Stockmeyer, L.: On the minimal synchronism needed for distributed consensus. Journal of the ACM 34(1), 77–97 (1987)
12. Veríssimo, P., Casimiro, A.: The timely computing base model and architecture. IEEE Trans. on Computers 51(8), 916–930 (2002)
13. Hiltunen, M.A., Schlichting, R.D., Han, X., Cardozo, M.M., Das, R.: Real-time dependable channels: Customizing qos attributes for distributed systems. IEEE Trans. on Parallel and Distributed Systems 10(6), 600–612 (1999)
14. Aurrecoechea, C., Campbell, A.T., Hauw, L.: A survey of qos architectures. ACM Multimedia Systems Journal 6(3), 138–151 (1998)
15. Gorender, S., Macêdo, R.J.A., Raynal, M.: An adaptive programming model for fault-tolerant distributed computing. IEEE Trans. on Dependable and Secure Computing 4, 18–31 (2007)
16. Macêdo, R., Gorender, S.: Perfect failure detection in the partitioned synchronous distributed system model. In: Proc. of the The 4th International Conference on Availability, Reliability and Security (ARES 2009), pp. 273–280. IEEE CS Press, Los Alamitos (2009)
17. Macêdo, R.J.A.: Fault-tolerant group communication protocols for asynchronous systems. In: Ph.D. Thesis, Department of Computing Science, U. of Newcastle upon Tyne (1994)
18. Macêdo, R.J.A., Ezhilchelvan, P., Shrivastava, S.K.: Flow control schemes for fault tolerant multicast protocols. In: Proc. of the IEEE Pacific Rim International Symposium on Fault-Tolerant Systems (PRFTS 1995) (1995)
19. Ezhilchelvan, P., Macêdo, R.J.A., Shrivastava, S.: Newtop: a fault-tolerant group communication protocol. In: Proc. of the 15th IEEE Int. Conf. on Distributed Computing Systems (ICDCS 1995), pp. 296–306 (1995)
20. Schneider, F.B.: Implementing fault-tolerant services using the state machine approach: a tutorial. ACM Computing Surveys 22(4), 299–319 (1990)
21. Lamport, L.: Time, clocks, and the ordering of events in a distributed system. Communications of ACM 21(7), 558–565 (1978)
22. Macêdo, R.J.A.: Adaptive and dependable group communication. Technical Report 001/2008, Distributed Systems Laboratory (LaSiD) - Federal University of Bahia, Salvador, Brazil (December 2008)
23. Cristian, F., Center, I., San Jose, C.: Agreeing on who is present and who is absent in a synchronousdistributed system. In: Digest of Papers of the 18th International Symposium on Fault-Tolerant Computing (FTCS-18), pp. 206–211. IEEE CS Press, Los Alamitos (1988)
24. Lundelius, J., Lynch, N.: Upper and lower bound for clock synchronization. Information and Control 62(2), 190–204 (1984)
25. Lehoczky, J.P., Sha, L., Strosnider, J.: Enhanced aperiodic responsiveness in hard real-time environment. In: Proc. of the 8th IEEE Real-Time Systems Symposium (RTSS 1987), San Jose, California, pp. 110–123. IEEE CS Press, Los Alamitos (1987)
26. Blake, S., Black, D., Carlson, M., Davies, E., Wang, Z., Weiss, W.: An architecture for differentiated services. RFC 2475 (December 1998)

# A Flexible Approach for Business Processes Monitoring

Diana Comes, Steffen Bleul, Thomas Weise, and Kurt Geihs

Distributed Systems Group, University of Kassel,
Wilhelmshöher Allee 73, 34121 Kassel, Germany
{comes,bleul,weise,geihs}@vs.uni-kassel.de
http://www.vs.uni-kassel.de/

**Abstract.** Business processes and their implementation as Web Service Compositions are not only dependent on Web Services and partners all over the Internet, but also on their failsafe execution. Service providers have to obligate their services to perform according to negotiated Quality of Service (QoS) parameters. For example, response time and throughput are important parameters to achieve fast and efficient services. Overloaded or failing services may compromise the reliability and execution of whole enterprise processes.

In this paper we introduce a flexible monitoring approach for the measurement of QoS in BPEL (Business Process Execution Language) processes. We propose a generic algorithm for QoS aggregation in BPEL processes. The novel generic aggregation algorithm applies customized aggregation functions for QoS dimensions. Furthermore, we present a BPEL monitoring system which supports ad-hoc sensor deployment and efficient runtime and offline data aggregation not only for whole process descriptions but also sections inside service processes.

**Keywords:** Business Processes, Quality of Service, BPEL, Web Services, QoS Aggregation, Monitoring.

## 1 Introduction

Web Services and BPEL processes are the de-facto standard for implementing business processes in SOAs. Enterprise software is encapsulated inside web services and offered to the partners over the Internet. Web services are composed into more complex BPEL workflows which thus implement business processes. The number of enterprises that adhere to this technology is rapidly increasing, since enterprises need to offer services across organizational boundaries to their partners. Since several services may provide the same functionality, the *Quality of Service* makes the difference between different offers for business processes.

In order to ensure fast executing business processes, the QoS of a service must fulfill the expectations of its client applications. If the business process does not meet the quality requirements, actions need to be performed in order to improve its behavior. Therefore the monitoring, measurement and evaluation of non-functional properties of the processes is imperative. The Business Process

T. Senivongse and R. Oliveira (Eds.): DAIS 2009, LNCS 5523, pp. 116–128, 2009.

Execution Language (BPEL) standard has emerged for the implementation of interaction between services over the Internet. BPEL enables the specification of Web Service orchestrations. However, BPEL does not contain any specifications regarding the QoS of a business process.

In this paper we address these non-functional requirements. We present a monitoring and assessment approach for the computing of QoS in business processes. Our assessment approach is flexible enough to fulfill the requirements of a continuously changing environment. So far, most research studies have not dealt with the following QoS issues in workflows: Automatic sensor deployment, replacing QoS parameters, customizable aggregation functions, and subsection aggregation. Thus, these related studies do not put enough focus on the needs of heterogeneous and dynamic changing environments.

The remainder of this paper is structured as follows. Section 2 presents the motivation for our flexible monitoring approach. Section 3 makes a short introduction to the WS-BPEL language and some of its main constructs. A formalization of our model can be found in section 4. In section 5 the generic algorithm for QoS computation of a business process is presented. The paper proceeds with section 6 where we give an overview of our monitoring framework. The evaluation of our framework can be found in section 7. We make a comparison to other works related to ours in section 8.

## 2   Motivation

A Service Oriented Architecture is a dynamic environment where services and respectively partners are continuously changing. We can describe the interaction between these services with BPEL, but BPEL does not include extensions allowing us to monitor or to ensure the performance. A SOA promotes the ability for flexibility and change, but this is not possible for the assessment of QoS related issues. At any time, new QoS dimensions like cost and bandwidth have to be introduced, measured and aggregated in order to allow a suitable evaluation for performance. We designed a flexible approach, where QoS parameters can be easily considered and aggregated with minimum effort on manual administration and no effort spent by the business process architect. In this paper we tackle the following issues:

**Automated Deployment:** A business process includes a set of activities in order to invoke Web Services and each activity performs at a certain QoS. In several research studies (e.g. [9], [10]), the BPEL process description is interweaved with comments and extra activities are inserted additionally to the BPEL process. These artifacts are used to define the required QoS parameters, its monitoring sources and their aggregation functions. Thus, every time the process description changes its behavior or partner services then the process architect has to adjust the whole QoS assessment artifacts. Our goal is not to alter the process description with artifacts for process monitoring.

**Aggregation Functions and QoS Parameters:** In contrast to the measurement of QoS for single Web Services, the business processes additionally consist of different activities such as if-conditions, loops and parallel invocations of Web Services. This is why the measurement of QoS in business processes needs to be treated differently as for web services. The QoS value of a business process is computed out of the QoS values of the building blocks inside the process.

Usually, the QoS requirements and implicitly, the corresponding QoS measurements for business processes, vary over time. Thus the QoS monitoring and measurements need to be done as flexible as possible. For example, a service provider must ensure a certain response time for his business process. If, for some reason, the response time of the process is not the expected one, the service provider is in charge for analyzing the bad performance of the process. As the response time may be compromised by the bandwidth, the provider may also want to introduce the new QoS dimension bandwidth in the monitoring. In our approach we introduce a generic QoS assessment algorithm where we must only provide a set of aggregation functions in order to make it work with newly introduced QoS parameters.

**Process and Section Measurement:** Within a process description, we also consider sub-orchestrations, which we call sections of a business process. By section, we refer to a part of a BPEL process which begins within one activity and ends with another activity, while the second activity is triggered after the first one. Also, a structured activity like a while loop may represent a section, contained within the beginning and the end of the structured activity. However, a section may contain sequential and concurrent activities as well. Performing measurements and monitoring in a section is important as we further need to specify QoS requirements and manage the process within sections. This way the business process architect has a better view on what sections of the business process may cause problems in the behavior of the entire process.

## 3    An Overview of WS-BPEL

WS-BPEL [11] is an XML-based OASIS standard for describing and executing business processes which consist of web services. BPEL allows arranging web services in sequences, loops, and to execute them in parallel. A process specified with BPEL begins its execution with a start activity such as a receive or a pick. The BPEL engine creates a new instance of the process when a certain message arrives. BPEL activities are triggered either sequentially or concurrently. With invoke, a single web service is executed while the values of variables are set with assign. The activities nested inside a flow element are executed concurrently. In contrast, the activities defined by elements nested inside sequence are triggered in the same order that they appear.

Besides the control flow, additional information such as partnerlinks for defining corporate bodies that participate in the business process and faultHandlers listing the activities to be executed in case of failures can be specified with BPEL as well. Additional aspects like defining QoS parameters and QoS aggregation cannot be specified with BPEL. To fill these gaps, we apply our model and algorithm.

# 4 Business Process Model Incorporating QoS

We have designed a generic model for monitoring a business process by computing its QoS properties by aggregating the QoS of its components. In this section, we will provide the definitions necessary to specify this approach. In our model, we divide all BPEL elements relevant in the context of QoS computation into two classes:

1. the set of simple element types $S = \{$receive, reply, invoke, assign, throw, wait, ...$\}$ and
2. the set of complex element types $C$ which are used for structuring the control flow like sequence, flow, if, while, and foreach, for example.

Thus, the BPEL activity types are members of the joint set $T = S \cup C$. The instances of a simple element contribute directly to the quality of service of the overall process. They do not contain any child elements from $T$. Complex elements, on the other hand, may contain arbitrary other complex or simple elements. They specify how these elements are to be executed and their QoS values can be computed by aggregating the QoS of their children.

For each element *elem* in a BPEL process specification which belongs to one of the types in $T$, a unique identifier $elem.id1 \in I1$, $I1 \subset \mathbb{N}$ will be assigned in the initialization phase of our system. We furthermore assume that *each single execution* of *elem* has an identifier $id2 \in I2$, $I2 \subset \mathbb{N}$ unique in the current process instance.

The quality dimensions $q$ which can be measured in our system, are subsumed in the set $Q$. One example for such a set $Q$ could be $\{$responsetime, availability, cost, bandwidth$\}$. For each quality dimension $q$, there exists a domain $d_q$ which defines the set of possible values of this QoS feature. For $q = $ cost $\in Q$, $d_{\text{cost}}$ would be $\{x | x \in \mathbb{R}^+\}$, for instance. We define the domain $D$ as the union of all the domains $d_q$. The computation of the actual quality of service values in our model is based on two functions:

1. $f_{value} : Q \times I2 \mapsto D$ which determines the QoS value of a single invocation of a simple element and
2. $f_{agg} : Q \times C \times D^* \mapsto D$ aggregating all QoS values of the elements nested inside a complex element (where $D^*$ is the set of spaces of vectors of arbitrary dimensionalities over the quality domains).

Whereas $f_{value}(\text{cost}, 9)$ would return the single value from $d_{\text{cost}}$ which resulted from the invocation of a simple element with $id2 = 9 \in I2$, we could define $f_{agg}(\text{cost}, \text{sequence}, X)$ as $\sum_{i=1}^{n} x_i$, where $X = (x_1, x_2, \ldots, x_n)$ is a vector in $d^*_{\text{cost}}$ and $n$ would be the number of elements in this vector. For $X = (0.01, 0.03, 0.08)$, $f_{agg}(\text{cost}, \text{sequence}, X)$ evaluates to 0.12, for instance.

In Table 1, a set of such aggregation functions are listed for representative quality dimensions. The vector $X$ contains the QoS values $x_i$ that correspond to a process execution, which means that the corresponding activities were executed. We adapted the aggregation formulas from [1] to our approach. Since [1] consider a stochastic model and we perform aggregations on running or completed instances, we set the probabilities of executing an activity to 1 and obtained the functions from table 1:

**Table 1.** Aggregation Functions

| QoS Dimension $q$ | $fagg(q, c, X)$ $c = $ sequence | $fagg(q, c, X)$ $c = $ switch | $fagg(q, c, X)$ $c = $ flow | $fagg(q, c, X)$ $c = $ while |
|---|---|---|---|---|
| $q=$responsetime | $\sum_{i=1}^{n} x_i$ | $\sum_{i=1}^{n} x_i$ | $\max_{i \in 1..n} \{x_i\}$ | $\sum_{i=1}^{n} x_i$ |
| $q=$cost | $\sum_{i=1}^{n} x_i$ | $\sum_{i=1}^{n} x_i$ | $\sum_{i=1}^{n} x_i$ | $\sum_{i=1}^{n} x_i$ |

# 5   The Quality of Service Aggregation Approach

In the following we present the generic algorithm for the QoS computation of the business process and its sections. We therefore assume that the values of the $f_{value}$-function for the simple elements within the process are known. The generic algorithm computes the QoS value of the entire business process and/or its sections. The QoS aggregation of the BPEL process is done in several steps and there are two ways for QoS aggregation possible: A) aggregation on stored monitored data and B) live aggregation. Our algorithm is applicable in both scenarios, QoS aggregation during runtime and also post-processing after the processes have finished their execution.

## 5.1   Startup Phase: The BPEL Tree

During the startup phase of our system, the BPEL documents are translated into tree prototypes which contain only nodes for BPEL elements which are instances of either simple or complex elements. Since $T = S \cup C$ only contains the types of elements which are relevant for the execution of the BPEL process, this tree prototypes $Tree$ do not contain nodes for partnerLinks, for instance. Each node $qnode$ of the tree has the same structure and contains

1. the type $qnode.elem \in T$ of the element representing the node,
2. a unique identifier $qnode.id1 \in I1$ of the element in the tree,
3. the list with $m$ quality dimensions $qnode.qDimensions \subseteq Q$ which are monitored or aggregated for this node,
4. a map $qnode.ChildrenValues \in D^{* \times n}$ which can hold the corresponding QoS values of the $n$ children of the node; we need this map due to the propagation nature of our algorithm,

5. the map *qnode.Value* holding a value *qnode.Value*($q$) for each of the quality dimensions $q \in qnode.qDimensions$ monitored for the element itself, and
6. a reference *qnode.parent* to the parent node of *qnode* (or **null** if *qnode* is the root node of the tree).

Both *qnode.ChildrenValues* and *qnode.Value* are initially empty and remain empty in the prototype tree *Tree*. For each instance of the business process, our monitoring system creates a new copy *tree* of *Tree*. In these copies, *qnode.ChildrenValues* and *qnode.Value* are filled in by the system. The result of quality measurement of a process instance is then a tree which contains the QoS values for each element of the business process in the field *qnode.Value* of the corresponding node *qnode*. We furthermore define the function **getQNode** (*tree, id1*) which returns the node *qnode* $\in$ *tree* with *qnode.id1* = *id1* (or **null** if such a node does not exist in *tree*).

We will call a node *qnode* a simple node if it has *qnode.elem* $\in S$. Analogously, we call a node *qnode* a complex node if it has *qnode.elem* $\in C$. Since simple elements cannot contain other elements, simple nodes are the leaves of the process trees.

## 5.2  Monitoring a Running BPEL Process

While the business process is running, our monitoring system records a list *execution* of records *execElem*, each holding

1. the unique identifier *execElem.id1* $\in I1$ of the element which was invoked,
2. the unique identifier *execElem.id2* $\in I2$ of the invocation itself,
3. and the measured quality of service values *execElem.Value* which provide the results of the $f_{value}$-function
$$\left(execElem.Value(q) = f_{value}(q, execElem.id2) \; \forall q \in Q\right)$$

for a single invocation of an element in the BPEL tree. While the process is running, whenever an activity corresponding to a node in the process tree is finished, a new *execElem* record is added to the execution list.

## 5.3  The QoS Aggregation Algorithm

The generic algorithm provides as a result the aggregated values for $m$ QoS dimensions of an execution path of a BPEL tree or its sections. As input, the algorithm expects the execution list *execution* and a copy *tree* of the BPEL prototype tree. The generic algorithm listed below can be applied for any type of QoS dimension if suitable aggregation functions are provided.

The QoS values *qnode.Value* of a complex node *qnode* are computed from the values of its direct children in the tree. By applying the aggregation functions $f_{agg}$ on the QoS values of the children nodes, we obtain the QoS values of *qnode*. The values of simple nodes are known from the *execElem*-records and given by the value of the $f_{value}$-function.

The Algorithm 1 starts with traversing the list *execution* of executed activities. Each record *execElem* $\in$ *execution* stands for a completed activity. Since

---

**Algorithm 1.** aggregateQoS(*execution, tree*)

---

**Input**: *execution*: the execution list
**Input**: *tree*: the process tree to be filled with QoS values

1  **begin**
    // analyze the complete execution list *execution*
2      **for** $i \longleftarrow 1$ **up to** *execution.length* **do**
3          *qnode* $\longleftarrow$ getQNode (*tree, execution*[$i$]*.id1*)
4          **foreach** $q \in qnode.qDimensions$ **do**
5              **if** $qnode.elem \in C$ **then**
                // the node *qnode* is a complex node
6                  $qnode.Value(q) \longleftarrow$
                $f_{agg}(q, qnode.elem, qnode.ChildrenValues(q))$
7              **else**
                /* the node *qnode* is a simple node and $f_{value}$ is
                    equivalent to *execElem.Value*          */
8                  $qnode.Value(q) \longleftarrow f_{value}(q, execution[i].id2)$
            // propagate this QoS value of this node to the parent
            node
9              addQToChildrenValuesOfParent (*qnode.parent, q, qnode.Value(q)*)

10  **end**

---

the QoS values of an activity can be computed in the moment the activity is finished, each record allows us to derive a set of QoS values. In the case of an *execElem* which denotes completion of an activity belonging to a simple node, the QoS values are the data directly stored in *execElem* corresponding to the $f_{value}$ function. If *execElem* belongs to complex node, its occurrence means that the QoS of this node can be aggregated from its child nodes since an activity can only terminate after all of its children have terminated. In both cases, the new QoS values are propagated to the parent node.

Because of this propagation nature, the steps 3 to 9 of algorithm 1 can also be executed online while the process is running. In other words, the quality of service of the process tree *tree* can be built on the fly. If this is done, components which supervise or enforce policies such as Service Level Agreements (SLA) or management components like our BPRules framework [6] for business process management, can be easily integrated.

## 5.4 Example

Figure 1 represents an example of a BPEL process execution. It is an example of QoS aggregation for *response time*. On the left side of the figure, the monitored values are represented. These are the *ids* of the executed activities, in the order of execution. Also we monitored the value of *response time* (which represent *fvalue*) for the simple elements (e.g.: receive, reply, assign, invoke). These represent the input data to the QoS aggregation algorithm.

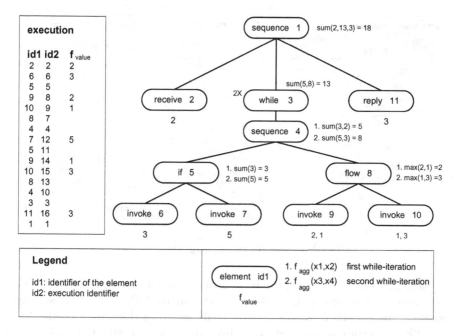

**Fig. 1.** Response Time aggregation

The while element *(id1=3)* performs two iterations. The activities inside the while have two values except for the if element *(id1=5)*. In the first iteration the first branch of the if-element is executed. The computation starts with the receive element, *id1=2*, $f_{value}$ *(responsetime,2)=2*, which is the first element that is completed. Then this value is added to the *Children Values* map of the parent node (sequence, *id1 = 1*). The process is continued with every completed element in the *execution* list. Finally, the last completed element is sequence with *id1 = 1*, which is also the root of the tree. By applying the aggregation function on the values of the children (the *Children Values* map) of the root node $(f_{agg}$ *(responsetime, sequence, X)* $= 2+13+3=18$), we determine the aggregation value of the *response time* for the entire tree.

## 6 Automated Deployment and Monitoring Framework

The main tasks of our framework are the automated deployment, monitoring and assessment of BPEL processes. For the monitoring purpose, previous to the deployment, sensors need to be associated to the BPEL process. The monitoring task is supported by the utilization of sensors which is a feature offered by the Oracle BPEL Process Manager engine, where our business processes are deployed. A sensor is associated to a BPEL activity and is fired during the execution of the activity and on the occurrence of certain events.

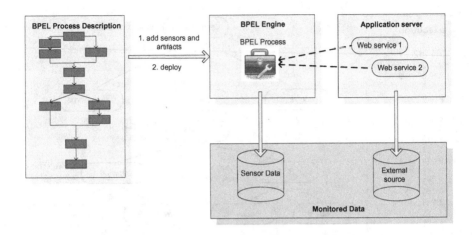

**Fig. 2.** The framework

Before process deployment, we dynamically associate sensors to each activity in the process. The sensors are declared apart from the BPEL process description inside separate XML files. We automatically generate these sensors files from the BPEL description. They are then interpreted by the Oracle BPEL engine for firing the sensors. The sensors provide valuable information, such as the timestamp when the associated activity was activated, completed or faulted. Figure 2 illustrates the deployment of a BPEL process and its associated sensors to the BPEL engine. The BPEL process and its web services may be monitored by different parties and the monitored data is stored into different sources.

Even if our generic algorithm takes advantage of the sensors offered by the Oracle BPEL Process Manager, it could also run with another BPEL engine as well. If the BPEL engine used does not support sensors similar to those the Oracle Engine provides, these software components should be additionally implemented. The premise that our algorithm runs on another BPEL engine is that its input data is delivered properly. The direct impact of sensors is on the creation of the *execution* list, which contains the identifiers of the activities in the order that they were triggered.

The main component of our assessment framework is the *QoS Aggregator* which performs the aggregation of the business process and its sections. Figure 3 illustrates the QoS aggregator component as well as its input and output data.

The flexibility of our monitoring framework is sustained by the use of plug-ins, which are software components. The advantage of using plug-ins is that they may be easily added. As the aggregation and value functions ($f_{agg}$ and $f_{value}$) are subject to modifications, we will use for each aggregation and value functions additional plug-ins. Plug-ins are reusable components. The $f_{agg}$ function plug-ins can be reused over several instances since they only depend on the type of BPEL activities. The advantage of the $f_{value}$ function plug-ins is that they can retrieve monitoring data from other sources as well, regardless where the monitoring actually takes place. An example for this is a situation where web

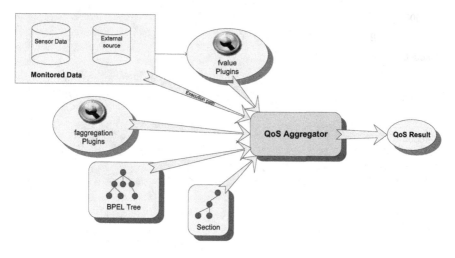

**Fig. 3.** The QoS Aggregator Component

services inside the BPEL process are monitored by the web service providers themselves and the monitored data is stored into a database different from the database where the data from the monitored BPEL *process* is stored. This has also been depicted in figure 2.

# 7   Evaluation

As example application, we have developed a *Bookshop* business process which is implemented with WS-BPEL. The *Bookshop* process is a regular business process for purchasing books at an online book shop. It interacts with four web services: the *Stock Service*, the *Distributor*, the *Accounting* and the *Bank Service*. It runs on the Oracle BPEL Process Manager and the web services are installed on the Oracle Application Server OC4J. The monitoring data, provided by the Oracle BPEL engine (e.g. instance data, sensor data) is automatically inserted into the Oracle Database. The assessment data is written into a custom MySQL database.

We performed several evaluation tests on the *Bookshop* process. The test system is a Lenovo R60 notebook with Intel Core 2 Duo processor T5600 (2x1,83GHz) with 2GB memory and Windows XP Professional Version 2002, Service Pack 2.

For the *Bookshop* process, we defined a section consisting of 20 elements, while the entire process consists of 46 elements. We measured the time consumption for the generic aggregation algorithm, by iteratively increasing the number of process invocations. Figure 4 represents the time in ms needed for the response time aggregation for the entire process. We observe a linear growth of time in relation to the number of instances that were aggregated. Since we wanted to test how our algorithm behaves if the memory is limited, we set the Java Heap size

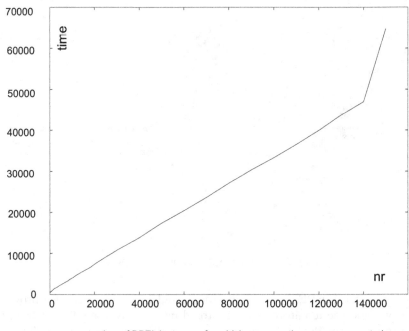

- nr:    number of BPEL instances for which responsetime was  aggregated
- time:  the time needed for the aggregations, expressed in ms

**Fig. 4.** Example Business Process Aggregation

at 90 MB. When the entire memory was allocated (at about 150000 of process instances), we also observe an abrupt increasing in the time consumption. This is an expected result and shows that the algorithm performs well but will fail if the resources of the system it is deployed on are exhausted.

## 8    Related Work

In his thesis [3], Cardoso describes a framework for estimating, predicting and analyzing QoS in workflows. For this QoS computation, he presents a mathematical model and a Stochastic Workflow Reduction (SWR) algorithm. The SWR algorithm uses six reduction rules: sequential, parallel, conditional, fault-tolerant, loop and network. These rules are iteratively applied on the workflow until one atomic task remains. The QoS value of this remaining task represents the QoS value of the workflow. Even if the rules apply on most workflows, for specific cases that may apply in a BPEL process, new rules have to be developed. Different from Cardoso's work, we do not focus on deriving a statistical model or to predict QoS values but only consider their measurement on a running system. Thus, our approach would be a possible input source from which estimators for future process behavior could be built.

In [4], Zeng et al. present a middleware platform for web service compositions from the QoS perspective. There are two approaches described for the selection of web services by satisfying the constraints set by the user on QoS attributes. Their approach is based on state charts and execution plans represented as DAGs (direct acyclic graphs). The authors define aggregation functions for price, duration, reputation, success rate and availability.

In [7], M. Jaeger presents a method of QoS aggregation for service compositions based on composition patterns. There were nine composition patterns identified that might occur in a workflow. A workflow structure is represented as a graph which is collapsed step by step due to the composition patterns that were identified in the workflow until one statement remains. The aggregations are performed on the level of composition patterns. Dependent on the pattern and QoS characteristic, aggregation rules are defined. Yet, the identification of the composition patterns on the workflow graph is not a trivial task.

Mukherjee et al. focus in their work [5] on the QoS computation in BPEL processes. They address three QoS dimensions response time, cost and reliability. They also utilize fault tolerance techniques (e.g. Recovery blocks, N-version programming) to study the impact on QoS. The computations are performed on an activity graph, which nodes represent BPEL activities and handlers.

Canfora et al. [1] adopt a similar approach to Cardoso [3] for QoS computation. They apply the same aggregation functions as Cardoso, except for loops. In our approach we used the same functions as Canfora but, as already stated, focus on measurement instead of prediction. Thus, probabilities for a certain control flow do not exist in our approach or, from another perspective, are always 1 or 0, since we aggregate the data a posteriori. In their work, Canfora et al. propose a solution with genetic algorithms for the service selection problem in service compositions.

In [10] Baresi et al. are also concerned with the monitoring of WS-BPEL processes. They add monitoring rules to the BPEL process by inserting them as comments to the source code. For monitoring purpose, we profit from the utilization of sensors that are directly triggered by the BPEL engine, and do not have to insert extra monitoring artifacts.

In our approach, we do not apply workflow patterns or reduction rules like [7], [3] and [1]. We represent the BPEL process as a tree and by only applying aggregation functions on the nodes values we are able to compute the QoS value of the entire business process. We also provide a generic algorithm that is applicable for any QoS dimension if appropriate aggregation functions are provided.

# 9   Conclusion

In this paper, we presented a flexible approach for the monitoring and computation of QoS in business processes. We have demonstrated the feasibility of our method on a business process that we implemented with WS-BPEL. We have developed a generic algorithm that performs the computation of any QoS dimension if appropriate aggregation functions are available. The algorithm may be applied both at runtime or after a business process terminated its execution. By executing the algorithm at runtime, the process is additionally observed whether it behaves as expected. Otherwise, appropriate management actions may be triggered to improve the process behavior. We also support QoS monitoring and computation on sections of the process, which permits detecting the sections of the process that cause problems and might lead to undesired QoS values of the process.

We take advantage of the utilization of sensors for the monitoring purpose. Sensors are dynamically associated with each activity of the BPEL process and the BPEL process description is not affected by extra monitoring artifacts. New QoS dimensions can be integrated with minimal effort by only specifying the aggregation functions.

# References

[1] Canfora, G., Penta, M., Esposito, R., Villani, M.L.: An approach for QoS-aware service composition based on genetic algorithms. In: Proceedings of the 2005 conference on Genetic and evolutionary computation, pp. 1069–1075. ACM, Washington (2005)

[2] Canfora, G., Penta, M., Esposito, R., Villani, M.L.: A Lightweight Approach for QoS-Aware Service Composition. Technical report, Research Centre on Software Technology University of Sannio (2004)

[3] Cardoso, J.: Quality of Service and Semantic Composition of Workflows, PhD thesis, University of Georgia, Georgia (2002)

[4] Zeng, L., Benatallah, B., Ngu, A.H., Dumas, M., Kalagnanam, J., Chang, H.: QoS-Aware Middleware for Web Services Composition. In: IEEE Transactions on Software Engineering, pp. 311–327. IEEE Press, Los Alamitos (2004)

[5] Mukherjee, D., Jalote, P., Nanda, M.: Determining QoS of WS-BPEL Compositions. In: Bouguettaya, A., Krueger, I., Margaria, T. (eds.) ICSOC 2008. LNCS, vol. 5364, pp. 378–393. Springer, Heidelberg (2008)

[6] Comes, D., Bleul, S., Zapf, M.: Management of the BPRules Language in Service Oriented Computing. In: 16th Workshops der Wissenschaftlichen Konferenz Kommunikation in Verteilten Systemen 2009, WowKiVS, Electronic Communications of the EASST, Kassel (2009)

[7] Jaeger, M.: Optimising Quality of Service for the Composition of Electronic Services, PhD thesis, University of Berlin, Berlin (2007)

[8] Charfi, A., Schmeling, B., Heizenreder, A., Mezini, M.: Reliable, Secure, and Transacted Web Service Compositions with AO4BPEL. In: Proceedings of the European Conference on Web Services (ECOWS 2006), pp. 23–34. IEEE Computer Society, Los Alamitos (2006)

[9] Baresi, L., Ghezzi, C., Guinea, S.: Smart monitors for composed services. In: Proceedings of the 2nd international conference on Service oriented computing, pp. 193–202. ACM, New York (2004)

[10] Baresi, L., Guinea, S.: Towards Dynamic Monitoring of WS-BPEL Processes. In: Benatallah, B., Casati, F., Traverso, P. (eds.) ICSOC 2005. LNCS, vol. 3826, pp. 269–282. Springer, Heidelberg (2005)

[11] Web Services Business Process Execution Language Version 2.0, OASIS standard, 2007, http://docs.oasis-open.org/wsbpel/2.0/OS/wsbpel-v2.0-OS.html

[12] Oracle BPEL Process Manager (2008),
http://www.oracle.com/technology/products/ias/bpel/index.html

# Distributed Contracting and Monitoring in the Internet of Services

Josef Spillner[1], Matthias Winkler[2], Sandro Reichert[1], Jorge Cardoso[2], and Alexander Schill[1]

[1] TU Dresden, Nöthnitzer Str. 46, 01187 Dresden, Germany
{josef.spillner,sandro.reichert,alexander.schill}@tu-dresden.de
[2] SAP Research CEC Dresden, Chemnitzer Str. 48, 01187 Dresden, Germany
{matthias.winkler,jorge.cardoso}@sap.com

**Abstract.** The recent approval of the EU Services Directive is fostering the *Internet of Services* (IoS) and will promote the emergence of marketplaces for business and real-world services. From a research perspective, the IoS will require a new bread of technological infrastructures to support the concepts of business service description, contract management from various perspectives, end-to-end marketplaces, and business monitoring.

The IoS is a vision referring to web service-based digital societies. When service hosting moves from best-effort provisioning to guaranteed service delivery, monitoring becomes a crucial point of proof for providers and consumers of such services. We present the uplifting of technical contract monitoring results to business effects based on the distributed service infrastructure developed in project THESEUS, use case TEXO.[1]

## 1  Introduction

The emergence of electronic marketplaces for services is driving the need to describe services, not only at the technical level, but also from business and operational perspectives. In this context, Service-oriented Architectures (SOA) and web services leverage the technical value of solutions in the areas of distributed systems, cross-enterprise integration, and enterprise architectures. While SOA and web services reside in an IT layer, organisations are requiring advertising and trading business services which reside in a business layer. Previous solutions for Service Level Agreement (SLA) negotiation and monitoring need to be adapted to provide suitable infrastructures for the monitoring of the business aspects.

The European directive on services in the internal market [1] will facilitate businesses to provide and use cross-border services in the EU. It will also strengthen the rights of consumers of services, for instance by enshrining the

---

[1] The project was funded by means of the German Federal Ministry of Economy and Technology under the promotional reference "01MQ07012". The authors take the responsibility for the contents.

T. Senivongse and R. Oliveira (Eds.): DAIS 2009, LNCS 5523, pp. 129–142, 2009.

right of non-discrimination and contract fulfilment protection. In business, a service is the non-material equivalent of a good. It is considered to be an activity which is intangible by nature and is provided by a service provider to a service consumer to create a value possibly for both parties.

Real world examples of domains with requirements to digitally describe and monitor business services and establish contracts include the software industry (e.g. SAP Business ByDesign Services and IBM Smart Market) and automobile industry (e.g. BMW Assist, and Mercedes-Benz TeleAid). In these use cases, providers as well as consumers face the problem of describing service offerings, which is of considerable importance since services are one of the least understood portions of the global economy [2,3].

This paper is structured as follows: in Sect. 2 we explain the advantages of the Universal Service Description Language (USDL) as our approach to describing business services, the creation of SLA templates from USDL service descriptions and the negotiation of SLAs. In Sect. 3 we present our monitoring architecture and illustrate different aspects of IoS monitoring. In Sect. 4 we show how monitoring data can be aggregated and used to evaluate SLAs. Finally, we describe how discovered problems can be handled in Sect. 5, followed by a summary of the novelties of our approach.

## 2    Descriptions of Services and Service Level Agreements

The description of services is a fundamental requirement for enabling offering, search and usage of services. SLAs are formal contracts between a service provider and consumer regulating the provisioning and consumption. In this section we argue for a need of suitable means for describing services and present USDL as our approach. We will also show how SLAs are created based on USDL descriptions.

### 2.1    Business Service Descriptions

Recently, the vision of the IoS [4] and service marketplaces have emerged and can be seen as a new business model that can radically change the way users discover and invoke services. The development of infrastructures to maintain electronic marketplaces for services will require the support for the contracting and monitoring of business aspects of services. In the IoS vision, services are seen as tradeable goods that can be offered on service marketplaces by their providers to make them available for consumers. Barros et al. [5] describe service marketplaces as one example of service ecosystems that represent "[...] a logical collection of [...] services whose exposure and access is subject to constraints, which are characteristic of business service delivery." On a service marketplace multiple providers may offer their business services, thus creating an ecosystem which enables competition as well as collaboration among service providers.

**Going beyond WSDL.** The notion of business service is broader than the well-known concept of web service. Web services have mainly an information technology (IT) perspective. They are technical software resources which are discoverable, invokable, platform independent, and self descriptive [6]. This type of service is mainly described by an interface definition (e.g., WSDL and other WS-* protocols) with a focus on technical service aspects. SLAs and monitoring consider the technical and infrastructure level. The IoS has different requirements from the ones fulfilled with WSDL. While the technical description of services is important for SOA, the business and operational perspectives on services have a significant importance for the IoS. Therefore, new service descriptions are needed to bridge business, operational and technical perspectives. A suitable service description needs to account for information that includes legal constraints, pricing strategies [7], resources consumed and produced [8], service scope and purpose, consumer benefit, participating roles and responsibilities, service level, operations, distribution channels, and marketing endeavours. A better description of the business and operational perspectives will bring to a marketplace an advantage over competitive platforms by being an added value for service providers and consumers. Based on this examination and requirements, we have devised a new specification language - USDL: the Universal Service Description Language - for services that will be hosted and traded in electronic marketplaces.

**Describing Services with USDL.** The Universal Service Description Language [10] enables the description of business characteristics exposed by an organisation for the purpose of providing a way for consumers to invoke and use services. The USDL schema defines three core clusters of information: business, operational and technical. Fig. 1 shows a simplified view of the USDL meta model. It can be seen that USDL has a strong emphasis on business and operations, while the technical perspective is reduced. The business cluster is used to describe information about the service provider and relevant consumers it is destined for, quality of service aspects, legal information, and marketing information such as pricing. Also, interaction aspects regarding service invocation and execution and bundling information is described. The operational cluster describes the offered functions of a service and provides a functional classification which supports the search for a service. Finally, the technical perspective allows the specification of different WS-* protocols for interaction. By defining the three clusters USDL goes beyond purely technical approaches such as WSDL. On the other hand it provides a well-understood and limited set of options for describing the most important aspects of business services. This approach is different from e.g. ontological approaches such as WSMO [9] which enable the user to model complex descriptions, but have the drawback of being difficult to handle by business users. More details on USDL can be found in [10].

**USDL: An example from logistics.** Listing 1.1 presents a simplified example of a USDL description (business and operational aspects) of a logistics service. The example describes the Truck Transport service that enables the transport of goods within the city limits of Dresden. It is classified as a logistics service according to the UN/SPSC standard[2]. The service will be executed within

---

[2] United Nations Standard Products and Services Code, http://www.unspsc.org/

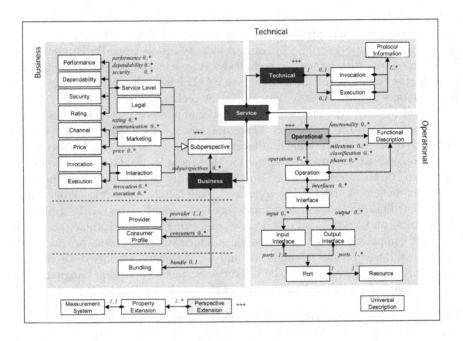

**Fig. 1.** Simplified view of the model behind USDL

3 hours and has an advertised reliability of 95%. This example will be used in the next section to exemplify how an SLA template can be generated automatically on behalf of the provider.

```
1  service {
2    serviceName Truck Transport
3    description Transport of goods within city area
4    business {
5      providerName Truck Transport Dresden GmbH
6      providerAddress Traubestr 17, Dresden, Germany
7      price 100 EUR
8      termsOfUse http://www.truck-dd.com/ToU.html
9      executionTime 3H
10     reliability 95%
11   }
12   operational {
13     classification_UNSPSC 80111623
14  }}
```

**Listing 1.1.** Sample USDL for logistics service

## 2.2    Deriving Service Level Agreements from Service Descriptions

In the IoS vision SLAs provide a formal base regulating the provisioning and consumption of services between service providers and consumers. These contracts are monitored to assure conformance to the agreement by both involved parties. Violations of the different service level objectives (SLOs) of an SLA need to be identified and reactions triggered.

Different technologies have been developed in recent years for negotiating and representing such formal contracts (e.g. WSLA [11], SLAng [12], WS-Agreement [13]). While WSLA and SLAng are not being developed any further, the WS-Agreement specification is driven by the Open Grid Forum. It provides a structure and language for specifying SLAs as well as a protocol for offering and negotiating SLAs. For our purpose we have chosen to implement SLA handling based on WS-Agreement and augment it with information from our USDL specification. The creation of SLAs is integrated with our service development process. A runtime component, called SLA Manager, encapsulates SLA syntax and handling. Its task is the negotiation of SLAs and making SLA information available to other components. In the following sections we will describe the extended WS-Agreement structure as well as the implementation of the SLA Manager.

**Specifying Service Level Agreements.** The SLA negotiation process, which follows the protocol specified by WS-Agreement, has an SLA template as its starting point. It is generated from the service description at the end of the service development process. During the negotiation process this template is refined first to an agreement proposal and finally to an agreement. The different WS-Agreement files are structured in mainly three sections: the *ServiceDescriptionTerms*, *ServiceProperties* and *GuaranteeTerms*. The *ServiceDescriptionTerms* section describes general information on the service and the functionality it provides including but not limited to the service name, pricing information, terms of use, and a functional classification. The *ServiceProperties* section defines measurable service attributes (e.g. execution time). The *GuaranteeTerms* section defines SLOs (e.g. min, max, average, or concrete values) which are guaranteed for service provisioning. They can be specified for the variables defined in the *ServiceProperties* section. A simplified SLA example is shown in Fig. 2. Due to the space limitations of the paper not all attributes are shown in the SLA.

In order to create SLA documents for services, a language for describing services is needed in addition to the language constructs of WS-Agreement. USDL provides such functionality. Thus, we have used it within SLA documents. Fig. 2 depicts examples of USDL code marked via the usdl namespace within an agreement.

Fig. 3 presents an overview of the SLA generation, negotiation, and monitoring processes which support tradeable services. In our implementation thereof, services are created using a service engineering workbench which is called ISE (Integrated Service Engineering). It implements a model-driven approach to service development and was developed based on the Eclipse platform. As a final step of the development process ISE generates SLA templates from the USDL service description. There are two ways for integrating information from a USDL

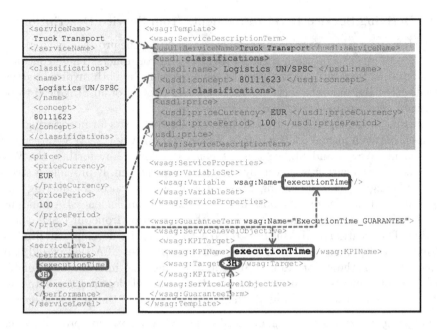

**Fig. 2.** Mapping USDL to a WSAG template

service description into an SLA template file. The first approach which we apply is to embed sections of USDL code into the WS-Agreement document structure. This is done in order to create the *ServiceDescriptionTerms* section, where a domain-specific service description language is needed. The second way of integrating service description information into the SLA is the mapping of USDL parameter names and values to WS-Agreement elements. This mapping is used for the generation of the *ServiceProperties* and *GuaranteeTerms* sections. Fig. 2 illustrates the mapping between USDL and a WS-Agreement template. Four simple USDL fragments (service name, classification, price, service level) are mapped to the different sections of the template. We implemented this transformation using openArchitectureWare [14]. The generated templates are then deployed to the SLA Manager where they are available for the negotiation process which is described in the next section. An approach of generating SLA templates from service descriptions was also described in [15]. It is limited to purely technical service aspects, while our approach, through the usage of USDL, allows to specify also business related service aspects such as rights and duties of the involved parties and penalties, to only mention a few.

**The SLA Manager.** The SLA Manager is a central component of the Service Management Platform (see Fig. 4), which handles a variety of tasks related to SLAs. First of all it provides interfaces for the deployment, update and removal of SLA templates. These interfaces are currently used e.g. by a deployment component which enables the deployment of newly modelled or changed services

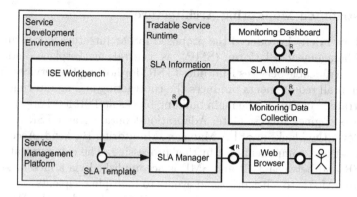

**Fig. 3.** Overview SLA generation, negotiation, monitoring

and related artefacts from the ISE workbench. The update functionality for SLA templates may also be used by other components, e.g. a monitoring component after realising that current SLAs are often violated and thus the SLA template needs to be refined accordingly.

The main task of the SLA Manager is to support the negotiation of SLAs which follows the approach defined by WS-Agreement. The negotiation is started by a user who intends to consume a service. The SLA Manager provides an SLA template which is presented to the consumer via a user interface as part of the Service Management Platform. It allows the consumers to make changes to the SLA template and submit it in the form of an agreement proposal. This document is validated by the service provider and accepted or rejected.

Another major task of the SLA Manager is the monitoring of the state of negotiated SLAs. While the evaluation of SLAs based on monitoring information is executed in a distributed fashion by the SLA Monitoring components at the Service Delivery Platforms (see Fig. 4), the SLA manager keeps track on SLO violation information from these components. It provides an interface for SMP components such as Billing to retrieve information regarding the state (SLA fulfilled, violated, not determined) of an SLA as well as the types of SLA violations that occurred.

Further interfaces are provided for information about contractual details which are needed by the SLA Monitoring components (SLOs to monitor) or by any subsequent pricing and billing components, e.g. for pricing information and consumer data.

## 3   Contract Monitoring

The task of contract monitoring is to collect all information necessary to realise the execution of tradeable services with respect to given guarantees (SLA) and to get usage data relevant for billing. On a technical level, service and system monitoring help reaching this goal. We present a monitoring architecture which integrates the flow of contracts.

### 3.1 Distributed Monitoring Architecture

In Sect. 1 we briefly introduced the proposed IoS architecture, consisting of one Service Management Platform (SMP) as central marketplace and several, distributed Tradeable Services Runtimes (TSR) for hosting the services. The consideration of all requirements produces the contracting and monitoring architecture illustrated[3] in Fig. 4. The main building blocks at TSR level are the Process and Service Engines, Access Gate, Adaptation Container and TSR Monitoring. At SMP level the blocks are SLA Manager, Monitoring Backend, Access Rights Management and components for further processing. The communication internal to TSR and between TSR and SMP is accomplished via a message-oriented middleware (MoM) to efficiently send events to multiple recipients.

When a new service is deployed, its code is transferred to the Process and Service Engines at the TSR. Once a customer has negotiated a contract via the SLA Manager's SLA Negotiation component, the resulting SLA is stored in the SLA Repository and the SLA Manager sends a message to the MoM that a new SLA is available. Subscribers of this type of message are SLA Monitoring and Monitoring Coordinator at TSR Monitoring. The latter then starts the appropriate Monitoring Sensors and Aggregators as described in the following sections. In case of an SLA violation, the SLA Monitoring triggers the Adaptation Coordinator to start one of the Adaptation Mechanisms described in Sect. 4.3.

Since complex business processes may consist of multiple services, deployed on distinct TSRs, a central Monitoring Backend at SMP level is needed to collect the monitoring data from single services and merge it into a central database. Consumers with further processing needs can access the monitoring data via Monitoring as a Service (MaaS). To keep SLA-related data private, MaaS checks the requester's identity and the access rights at every request.

In the following subsections we highlight the challenges of the various Monitoring Sensor types. We distinguish between monitoring on the system and execution container level (Sect. 3.2) on the one hand, and individual service monitoring on the other one. A further difference exists in that some of the service properties can be monitored from the outside (Sect. 3.3), e.g. by observing its message transmission behaviour, while other properties can only be measured with explicit support within the execution container (Sect. 3.4). Finally, the sensor data is converted to business objects (Sect. 3.5) and linked to contract objectives.

### 3.2 System Monitoring

IT system monitoring is a well-established activity ranging from single desktop computers to large data centres. Usually, the overall health status of distributed hardware and software is determined by measurement with agents, e.g. using SNMP or Nagios [16], and controlled from a central monitoring location. In scenarios of contract-bound service execution, determining the status and available resources of the execution servers is mandatory for creating realistic SLA offers.

---

[3] FMC-notation, see http://www.fmc-modeling.org

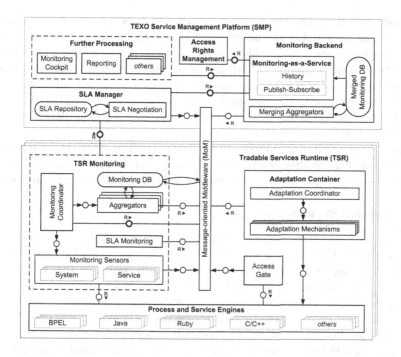

**Fig. 4.** Contracting and monitoring architecture for the IoS

In our approach, system monitoring controls the overall system health by keeping track of typical system parameters, e.g. system load, network performance,
CPU and memory usage. For each SLO parameter found in active SLA files,
the Monitoring Coordinator initialises a System Sensor which then transmits its
measurements to the Monitoring DB, and the Aggregators for further processing,
see Sect. 4.3.

In contrast to the system monitoring where only system-wide parameters are
monitored, the following two categories covers all monitoring mechanisms which
observe service specific parameters.

## 3.3   External Service Monitoring

External service monitoring mechanisms observe a service without the need for
platform support. Parameters like the availability of a service can be probed
by a third instance. Since these parameters are of a high importance to service providers, our monitoring framework possesses sensors and aggregators to
monitor these non-functional properties of services.

An instance for external monitoring is the Access Gate. It represents a service
by a transparent proxy which asynchronously intercepts all service invocations.
In a first step, it checks the caller's identity by an authentication mechanism.
In a second step, the Access Gate checks whether the caller is authorised to
send this request. If positive, it forwards the intercepted message to the service

originally called, awaits the answer and sends it back to the originator of the request. The gathered usage information is sent to the MoM and will be used for billing purposes. Besides this, the Access Gate measures the response time, calculates the throughput of a call and sends the monitored value to the local Monitoring DB. If the caller can not be identified or is not allowed to send the particular request, an appropriate error message is sent to the MoM. The separation of concerns is maintained by encapsulating the authentication and monitoring code.

All of these monitoring operations are driven by SLAs which include both the objectives and the quality and therefore frequency of the monitoring probes. Due to often overlapping objectives, the probes are optimised by combining them.

### 3.4  Internal Service Monitoring

Going step by step closer from System Monitoring (see Sect. 3.2) to the services, parameters like CPU load or memory consumption are available at a more fine grained level for execution containers, e.g. a web server or the Java Virtual Machine, where all services share the same address space.

To gain even more knowledge about the status and behaviour of services, several techniques are available to inspect service instances at runtime. Most of them are based either on prior instrumentation, e.g. addition of monitoring status calls from within the service or opening up a shared memory structure to give insight into data structures, or on run-time instrumentation with tracing support from the execution environment (virtual machine, operating system). Tracing can be used to monitor the SLA compliance of a potentially untrusted service [17] whereas instrumentation is typically used for profiling and performance measurement. Either technique leverages the IoS concept of combining rapidly developed services with powerful execution platforms, leaving the measurement and management of services with specialised providers.

### 3.5  Business Monitoring

Based on the various available techniques for technical monitoring, higher-level business objectives in SLAs can also be monitored. Provider objectives like service popularity or increasing numbers of value contracts can easily be aggregated from existing sensor data. Consumer objectives like SLA compliance can likewise be controlled by using monitoring data. Therefore, we see the need to introduce aggregators and SLA checks on top of the already mentioned components.

## 4  Aggregation and SLA Status Determination

While the collection of monitoring data is a continuous process, a parallel activity to find out the interesting events and correlations is needed in order to determine the fulfilment of SLAs. We present an aggregation mechanism and an algorithm for SLA violation detection, and include methods to avoid SLA violations from happening at all.

## 4.1   Aggregation

On each service execution host, we assume the presence of one monitor. Sensors and aggregators run side-by-side as part of each monitor. While sensors collect data from various sources, aggregators turn such streams of data into higher-level indicators. To identify meaningful or complex events, reduce the amount of low-level events, and ensure the scalability of our system, we use existing complex event processing techniques. The uptime of a service is a good example for a non-measurable value which can only be calculated based on a series of individual test calls.

Since we assume a decentralised architecture with a central marketplace, another instance of the monitoring framework with special configuration runs on the marketplace. It only contains aggregators to further refine the results and produce cross-host metrics like the overall reliability of services available from that marketplace. In the previously introduced example of service guarantees in logistics, this can be seen in Fig. 5. Suppose that each incoming connection (1) gets redirected by a proxy to the service (2), while at the same time information about start and end times is measured (3) and broadcast across the monitoring infrastructure (4), (5). If the guaranteed response time of 3 hours is not met in at least 95% of all cases within a month, the aggregator sends an additional event (6) to the SLA Monitoring, which can then check the SLA violation status and transmit this information (7), (8) to the SMP to make it available to the user in a monthly report (9).

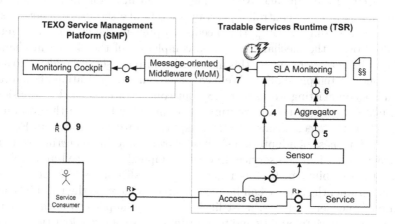

**Fig. 5.** Example of event propagation leading up to SLA violation

## 4.2   Determining SLA Conformance

We are currently developing a component for monitoring SLA conformance. Its task is to validate available monitoring information against negotiated SLAs. The SLA Monitoring component receives monitoring information via the MoM. Information on negotiated SLAs is requested from the SLA Manager. When the violation of an SLO of an SLA is detected, an SLO violation message is sent to the MoM. From there the information is available to other components for triggering further actions (e.g. informing a responsible person) or displaying the information in the monitoring cockpit. An additional step following the monitoring could be the analysis of the effects of SLO violations. In service compositions, services are not isolated from each other. Instead, SLO violations of one service may lead to situations where other services cannot be provided any more. Monitoring such effects at runtime would help to improve the provisioning of services in compositions.

### 4.3   SLA Violation Prevention through Adaptation

Monitoring is not just an end in itself; rather, the collected and calculated data serves a very special purpose: to improve the quality of the service delivery. We distinguish between passive observation of monitoring data and active use for service adaptation, and argue for the necessity of adaptation to avoid contract violations.

Based on the information provided by the MaaS, the SLA Manager component decides if an SLA has been violated or is at risk of being violated in the near future as predicted by a probability-based forecast function. In such cases, adaptation can help avoiding the violation. Adaptation strategies include scaling-up by dynamically adding computing resources such as CPUs, memory or hard disk space, and scaling-down by reconfiguring the services or cutting down on some aspects of the contract. Adaptation mechanisms implement the strategies on a technical level by controlling certain targets like services or contracts. An Adaptation Coordinator (Fig. 4) is needed to prevent the collision and mutual neutralisation of the mechanisms. Upon completion of the chosen mechanisms, an adaptivity reasoner conveys this information into the service registry to adjust future contract template offers. We have based our categorisation of adaptation mechanisms on existing works, e.g. [18], but concentrated on a clear division between matchmaking time and runtime. The interplay between the coordinator, the reasoner, the mechanisms and the adaptation targets is shown in Fig. 6.

The effectiveness of adaptation shall be shown using the recurring example of a contract with a logistics service. In case an implied and agreed-upon tolerance region of a reliability of 95% is reached, e.g. at 96% after 50% of the associated time frame, the service can be reconfigured to increase the reliability at the expense of another property, most likely cost. This applies to both a technical sense of web service reliability and to a business sense of truck logistics reliability. In the given business-level example, assuming the main cause for belated transport is traffic congestion, the mechanism in question would modify the booking of trucks to insist on using faster, but more expensive, vehicle toll roads. Depending on the contract tariff scheme, this trade-off between toll and contract violation compensation can be an economic and reputation gain, as shown in Table 1.

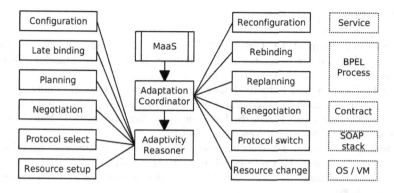

**Fig. 6.** Adaptation coordinator, reasoner, mechanisms and targets

**Table 1.** Cost-based adaptation trade-off

|  | Tariff without toll | Tariff with toll |
|---|---|---|
| Cost per transport | 30 EUR | 32 EUR |
| Probability of traffic congestion | 7% | 3% |
| Congestion compensation fee | 50 EUR | |
| Resulting average cost | 33.50 EUR | 33.50 EUR |
| Effect on reputation | lowering | raising |

## 5  Conclusion

We have designed and partially implemented a technical foundation for distributed service contracting and monitoring. A novel aspect of linking it to the business level was introduced. It allows consumers to rely on the advertised functionality of business services. The resulting architecture is built around USDL service descriptions and WS-Agreement based SLAs. Through a division into user-visible marketplaces and execution servers, it scales well enough for operation in an Internet of Services. The pervasive use of contracts and the enforcement of contractually guaranteed terms increases the acceptance among business users and makes it feasible to establish the excogitated service marketplaces.

## Acknowledgements

The information in this document is proprietary to the following Theseus Texo consortium members: SAP AG and Technische Universität Dresden. The information in this document is provided "as is", and no guarantee or warranty is given that the information is fit for any particular purpose. The above referenced consortium members shall have no liability for damages of any kind including without limitation direct, special, indirect, or consequential damages that may result from the use of these materials subject to any liability which is mandatory due to applicable law. Copyright 2009 by the Theseus Texo consortium.

# References

1. European Parliament: EU Directive 2006/123/EC of the European Parliament and of the Council of 12 December 2006 on services in the internal market. Technical report, European Parliament (December 2006)
2. OECD: Business and Industry Policy Forum on the Services Economy. Technical report, Organisation for Economic Cooperation and Development (OECD) (2000)
3. Riddle, D.: Service-Led Growth. The Role of the Service Sector in World Development. Praeger Publishers, New York (1986)
4. Schroth, C., Janner, T.: Web 2.0 and SOA: Converging Concepts Enabling the Internet of Services. IT Professional 9(3), 36–41 (2007)
5. Barros, A.P., Dumas, M.: The Rise of Web Service Ecosystems. IT Professional 8(5), 31–37 (2006)
6. Ameller, D., Franch, X.: Service-oriented computing: Concepts, characteristics and directions. In: WISE 2003: Proceedings of the Fourth International Conference on Web Information Systems Engineering, pp. 3–12. IEEE Computer Society Press, Washington (2003)
7. O'Sullivan, J., Edmond, D., Hofstede, A.: Formal description of non-functional service properties. Technical report, Queensland University of Technology (2005)
8. Dietrich, B.: Resource planning for business services. Commun. ACM 49(7), 62–64 (2006)
9. Roman, D., Lausen, H., Keller, U., de Bruijn, J., Bussler, C., Domingue, J., Fensel, D., Hepp, M., Kifer, M., König-Ries, B., Kopecky, J., Lara, R., Oren, E., Polleres, A., Scicluna, J., Stollberg, M.: D2v1.3. Web Service Modeling Ontology (WSMO). WSMO Working Draft (October 2006)
10. Cardoso, J., Winkler, M., Voigt, K.: A Service Description Language for the Internet of Services. In: Proceedings of ISSS 2009 - International Symposium on Services Science (March 2009)
11. Ludwig, H., Keller, A., Dan, A., King, R.P., Franck, R.: Web Service Level Agreement (WSLA) Language Specification. Technical report, IBM (2003)
12. Lamanna, D., Skene, J., Emmerich, W.: Specification Language for Service Level Agreements. EU IST 34069 deliverable D (2003)
13. Andrieux, A., Czajkowski, K., Dan, A., Keahey, K., Ludwig, H., Nakata, T., Pruyne, J., Rofrano, J., Tuecke, S., Xu, M.: Web Services Agreement Specification (WS-Agreement). Technical report, Open Grid Forum (2007)
14. openArchitectureWare.org: openArchitectureWare. Project page
15. Reichert, J.: Serviceabhängige Qualitätsparameter in Dienstgüteverträgen. Java Spektrum (6), 29–33 (2008)
16. Toland, C., Meenan, C., Warnock, M., Nagy, P.: Proactively Monitoring Departmental Clinical IT Systems with an Open Source Availability System. Journal of Digital Imaging 20, 119–124 (2007)
17. Spillner, J.: Privacy-enhanced Service Execution. In: Westnik DUIKT - Proceedings of the International Conference for Modern Information and Telecommunication Technologies, Livadia, Krim, Ukraine (September 2008)
18. Meyer, H., Kuropka, D., Tröger, P.: ASG–Techniques of Adaptivity. In: Proceedings of Autonomous and Adaptive Web Systems, Dagstuhl, Germany (June 2007)

# Dependency Management in Smart Homes

Daniel Retkowitz and Sven Kulle

Department of Computer Science 3 (Software Engineering)
RWTH Aachen University
Ahornstr. 55, 52074 Aachen, Germany
retkowitz@i3.informatik.rwth-aachen.de,
svekul@i3.informatik.rwth-aachen.de

**Abstract.** In future smart homes functionality will be provided to the
inhabitants by software services decoupled from the underlying hardware devices. While this will enhance flexibility and will allow to provide
cross-functionalities across multiple devices it will also lead to resource
conflicts. Future devices will provide basic functionalities which are used
by separate higher level services. Each person will use a number of different services and each environment can be inhabited by multiple users
at the same time. All respective services have to be executed based on a
limited number of devices, which will result in resource conflicts. In this
paper we describe how we extended our existing dependency management approach for smart home services with a mechanism for monitoring
service bindings and handling access control based on priority groups.

## 1 Introduction

Today computing is associated with desktop or laptop computers. Research in
the field of ubiquitous computing aims at integrating small computing devices
into almost anything that surrounds us in our everyday life. While being unaware
of the individual devices, users will be supported in different ways by software
services running on such devices. Smart Homes, or *eHomes* as we call them,
are smart environments based on the ubiquitous computing paradigm especially
focusing on home environments, e. g. private residential buildings.

Component-based software engineering allows to reuse existing software easily
and facilitates dynamic composition. These characteristics are especially important for eHome systems. To make low-cost eHomes available to a broad market,
ready-made components are used that are composed dynamically according to
the user's needs and the current context. Typically an underlying middleware
infrastructure is used to support the development of service components. By
making use of middleware technology, the service development effort can be
greatly reduced as the developers can focus on the services' application logic instead of implementing infrastructure functionality, e. g. life cycle and dependency
management, time and again for each service. This way service development is
simplified and development costs are reduced. In addition, more consistency is
gained by moving cross-functionality to the middleware layer.

T. Senivongse and R. Oliveira (Eds.): DAIS 2009, LNCS 5523, pp. 143–156, 2009.

The idea of ubiquitous computing implies a separation of application functionality and the devices used for realizing this functionality. Todays consumer electronics are typically based on a tight coupling of functionality and hardware. Either the functionality is directly implemented in hardware or it is implemented as an embedded system, i.e. a specific software hardware composition. Ubiquitous computing will lead to more general purpose devices and less highly integrated devices incorporating very specific functionalities. Thereby the direct relationship between functionality and the corresponding hardware used for its realization will disappear. While this will lead to positive effects in general, it will nevertheless create problems with respect to resource usage. Each eHome user can use a number of different services and different users can share the same environment within an eHome. The numerous services on the one hand and the limited number of hardware devices on the other hand will result in a disproportion. Therefore services usually will have to share the resources available in the respective environments. But in general not all resources may be used by multiple services at the same time. If e.g. a speaker system is used by lots of services at the same time, the user would only hear a chaotic noise. On the other hand, if one service exclusively uses the speaker system for a longer period of time, all other services depending on the speaker system will be blocked and can only proceed after the speaker system is released. This may not be reasonable in many cases.

To prevent such situations of resource conflicts a dynamic dependency management and resource allocation mechanism is needed to find a feasible trade-off between getting exclusive usage access to devices and sharing resources with other services. In this paper we will present our approach to tackle this issue and we will describe how we manage the service bindings at runtime with respect to concurrent use of resources. This approach is based on a fine-grained notion of bindings and corresponding usage relations, which enables interleaved resource access. Furthermore, our approach includes a priority management mechanism for service bindings, which is used to solve resource conflicts by prioritizing certain services over others. This is especially useful in case of security related services.

The paper is structured as follows. In Section 2 we describe previous work in our project that is used as basis for the dynamic dependency management introduced in this paper. The following Section 3 constitutes the main part of the paper in which we describe the extensions we made regarding binding types, priorities, and the application of both at system runtime. In Section 4 we explain the mechanisms used to implement the extensions. Furthermore we give an overview on some related work in Section 5. Finally, in Section 6, we conclude the paper with a summary and an outlook.

## 2    eHome Systems

Inhabitants of future smart home environments will use services from different domains as comfort, entertainment, communication, security, health care, or time and energy saving. To facilitate services in these areas a powerful infrastructure is needed to support development and later execution of services. Important challenges we addressed in previous work are handling the dynamics that occur in smart environments and enabling adaptivity and interoperability of heterogeneous services. In the following we give a brief description of our project and the underlying system architecture.

## 2.1  System Architecture

In our prototype realization, we use the OSGi Service Platform as a component-based service architecture for the implementation of eHome services [1]. In OSGi software components are called bundles which are deployed onto a service platform. OSGi provides different capabilities needed to build and run a component-based software system. Most importantly OSGi offers a concept for modularization, which is only supported insufficiently in pure Java. Furthermore it offers life-cycle management, allowing to add or remove bundles at system runtime. A service registry allows to find and use registered services from other bundles.

While OSGi offers these important capabilities it provides only limited support for a dynamic and context-aware dependency management, which is needed for services in the area of smart environments. For eHomes we need a more sophisticated model to handle special requirements like which service instance is assigned to which room and how many devices of a certain type are available in a room and are ready to use. Furthermore the user requirements change often and the eHome system has to be reconfigured accordingly. These characteristic requirements affect the configuration process of such systems.

Our system is based on a three-layered architecture of eHome services. The upper layer consists of so-called top-level services. These are application services that provide their functionality directly to the user. To provide this functionality they typically rely on driver or integrating services. Driver services build up the bottom layer. They provide access and control of available hardware devices in the eHome. Integrating services are used in an optional intermediate layer which allows to provide different steps of abstraction to connect top-level services to driver services.

## 2.2  Dynamic Dependency Management

Any service which requires a certain functionality needs a corresponding service providing that functionality. This relationship between services constitutes a *dependency*. At runtime, when service instances are created, these dependencies have to be fulfilled to allow the execution of the service instances. Dependencies are fulfilled by creating a *binding* between service instances. We call this process *configuration*. The purpose of the configuration process is to create a service composition that matches the user requirements and the available device environment on the one hand and tries to meet all service dependencies if possible on the other hand. The service specification affects the dependencies to other services. For each dependency the composition behavior can be influenced by so-called *binding policies*. These policies define whether a dependency is to be fulfilled automatically or manually and whether to bind as many services as possible or to bind only the minimum requirements. Furthermore, *binding constraints* impose restrictions on the service matching and thereby imply more specific service dependencies. Binding constraints are defined in the service specification for each required functionality. This way dependencies that relate to the current context of the environment can be realized.

We developed a prototype tool called *eHome Tool Suite* to support dynamic dependency management of eHome services as described above. Besides an editor for service specification the eHome Tool Suite also comprises a graphical editor for managing the runtime phase of the eHome system. Runtime management is implemented according to the so-called *SCD Process* [2] which consists of the three phases specification, configuration, and deployment. The specification can be modified by the user at any time using the graphical editor, e. g. moving services from one location to another or by manually adjusting service bindings. Based on this and the selected services' specifications the configuration of the system is generated or adjusted by the dependency management system described above. Finally the (modified) system configuration is deployed to the OSGi runtime environment in the deployment phase. This includes loading the corresponding bundles, creating service instances, and setting the service references according to the configured bindings. In contrast to other approaches aiming at a fully automatic system management, we provide the eHome Tool Suite as a means to visualize the current system state and to apply manual modifications to this state. In our view such means will be essential in future eHome systems to keep the users in control of their environments.

### 2.3   Example Scenario

In the rest of this section we will describe an example scenario to illustrate the problems evolving from the disproportion of used services and available resources.

Peter lives in an eHome and uses a web-enabled speaker system allowing to play different audio streams from network resources. The speakers are placed in the different rooms of Peter's apartment. His speaker system is used by several services, e. g. an alarm service for intrusion detection, a music service, a wake-up service, and a TV service. All these services depend on the speaker system.

Coming home from work, Peter's personal music service starts to play his favorite music. While walking through his apartment the music service is following automatically to his current location. After a while Peter wants to watch the news on TV. Because the music service has bound all speakers in the living room, he has to perform several manual reconfiguration steps such that the music service is stopped and the TV gets connected to the speakers. He also configures his wake-up service to wake him up at 6.00 am the next morning because he has an important meeting that day. After watching TV for a while Peter falls asleep in the living room. In the morning Peter wakes up at 6.30 am, fortunately not yet too late, wondering why he did not notice the wake-up call. The wake-up service could not use the speakers because they are still in use by the TV service and therefore could not be used by the wake-up service.

This problem also applies to other categories of resources. Considering a general heating service which keeps the temperature of a room at a certain level depending on the time of the year and the day we can easily imagine conflicts with personalized services relying on heating functionality. The wake-up service e. g. should be able to increase the bathroom temperature shortly before waking up the user. Therefore it needs to withdraw resources from the heating service.

These examples show that there will be a lot of standard services in future eHomes which make use of common resources. Even more services have to be taken into account if several users live in an eHome together. Especially an alarm service should be active at all times without requiring a constant manual reconfiguration of the system. It should always get access to resources that are currently used by other services due to the high security relevance.

# 3   Dependency Management

As we have seen in Section 2 the eHome prototype deals with common dynamic situations, like the dynamic reconfiguration of a user's music service to adapt to his movement. The reason for the occurrence of resource conflicts lies in the limited number of available resources. At some point, required resources will be unavailable which will lead to conflicts. But services do not need required resources during their entire runtime. If services would share resources efficiently during the time they are unused a lot of conflicts could be avoided. Based on this idea we present a solution to address this problem in the following.

## 3.1   Different Binding Types

The service developer enriches each service with a specification consisting of functional and non-functional meta-data, e. g. the service dependencies. This information is required for the (re-)configuration of an eHome system. Figure 1 illustrates the specification and configuration of the music service scenario and a wake-up service. On the left hand side the specification is shown. Both services require the functionality *Audio Output* provided by the speaker driver service. On the right hand side both services are installed in the living room. The music service is not usable and marked as invalid due to unavailable speakers. On the contrary the wake-up service is valid and can be used. Furthermore the wake-up service can use the speakers and the corresponding bindings respectively at any point in time until it gets undeployed. One resulting problem is the permanent locking of the speakers even though the wake-up service uses them only for a few minutes per day, e. g. in the morning when the user wants to be wakened. This problem does not only apply to the wake-up service. Most services do not use their assigned resources permanently. Nevertheless services cannot use resources bound by other services whether they are actually in use at the moment or not.

Since this is not a preferable solution, we extended our existing dynamic binding concept to allow a shared resource usage. Instead of only having bindings reserving resources permanently, we suggest an additional type of bindings which

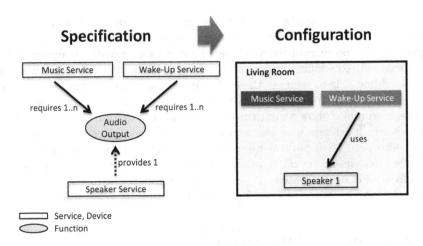

**Fig. 1.** Exemplary specification and configuration of eHome services

only locks a resource during the time it is actually using it. Bindings, allowing the shared use of resources are called *concurrent bindings* while bindings, only allowing the exclusive use of resources are called *exclusive bindings*. The extended dynamic binding concept is based on three main ideas: (1) Concurrent bindings get established independently of the actual availability of a resource. This is a substantial difference to exclusive bindings. As a consequence the availability of a service is computed differently. Unlike exclusive bindings concurrent bindings consume a provided functionality only while the binding is actually used. (2) If a service actually tries to use a concurrent binding the service framework must examine whether it is currently available or not. This binding check is performed by a so-called interceptor component. (3) Services trying to use a concurrently bound resource which is momentarily unavailable get notified about the failed use attempt. They are notified again when the resource becomes available again.

The three concepts mentioned above are implemented by the two newly introduced binding types. Exclusive bindings grant an independent and permanent access to the resource. But if no providing service is available no binding can be established. In that case the corresponding service is invalid if the binding is not specified as optional. In Figure 1 this applies to the music service which is invalid and cannot be used. Concurrent bindings always can be established but are not permanently usable, therefore each single attempt to use a concurrent binding is monitored and can either proceed or fail.

As mentioned above concurrently bound resources are locked temporarily depending on the actual use by other services. One important question is how to determine the time frame a concurrent binding is used. An idea coming first to mind is that the use of a binding begins with a call of a method and ends when the execution of the method is finished. But regarding the music service as an example, this would imply that after pressing the play button the bound speakers become instantly available to other services. This is because the music service is calling control operations on other services and resources. In case of the speaker

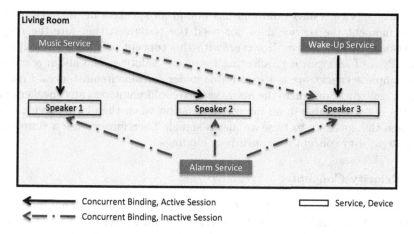

**Fig. 2.** Runtime configuration based on the extended dynamic binding concept

system the music service would pass certain parameters like the URL of a music streaming resource. Most top-level services have a controlling character like the music service. This means the actual playback of the music does not involve the controlling service itself and the time period during which the binding is actually used by a method call is very small. In most cases the resource is required for a much longer period of time. In case of the music service pushing the button is only a point in time but playing the song is not.

To overcome these difficulties, the dynamic binding concept has been extended to include a session concept. An active session indicates that the concurrent binding is used and therefore the availability of the resource is limited for other services. On the contrary, an inactive session indicates that the concurrent binding is not used and therefore the resource is available to other services. In previous work we introduced a concept allowing to map service functionalities onto a domain-specific ontology to enable semantic matching and service adaptation [3]. This concept is further used for semantical tagging of methods and in this context we use it for *begin session* and *end session* annotations. This way the service developer can express that with pressing the play button a session begins and the speakers are used by the music service until the user presses the stop button and the session ends. If the user pauses the music or changes the track then the session status remains unchanged. This also means that a resource can only be used if the session is already active or some method is called which starts a session. If the user e. g. pushes the next track button while no music is played there is no active session and nothing will happen.

Figure 2 shows a runtime configuration of three eHome services based on the extended dynamic binding concept. For the time being all three services have bound speakers and are therefore valid. The wake-up service is bound concurrently to the third speaker and also uses this speaker at the moment. All three speakers are bound to the music service but only speakers one and two are used by the service since the third speaker is already occupied by the wake-up service.

The alarm service is also valid and has bound all speakers in the environment. At the moment the service does not need the resources, therefore the respective sessions are not active. However, with this concept problems can still arise. Some types of services, e. g. affecting the users' safety as the alarm service in our example scenario, are not executable under certain circumstances. Figure 2 shows a configuration where the alarm service could not access any speaker at all which is not acceptable in an intrusion situation when the alarm service needs to access the speakers to raise an alarm signal. Therefore we use a simple but effective priority concept for concurrent bindings.

## 3.2   Priority Concept

The priority concept is based on a ranking of the installed eHome services. If required this ranking can be used to determine which service is allowed to use a shared resource. In Figure 2 the alarm service should have the highest priority so that the service can use all the speakers if needed. It is not reasonable to assign a priority number to each eHome service at development time. eHomes are dynamic systems and at specification time it is not known which services are installed later on that have to share common resources at runtime. Therefore no ranking can be specified beforehand. Instead we have to regard the specification of a function and the respective providing and requiring services in the service setup of a specific eHome system. At runtime the user can create an individual ranking and assign to each providing functionality of a service a corresponding priority list consisting of the installed services requiring this specific functionality. This is shown at the top of Figure 3. The leftmost service has the highest priority and the rightmost service has the smallest one. For practical reasons the services can be arranged in priority groups. Services within the same group also have the same priority. This means it is not determined which service is of higher priority and thus no service can withdraw resources from other services of the same group. If a higher priority service accesses a resource in use by a lower priority service, the resource is withdrawn from the lower priority service and reassigned to the higher priority service. The lower priority service then receives a notification and the corresponding session is closed. This procedure is based on the assumption that resources are fully interruptable and hence the withdrawal of concurrently bound resources is always possible. Anyway, the concurrent bindings remain established while resources are reassigned. When a required resource becomes available again a waiting service is notified and can continue using the resource.

## 4   Implementation

This section briefly describes the implementation of the extended dynamic binding concept. As mentioned before an interceptor component is used to monitor concurrent bindings at runtime. This component consists of two parts: The first part is responsible for detecting the actual use of a binding. The second part deals with access control, session handling, and the priority management.

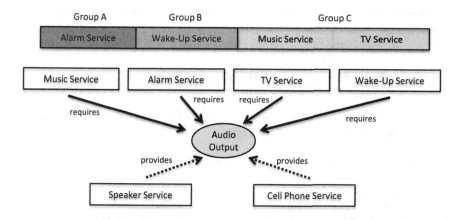

**Fig. 3.** Connection between services, functions, and priorities

Resources get accessed through method calls, e. g. `playMusic()` for the music service. After such a call is detected the eHome framework must decide whether the method call should be allowed or rejected. As explained above the use of a dynamic binding depends on the resource's actual usability. This check is related to the second part of the interceptor. According to the interceptor's result the method call can proceed or is rejected. In the second case, the service needs to be notified about the invalid access to be able to react correctly. For that purpose we use Java's exception mechanism. Similar to other frameworks like e. g. iPOJO [4] the eHome services mostly implement pure application logic. In general the service developer does not need to know much about the eHome framework to be able to develop services. In this case the developer must only be aware of the fact that some binding may not be usable and an exception is thrown. But this is a general requirement anyway in ubiquitous computing and especially eHome systems. Due to the dynamics in such environments, required resources may not be available or accessible at all times.

To monitor concurrent bindings we use aspect-oriented programming [5]. In our case the aspect-oriented language AspectJ is used, which is a seamless extension of the Java programming language. AspectJ enables a clean modularization of cross-cutting concerns such as error checking, logging, monitoring etc. We use especially the load-time weaving mechanism of AspectJ to implement the interception mechanism. This feature enables code injection into bundles that are already loaded and running.

In line 1 of Listing 1.1 the pointcut *functionMethods* is defined, which is responsible for the method call detection. Each call of a method within the *ehome.interfaces* package will be intercepted. These calls correspond to using a service binding. Pointcuts only match specific points in the control flow of a program, which are called join points. To actually inject code or implement cross-cutting concerns an advice is used. If a join point is reached corresponding advices are executed. AspectJ supports different kinds of advices. Line 3 shows an around advice which interrupts execution at respective join points and executes

```
1  pointcut functionMethods(EhService usedSrv) : target(usedSrv)
       && call(public * ehome.interfaces.*.*(..));
2
3  Object around(EhService usedSrv) throws
       BindingUnusableException : functionMethods(usedSrv) {
4      ...
5      String rString = interceptor.intercept(usingSrv, usedSrv,
           methodSig, interfaceName);
6
7      if (...) { // if binding usage is allowed
8          ...
9          proceed(usedSrv);
10     } else { // binding is not usable, raise an exception
11         int hashCode = Integer.valueOf((rString.split(";")[1]));
12         throw new BindingUnusableException(usingSrv.toString()+",
               "+usedSrv.toString(), hashCode);
13     }
14  }
```

**Listing 1.1.** Aspect intercepting service communication

the advice instead of the original method call. The given parameter *usedSrv* is the service which requests to use the binding. In line 5 the interceptor component checks if the service *usingSrv* is allowed to use the binding. If access is granted, line 9 redirects to the original method call. Otherwise the around advice throws an exception in line 12 to notify the calling service about the invalid access.

The second part of the interceptor component is called from within the advice discussed above and is modeled as a Fujaba story diagram. Fujaba is a UML-based development tool which allows to generate Java code from UML diagrams [6]. Besides the data model so called story diagrams, which are a combination of UML activity and collaboration diagrams, are used to model the application logic. This way executable Java code can be directly generated from the model. Since the whole story diagram modeling the interceptor component is quite complex, we will discuss a simplified view depicted in Figure 4. The interception process consists of four important steps. First the binding in question must be determined. The interception process only continues if the binding is a concurrent one, otherwise it returns with *proceed* which means the original method call will be executed by the around advice. The next steps depend on the state of the session and the binding's current usability. If the session is already established (cf. diamond *Active Session?*) then the method call is valid and can be allowed to execute. But before that, the interceptor checks if the session is to be closed. Like explained in Section 3 it is possible to semantically annotate methods with an *end session* tag. This annotation is read by the interceptor. If a service requests to use a resource and the session is not active then the interceptor must check if a session is to be opened (cf. diamond *Open Session?*). If this is not

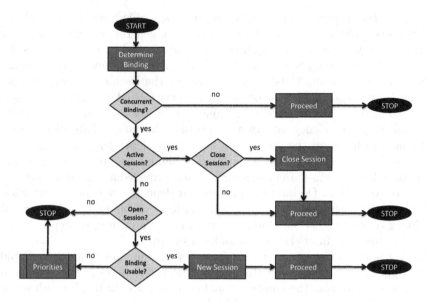

**Fig. 4.** Evaluation of intercepted service communication

the case the around advice rejects the method call. Otherwise a usability check is performed (cf. diamond *Binding Usable?*). The interceptor counts the active sessions and exclusive bindings to determine if a binding can be used. If no more active sessions are allowed, service priorities are taken into account to check if some active session has to be withdrawn from a service with lower priority. If the binding is still not usable the method call will be rejected. Otherwise a new session is opened and the method call is executed.

The described mechanism has been implemented and integrated into our prototype system. So far, we only performed a qualitative validation based on the *eHomeSimulator*, a software tool we developed to simulate different smart environments [7]. The results show that our approach actually allows to resolve resource conflicts. However, a quantitative evaluation is still pending.

## 5 Related Work

In service-oriented architectures, applications are composed from several services which often appear or disappear dynamically. Dependency management is therefore a key aspect and a lot of research is going on in this field.

A number of approaches are based on the OSGi Service Platform which also provides dependency management. Dependencies between bundles and dependencies between services are handled differently in OSGi. The first ones are package dependencies and are related to the OSGi module layer. The bundle developer specifies these dependencies in the bundle manifest. The OSGi framework resolves these bundle dependencies and only if all constraints are satisfied the bundle can be loaded. Service dependencies on the other hand are related to the service layer. An OSGi service is a normal Java object registered at the service registry under one or more Java interfaces. In general, a service can use the service registry to search for required services registered by other bundles. But this type of dependency management does not support automatic resolution.

Since release 4 of the OSGi Service Platform, the Declarative Services specification is available which evolved from the Service Binder project [8]. It separates two important responsibilities: Implementing the application logic on the one hand and dependency management on the other hand. This allows service developers to focus on the application logic while dependency management is outsourced into a special framework bundle. Similar to our approach bundles get enriched with meta-data descriptors of their provided and required functionalities. In contrast to Declarative Services, our dependency management allows to bind services depending on context information, e. g. bind only services within the living room. Further on, OSGi does not provide a priority concept, which is needed in the domain of eHomes as we have shown.

In [4] Escoffier et al. propose a service-oriented component model to simplify OSGi application development. Like with Declarative Services the application logic is separated from the non-functional requirements. In iPOJO each service is encapsulated inside a container, which is used to inject non-functional requirements to manage e. g. service bindings or the service lifecycle. Each container is composed by handlers managing these non-functional requirements. If a required service becomes available, the appropriate handler directly injects the needed objects. If a required service disappears and cannot be replaced, the depending services become invalid. Since iPOJO employs a decentralized composition approach, each container has its own dependency manager. Thus no global view is available and features like our resource management based on priority groups cannot be supported.

In [9] Bottaro et al. discuss several requirements for software architectures in home environments. The requirement of *service continuity* addresses rebinding problems due to stateful services. If a resource has an internal state and is replaced by another resource at runtime, the state information has to be transferred to the new resource. The authors propose to handle state transfer on the application level since an automatic approach is only possible in specific applications. This is also the case in our approach. However, the problem of how to handle the rebinding of services in the first place while allowing shared resource usage is not addressed in [9].

In [10] the problem of disconnections regarding component bindings in distributed environments is addressed. The authors argue that top-level components are rarely usable if disconnections occur frequently. The proposed solution is to activate and deactivate required interfaces according to their current availability and to allow component execution even if some required interfaces are deactivated. In that case the top-level component may still be usable though with restricted functionality. In contrast to our approach, the component developer is required to take care of testing the interface status before invoking methods. Our mechanism does not require such tests. However, the developer has to handle events in case of failed use attempts in our approach.

In [11] the authors describe an approach called COMITY for runtime conflict detection in pervasive computing environments based on the PCOM component model. The presented approach analyzes the effects that pervasive applications take on the environments they are executed in and how this affects other applications and users. The proposed system consists of a conflict manager component connected to a database that stores a context model representing the current state of the environment. A second database stores conflict specifications which determine what kind of situations are considered to be conflicting. Based on this, the conflict manager detects conflicting situations at runtime. In contrast to our approach COMITY does not focus on conflicts regarding resource usage but rather on conflicts resulting from different user interests. We do not address these conflicts as we believe they will require manual resolution by the users in most real-life scenarios.

In previous work at our department an approach to rule-based conflict detection has been developed [12]. The presented conflict detection mechanism assumes that each resource in the system is specified in form of an $\omega$-automaton describing its behavior. Together with a set of rules which formalize the different conflict types a monitor component can detect conflicting situations at runtime. This approach is similar to COMITY but it is based on a different infrastructure. It requires services to provide a semantic specification describing their behavior and it forces top-level services to be realized in a rule-based approach. We do not impose such strong requirements on service development, instead service developers can focus on the core task of implementing application logic.

# 6 Summary and Outlook

In this paper we described our approach to support dependency management for eHome systems dealing specifically with the resource constraints arising in ubiquitous computing scenarios. The general idea of our solution is to monitor and manage service communication based on the current state of the system configuration. All this is realized with minimal impact on the service implementation, so that the service development process is not affected unnecessarily. We introduced a session concept based on tagging service methods. Together with the interception of service communication this information is used to manage the utilization of bindings at runtime. In addition to that we allow to define priority groups at runtime to allow an automatic resolution of conflicts.

There are several issues which are to be addressed in future work. Up to now, we tested our approach using a testbed fully implemented in software. We still need to perform a quantitative evaluation in a larger scenario to analyze the scalability of our implementation. Furthermore, it is still an open question how to simplify the definition of priority groups to support automatic conflict resolution. In real-world systems we also need a simple but useful mechanism for solving conflicts manually at runtime without bothering the users with permanent requests for interaction.

# References

1. The OSGi Alliance: OSGi Service Platform Core Specification. Release 4.1 (April 2007), http://www.osgi.org/Specifications/HomePage#Release4
2. Retkowitz, D., Stegelmann, M.: Dynamic Adaptability for Smart Environments. In: Meier, R., Terzis, S. (eds.) DAIS 2008. LNCS, vol. 5053, pp. 154–167. Springer, Heidelberg (2008)
3. Retkowitz, D., Pienkos, M.: Ontology-based Configuration of Adaptive Smart Homes. In: Taïani, F., Cerqueira, R. (eds.) Proceedings of the $7^{th}$ Workshop on Reflective and Adaptive Middleware (ARM 2008) held at the $9^{th}$ International Middleware Conference, pp. 11–16. ACM, New York (2008)
4. Escoffier, C., Hall, R.S., Lalanda, P.: iPOJO: an Extensible Service-Oriented Component Framework. In: IEEE International Conference on Services Computing (SCC 2007), pp. 474–481 (July 2007)
5. Kiczales, G., Lamping, J., Mendhekar, A., Maeda, C., Lopes, C., Loingtier, J.M., Irwin, J.: Aspect-Oriented Programming. In: Aksit, M., Matsuoka, S. (eds.) ECOOP 1997. LNCS, vol. 1241, pp. 220–242. Springer, Heidelberg (1997)
6. Fischer, T., Niere, J., Torunski, L., Zündorf, A.: Story Diagrams: A new Graph Rewrite Language based on the Unified Modeling Language. In: Engels, G., Rozenberg, G. (eds.) TAGT 1998. LNCS, vol. 1764, pp. 296–309. Springer, Heidelberg (2000)
7. Armac, I., Retkowitz, D.: Simulation of Smart Environments. In: Proceedings of the IEEE International Conference on Pervasive Services 2007 (ICPS 2007), pp. 257–266. IEEE, Los Alamitos (2007)
8. Cervantes, H., Hall, R.S.: Automating Service Dependency Management in a Service-Oriented Component Model. In: Crnkovic, I., Schmidt, H., Stafford, J., Wallnau, K. (eds.) Proceedings of the $6^{th}$ ICSE Workshop on Component-Based Software Engineering (CBSE6), pp. 379–382 (May 2003)
9. Bottaro, A., Gérodolle, A., Lalanda, P.: Pervasive Service Composition in the Home Network. In: $21^{st}$ International Conference on Advanced Information Networking and Applications (AINA 2007), pp. 596–603 (May 2007)
10. Hoareau, D., Mahéo, Y.: Constraint-Based Deployment of Distributed Components in a Dynamic Network. In: Grass, W., Sick, B., Waldschmidt, K. (eds.) ARCS 2006. LNCS, vol. 3894, pp. 450–464. Springer, Heidelberg (2006)
11. Tuttlies, V., Schiele, G., Becker, C.: COMITY – Conflict Avoidance in Pervasive Computing Environments. In: Meersman, R., Tari, Z., Herrero, P. (eds.) OTM-WS 2007, Part II. LNCS, vol. 4806, pp. 763–772. Springer, Heidelberg (2007)
12. Armac, I., Kirchhof, M., Manolescu, L.: Modeling and Analysis of Functionality in eHome Systems: Dynamic Rule-based Conflict Detection. In: Proceedings of the $13^{th}$ Annual IEEE International Symposium and Workshop on Engineering of Computer Based Systems (ECBS 2006), Washington, DC, USA, pp. 219–228. IEEE, Los Alamitos (2006)

# SoundPark: Towards Highly Collaborative Game Support in a Ubiquitous Computing Architecture

Romain Pellerin[1], Nicolas Bouillot[2], Tatiana Pietkiewicz[1],
Mike Wozniewski[2], Zack Settel[3], Eric Gressier-Soudan[1],
and Jeremy R. Cooperstock[2]

[1] Conservatoire National des Arts et Métiers,
Paris, France
{romain.pellerin,eric.gressier_soudan}@cnam.fr
[2] Centre for Intelligent Machines,
McGill University, Montreal, QC, Canada
{nicolas,mikewoz,jer}@cim.mcgill.ca
[3] University of Montreal,
Montreal, QC, Canada
zs@sympatico.ca

**Abstract.** Ubiquitous computing architectures enable interaction and collaboration in multi-user applications. We explore the challenges of integrating the disparate services required in such architectures and describe how we have met these challenges in the context of a real-world application that operates on heterogeneous hardware and run-time environments. As a compelling example, we consider the role of ubiquitous computing to support the needs of a distributed multi-user game, including mobility, mutual awareness, and geo-localization. The game presented here, "SoundPark", is played in a mixed-reality environment, in which the physical space is augmented with computer-generated audio and graphical content, and the players communicate frequently over a low-latency audio channel. Our experience designing and developing the game motivates significant discussion related to issues of general relevance to ubiquitous game architectures, including integration of heterogeneous components, monitoring, remote control and scalability.

## 1 Introduction

Our research is oriented toward the use of distributed architectures to support high-level group interaction in computer-mediated environments, in particular, involving virtual and mixed reality. The applications we are exploring require an engaging level of interaction between multiple users and their environment, in which cooperation, coordination, and mutual awareness are critical. As we explain in further detail below, a ubiquitous computing architecture is not only

T. Senivongse and R. Oliveira (Eds.): DAIS 2009, LNCS 5523, pp. 157–170, 2009.
© IFIP International Federation for Information Processing 2009

appropriate for such requirements, but offers several further benefits of mobility and context-awareness, where context includes location, time, user activity, physical environment [1], as well as execution environment [2].

Ubiquitous computing and physical interaction with mobile device have proven to be significant factors in improving social relationships in teams working toward a common goal. Examples include children playing [3] or tourist groups visiting an unfamiliar museum [4]. However, when team members interact remotely, mutual awareness is often highly constrained. Existing ubiquitous games have addressed this shortcoming in part, but with an emphasis primarily on location awareness. We believe that significant opportunities remain untapped to improve the communication between players and interaction with the environment. Specifically, these aspects of game play can benefit from the use of personalized rendering of audio and graphics displays that enable continuous awareness between the team members and of their augmented environment.

To support our exploration of this potential in the context of a new mixed-reality multi-player game, *SoundPark*,[1] we developed three novel services intended to improve the degree of engagement and interaction between players: a framework for immersive spatial audio performance; a low-latency, high-fidelity streaming engine; and a service-oriented middleware for ubiquitous games. SoundPark takes full advantage of these generic services, including structured session management, continuous audio and graphic rendering, sensor management and low-latency communication. As anticipated, the integration of these components resulted in an unavoidable increase in implementation complexity.

The remainder of this paper is organized as follows. Section 2 summarizes and compares the present work with other games in this category. Section 3 describes the details of our own service architecture, addressing the issue of complexity. Section 4 is dedicated to the design of SoundPark, and reviews some of the lessons learned from the associated implementation effort. Section 5 summarizes lessons learned and discusses the implications of this work to supporting continuous mutual awareness in a ubiquitous computing environment. Section 6 concludes with suggestions for the development of future ubiquitous game architectures.

## 2    Related Work

The infrastructure of multiplayer ubiquitous games is typically based on computationally limited devices such as mobile phones, PDAs, and portable game systems, that delegate the complexity of group communication and state management to servers. In this context, mobile devices have traditionally enabled ubiquitous mixed reality by providing geo-localization, either to provide players' position or to collect virtual objects in the environment [5]. Examples include Botfighter [6], CanYouSeeMeNow [7], Mogi [8], and CatchBob [9].

A seminal example is Cheok's *Human Pacman* [10], which inherits its design from the eponymous arcade game of the early 1980's, but consists of human

---

[1] A sample video is available at
http://www.audioscape.org/twiki/bin/view/Audioscape/MobileAudioscape

**Table 1.** A comparison of notable mobile pervasive computing games

| game | description | localization technology | networking |
|---|---|---|---|
| BotFighters [6] | multiplayer city game using text messages to seek enemies. Browser game interface is provided for audience in order to monitor the game state | GSM network cell identification | GSM network |
| CanYouSeeMe [7] | multiplayer outdoor game using 2D graphical display on a PDA to seek other players. Audio communication between player using walkie-talkies | GPS | Wireless LAN |
| CatchBob [9] | multiplayer game where users collaboratively discover information necessary to catch Bob, a virtual object. Information is localized and displayed on a tablet PC using a 2D map overlay | radio beacon | Wireless LAN |
| Myht (Meet your heartbeat twin) [14] | multiplayer game continuously using players' heart rates to determine couples that have to meet. PDAs are used to display twin location | GPS | General Packet Radio Service (GPRS) |
| Pac-Lan [11] | multiplayer campus game using RFID tags to seek other players. For localization, graphical 2D display on mobile phone is provided to players and audience | RFID-based | General Packet Radio Service (GPRS) |
| Human-Pacman [10] | augmented reality (3D overlay on real images) campus game using HMD and backpack computers. Human helpers communicate with player using text messages to help them find each other. Bluetooth cookies are used for real world augmentation. | GPS | Wireless LAN |

players wearing head-mounted displays (HMD) and playing the role of *pacman* or *ghosts*. Human Pacman has been extended by different projects, including Pac-Lan RFID [11], where both game objects (pills, super-pills, and ghosts) and human players have associated RFID tags. Such tags, increasingly popular in entertainment applications, are used for location, identification and content delivery [12,13]. In addition to simple geo-localization, certain recently proposed games, such as MeetYourHeartTwin [14], propose the additional integration of biosensors to establish social relationships between players. In this example, players are able to use their PDA displays to see others who share their heartbeat characteristics, e.g., within a similar frequency range.

Table 1 provides a general description of previously mentioned games. While various localization technologies provide more or less accurate tracking, team coordination is typically restricted to simple mechanisms such as position visualization, text messages or standard walkie-talkies.

The architecture presented here shares many characteristics with these earlier works. However, rather than focusing only on visualization of position, we emphasize audio interaction for communication between players, for rendering various aspects of game state, and for enabling decision-making related to choices that affect the virtual world. Further, in contrast with the games described above, where little contextual information is exchanged between players, we integrate localization, low latency audio and other sensorially acquired data to support richer mutual awareness. In turn, our experience highlights the important trade-off between wireless communication over a large physical scale, where network access may be discontinuous, and tasks mandating a high level of connectivity. Needless to say, this remains a challenge that future related middleware will continue to face.

At the level of interaction design, our approach is distinguished by its emphasis on continuous modeling and perception of the overlaid virtual world. The positions and states of virtual objects are dynamically updated and may be manipulated through lightweight, mobile devices. Moreover, the nature of continuous audio perception, as it relates to geo-localization of the players, requires significantly greater accuracy of sensing than provided by GSM network cell identification, RFID or standard GPS, in addition to nearly continuous network connectivity.

## 3    Architecture

Support for mutual awareness and context awareness as relevant to user-level collaboration requires integration of various functionalities, leading to a complex combination of hardware and software components. This necessitates an extensible architecture, so that missing functionality can be enabled as required, and raises several design decisions that must be addressed. Foremost among these is the tradeoff between a distributed computing ideal, with all computation performed in a distributed manner, versus a more centralized, and likely less scalable, architecture. While high-end mobile devices may have the necessary processing capacity to support general-purpose applications, most highly portable platforms remain less suitable for the demands of real-time computation, such as user-specific multi-source audio spatialization or merging of virtual graphical content with the physical world in a mixed reality framework.[2]

Faced with the processing constraints of mobile devices, we were required to proceed with a centralized architecture, allocating the demanding computations to more powerful servers. On the positive side, our service-oriented approach enables extensions and supports reusability of already implemented components. In particular, our architecture allows for the separation of application- and device-specific code. As can be understood from the following description, this facilitates rapid prototyping of many applications requiring mutual awareness between users and context-awareness of both their states and that of the environment. Moreover, because the middleware provides connectors to handle data from any type of sensor, it is well suited for the integration of mobile devices with additional sensor inputs.

## 3.1 Overview

Our architecture is shown in Figure 1. The server is dedicated to global state management, user-customized audio, and graphical rendering of the virtual environment. It consists of two components: Audioscape for real-time rendering of audio and 3D graphics, and the uGASP server, based on our middleware that targets ubiquitous multiplayer gaming. The uGASP server, compliant with the OSGi specification[3], is the master component of the architecture. It handles high-level application events, that can be triggered by Audioscape for rendering the virtual environment. Existing uGASP services are used for coordinating scenario, session, and sensor management with a game engine.

Mobile clients support sensing of the user and the surrounding environment, as well as local delivery of audio and graphics. User input components, for physical mobile interaction, include GPS, Wiimote and RFID support. Although presented together in Figure 1, due to the limited functionality of current mobile products, the client features are actually deployed on two separate mobile devices, as described in Section 4.2.

## 3.2 uGASP

The uGASP[4] [15] middleware implements the Open Mobile Alliance Games Services (OMA GS) working group specifications that deal with multiplayer game management on embedded devices. uGASP, implemented in Java J2ME, is based on the Open Services Gateway Initiative (OSGi) component framework,

---

[2] The Human Pacman game [10] (see Section 2) is no exception: although local 3D visual rendering is performed locally to the user, the equipment includes a personal computer carried in a back-packed and a HMD. These requirements dramatically reduce the user's long-term mobility.

[3] OSGi Service Platform Release 4 specifications, http://www.osgi.org

[4] uGASP is available under the L-GPL license from
http://gasp.objectweb.org/ubiquitous-osgi-middleware.html

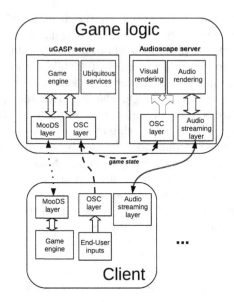

**Fig. 1.** SoundPark Middleware Architecture Overview

and more specifically on the iPOJO OSGi layer that provides additional modular, dynamic and configurable services through the creation, deployment and calling of a bundle[5]. Interestingly, this allows for deployment, optionally dynamic, of specific optimized instances of the middleware, freeing the binary code from unwanted functionality.

uGASP is composed of multiple families of services, including network communication, session management, a game server engine that handles game logic, ubiquitous services and system services. Game logic is implemented as a Java class that implements the Server interface. During implementation of the server, the required uGASP services are specified by the developer. These are then instantiated automatically as appropriate during initialization of a game session.

Existing bundles have been extensively employed in server and client implementations. For example, the uGASP location manager bundle is used to compute projections of player positions for both 2D and 3D displays, described later. Another bundle was deployed on mobile phones for handling RFID tags. The middleware was also improved with a bidirectional network communication connector, supporting more efficient exchanges than were available with the pre-existing HTTP connector. As seen in Figure 4, this new connector provides the communication layer used between the mobile phone and the Gumstix computer. Similarly, an OSC protocol (see Section 3.4) bundle was developed for the purpose of handling data acquired from various sensors and interpreting events necessary to manage the scenario.

---

[5] In OSGi terminology, a software component providing a specified service is denoted as a bundle.

uGASP, in addition to being a key part of the SoundPark architecture, provides a bundle for deploying a client side game engine. A 2D map display on mobile phones extracted from our SoundPark prototype illustrated by Figure 2, is used to show the locations of other players and virtual objects. In this application, the deployed byte-code contains only the necessary bundles, providing an optimized application memory footprint, as required for deployment on the resource constrained device.

**Fig. 2.** A 2D virtual world view appearing on a mobile phone display, extracted from our SoundPark prototype. Shown are two player avatars, a sound loop virtual object indicated by the musical note, and a player (Zack), approximately in the middle of the goal line of the football field (anchored at his feet). The yellow circle represents the staging area.

### 3.3   Audioscape

Ubiquitous mixed reality interaction leads naturally to context aware rendering of graphical and audio content. This is delegated to the *Audioscape* platform [16] that models the location of predefined sound sources, including both virtual objects and users, in a 3D representation of the physical environment. Using game events received through the uGASP server, the Audioscape server's role is to maintain the state of the virtual 3D environment, and compute spatialized audio renderings for each user, including real-time processing based on directivity of sound specification, radiation pattern, and realistic effects such as reverberation and Doppler shift.

Despite its name, Audioscape is also used for 3D *visual* rendering of the scene for monitoring the application, and optionally for visualization by an audience, as described below. This is accomplished with a customized graphics engine built with OpenSceneGraph[6], which represents users and virtual objects as arbitrary 3D models, as illustrated in Figure 3. This allows for monitoring of the actions of users, represented as dynamic 3D avatars, and the application status, on a virtual display.

---

[6] http://www.openscenegraph.org

**Fig. 3.** 3D virtual world view, in which two players, the hunter and scout, can be seen. Sounds are spread over the field.

In their current version, the Audioscape 3D audio and graphical engines are integrated into Pure Data (PD) [17], a pseudo real-time environment dedicated to (simulatenously) programming and executing interactive multimedia applications. The PD internal design provides an interface allowing the development of additional processing components, called *externals*. At the client side in our architecture, our PD externals are executed by *Pure Data anywhere* (PDa) [18], a rewritten fixed-point version of PD.

### 3.4    Communication

Communication between software running on the servers and mobile devices uses three different protocols. The first one, the MooDS protocol [19], providing binary serialization process within uGASP, is dedicated to optimized and reliable object-oriented communication with J2ME enabled devices. It was therefore considered suitable for game event dissemination.

Open Sound Control [20] (OSC) is a character-oriented data exchange protocol for real-time control of media processing, (initially sound processing) that has gained considerable popularity in the distributed audio community. It provide namespaces and is optionally encapsuled inside the UDP protocol, making it suitable for rapid prototyping of applications that require low-latency transmission of data, but that can tolerate sporadic data losses. This is particularly well-adapted for periodic data, such as those acquired by sensors.

Finally, the high-fidelity audio streaming protocol, *nStream*,[7] provides bi-directional low-latency audio communication. Its development was motivated in a large part by the high latencies and computational complexity associated with typical compressed audio formats, and the unsuitability of traditional RF

---

[7] *nStream* is a Pure Data component, compatible with Pure Data's fixed-point version. *nStream* source code, distributed under the GNU General Public Licence, is available within the Audioscape SVN repository, accessible at http://www.audioscape.org.

solutions given their limited range, high power draw, and signal interference issues. Low-latency,[8] generally required for remote audio interaction, is particularly important in our architecture, where all user audio rendering and team communications are computed remotely by the Audioscape server.

# 4   SoundPark

In order to evaluate our architecture, when supporting a deep level of player collaboration in a ubiquitous game context, we enabled very precise location tracking, powerful yet power frugal mobile computing resources, and low-latency audio connectivity between the players. This section describes the SoundPark game design and how it emphasizes player collaboration in a mixed reality environment, then covers the technical game implementation.

## 4.1   Game Design

The SoundPark game was designed for the Jeanne Mance park, an area covering 630x190 meters in the city of Montreal. The physical park environment was augmented with (physical) RFID tags and (virtual) audio objects, which were initially placed at pre-determined locations. Consistent with the theme of a mixed reality environment, game objects typically exist as both real (physical) and virtual entities: clues are represented by their associated bollards and RFID tags, but reveal their content graphically on a mobile phone display. Sound loops are only heard by users via directed listening, i.e. when close to the corresponding location, and only once the associated clue has been discovered. Although sound loops are only perceived in the virtual domain through the players' headsets, they can also be moved from place to place. In addition, audio spatialization is used to guide users toward the sound loop location, which becomes better audible with the use of volume level mapped with user's actual distance to the virtual sound location.

A team is composed of two player types, whose combined goal is to create a musical arrangement of multiple sound loops, assembled in a staging area, or home base. Walkie-talkie-like communication is used to coordinate their activities. Action is initiated by the *scout*, who discovers clues by reading the RFID tags distributed throughout the game area, and then observes the associated sound loop locations through a mobile display that also provides continuous updates of player locations (see Figure 2). Once the clue has been discovered, the associated sound loop appears in the virtual world, and can be heard by *hunters* who pass near to its physical location. The scout's role is then to guide the hunter near the sound loop, which is optionally acquired and then attached to the hunter, who must carry it to the staging area. After the sound loop is deposited, it becomes part of the target musical arrangement, composed of the

---

[8] With nStream, and by using recording software to capture both the original audio source signal as it is supplied to the mobile sender and the output audio from the receiver, we measured a total end-to-end delay of 14.4ms.

combination of all sounds acquired by the team. The game ends when one of the teams has successfully collected all its required sound loops.

To increase the challenge of the game, clues indicate the location of individual sound loops, but not their musical properties, which can only be discovered by the hunters as they draw near. Furthermore, not all sound loops will fit with the theme of a target musical arrangement. For example, a baroque guitar loop cannot be part of a jazz arrangement. Attempts to deposit such a sound loop in the staging area fail with an appropriate feedback message.

### 4.2  Implementation

During development, we extensively employed the services and components of our architecture. The game design itself was programmed with only a few (455) lines of code within the server, taking advantage of game engine and management services provided by uGASP. The most demanding part of creating the game itself was modeling and calibrating the park for 3D and 2D visualization, followed by creating the audio content.

In terms of user interface hardware for the players, our game requires only small form factor devices, such as the Gumstix, described later, and near-field communications (NFC)-enabled Nokia 6131 mobile phones. Players in Sound-Park use role-specific hardware: a *scout* player carries a mobile phone that displays a map of a section of the game environment, and with an NFC-RFID reader. Although RFID tags could contain game information in their own memory,[9] we simply use their Universal Identifiers (UID) to index data into the game database, hosted on a server. On the other hand, *hunters* do not require mobile phones, but rather, play with a Wiimote controller used for sound loop acquisition and deposit, accomplished by pressing the buttons on the controller.

As seen in Figure 4, we selected the Gumstix computer platform[10] as the central mobile device for all players. It consists of a Verdex XM4-bt main board with expansion boards for memory, 802.11g (WiFi) communication, bidirectional high-quality audio I/O, and differential GPS. It supports Linux and is powered by a portable USB power pack. Connectivity to other devices (e.g., mobile phone and Wii controller) has been enabled via Bluetooth.

Our software hosted by the Gumstix was implemented in C, as a set of PD externals (see section3.3). We used our already existing, adapted and cross-compiled externals including the OSC protocol, Wiimote controller access, and nStream engine. The code for handling GPS's standard NMEA data format has been added for the purpose of game development.

## 5  Lessons Learned and Discussion

The SoundPark implementation has effectively shown that our architecture requires few lines of code to develop a complete, working application. In addition,

---

[9] We are using Mifare 1k RFID tags, which provide 1 kB of storage capacity.
[10] http://www.gumstix.com

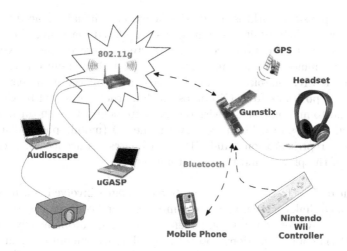

**Fig. 4.** SoundPark devices overview. Note that several of the components are unique to particular player roles (e.g., mobile phone for scouts, and Wii controller for hunters).

services added to the architecture are reusable for future application implementation. While this significantly reduced the necessary effort during application design and deployment, many issues remain. In this section, we discuss various related aspects of our experience: the use of mobile devices for the user interface, difficulties encountered during physical world modeling, integration, control and monitoring of the software components, and scalability.

**Mobile devices for the user interface.** Mobility requirements imposed hard limits regarding weight, size, and power autonomy. Solutions had to be found to extend battery life for all of the the various components, ranging from the Gumstix to the WiFi network and field servers, while still maintaining adequate processing and transmission power. In terms of logistics, the equipment *worn* by players should be mounted solidly and be well-protected from physical damage, but still have sufficient ventilation so as to not overheat. Our prototyping experience quickly demonstrated that sealed boxes of electronics and a hot summer day do not mix well. Ideally, the gear should be fixed securely to each player, yet still be easy to put on and take off. Future experiments will need to better cope with the constraints introduced by wearable computing hardware [21].

**Modeling physical world.** In order for 3D modeling to serve as an effective representation of the game state, each physical element (tennis courts, baseball diamond, walking paths, football posts, etc.) had to be modeled precisely with respect to its actual dimensions and physical location in the game area. Otherwise, the 2D and 3D displays, and in particular, the placement of player avatars within it, would not correctly correspond to the observations of the players and audience when viewing the real, non-virtual park. This effect, in addition to having a potential negative effect on the spatialized audio rendering, could also impact communication within the team.

Once the physical world is modeled, players are virtually placed within the 3D model, with their positions continuously updated via conversion of actual GPS coordinates to the model coordinate system. However, the uneven nature of GPS performance must be taken into account. Although our differential GPS sensors provide reasonable precision for most areas of the game environment, the extracted positions from GIS maps (such as those provided by Google and Yahoo!) lead to mapping errors with our measurements. This, in turn, frustrates our manual process of calibrating between the 2D (mobile phone display), 3D (Audioscape representation), and GPS coordinates, as needed for a consistent rendering of the players and their environment.

**Integration.** Due to the many disparate technologies involved, our middleware, uGASP, has to link together all these components and continuously compute the game state. However, several components, operating autonomously, are linked to uGASP via communication protocols, disabling their monitoring and control by uGASP internal interface. In contrast to uGASP components, nStream, Audioscape and PDa externals that access the GPS and the Wiimote devices are controlled and monitored through their own interface.

Global observation of all of the components is continuously enabled, in addition to uGASP built-in monitoring provided by the iPOJO layer, throughout the 3D environment. For instance, sensor states, such as player positions, are displayed, and 3D graphical vu meters are used to monitor audio communications. Our experience has shown that these metaphors are useful for understanding the status of the system. While our current implementation integrates mainly high level observations, such as user positions, it can be easily extended with lower layer ones, such as GPS signal conditions, and thus possible loss of accuracy. With such data attached to the client avatar and displayed on a dedicated 3D rendering, monitoring of the entire application can be achieved using traditional game-like navigation in the virtual environment.

The control and orchestration of the overall application were also significant challenges: control mechanisms for the various components include manual user control, OSC messages, and ssh. This heterogeneity complicates the task of orchestrating the full life cycle of an entire game. We are currently developing an orchestration component that abstracts access to, and functionality of, the components within the framework of a high level control infrastructure.

**Scalability issues.** As mentioned in Section 3, the computational restrictions of most existing mobile devices leads to a centralized architecture, where user-personalized audio rendering and game management are achieved with a server. Evolving towards a more distributed architecture, where mobile devices will operate autonomously by rendering the game state locally will significantly enhance scalability, since the number of users will not be limited by server capabilities. Although it would improve scalability, a more distributed architecture will also introduce additional challenges for global state management, player communication, consistency, and overall orchestration and coordination. These issues will become increasingly significant as more players participate in the game.

Moreover, in SoundPark, client-server interaction is supported by a single wireless network configured in managed mode that covers the entire game space. While robustness was sufficient to support the traffic generated by our application, this single network architecture restricts the game space to a static area. This constraint motivates us to investigate a more dynamic configuration that uses an ad-hoc networking strategy, as well as higher level protocols for managing group communication and low-latency transmission of data on overlay networks. In addition, and toward a more scalable and autonomic solution, we are also investigating adaptive protocols for the exchange of periodic data (audio and sensor), possibly at non-trivial bandwidth, and that better tolerate network performance variations and disconnections.

## 6   Conclusion

We presented a ubiquitous game architecture that eases the integration of heterogeneous components required for highly collaborative applications. This was used to support our mixed-reality game, SoundPark, which runs in a fully continuous and physically modeled environment with multimedia content and communication. The game further integrates user-personalized audio spatialization and low-latency audio streaming. As SoundPark delegates the players to different social roles, it vividly illustrates the possibilities of a ubiquitous computing architecture to support the demands of a highly engaging social activity.

SoundPark required only three months of development, taking advantage of the many reusable components of our service-oriented architecture. This amount of time is remarkably short, especially given that the members of the SoundPark team had not worked all together on any previous projects. Although we implemented several components of the architecture, many of them are reusable, while game-specific code contains few lines.

Finally, we provided details about lessons learned: in addition to several application specific issues, we discussed integration of heterogeneous components, their monitoring and control, as well as architecture scalability.

## References

1. Schmidt, A., Beigl, M., Gellersen, H.W.: There is more to context than location. Computers and Graphics, 893–901 (1999)
2. Schilit, B., Adams, N., Want, R.: Context-aware computing applications. In: Workshop on Mobile Computing Systems and Applications (December 1994)
3. Leichtenstern, K., Andr, E., Vogt, T.: Role assignment via physical mobile interaction techniques in mobile multi-user applications for children. In: Schiele, B., Dey, A.K., Gellersen, H., de Ruyter, B., Tscheligi, M., Wichert, R., Aarts, E., Buchmann, A. (eds.) AmI 2007. LNCS, vol. 4794, pp. 38–54. Springer, Heidelberg (2007)
4. Stahl, C.: The roaring navigator: a group guide for the zoo with shared auditory landmark display. In: MobileHCI 2007: Proceedings of the 9th international conference on Human computer interaction with mobile devices and services, pp. 383–386. ACM, New York (2007)

5. Natkin, S., Yan, C.: Adaptive narration in multiplayer ubiquitous games. In: IJCiNi. IGI Publishing (2007)
6. Sotamaa, O.: All the world's a botfighter stage: Notes on location-based multi-user gaming. In: Mäyrä, F., Tampere, E. (eds.) Proceedings of Computer Games and Digital Cultures Conference CDGC 2002, Finland (June 2002)
7. Flintham, M., Benford, S., Anastasi, R., Hemmings, T., Crabtree, A., Greenhalgh, C., Tandavanitj, N., Adams, M., Row-Farr, J.: Where on-line meets on the streets: experiences with mobile mixed reality games. In: CHI 2003, Proceedings of the SIGCHI conference on Human factors in computing systems, pp. 569–576. ACM, New York (2003)
8. Joffe, B.: Mogi, Location and presence in a pervasive community game. In: Proceedings of the Seventh International Conference on Ubiquitous Computing, Ubicomp. Ubiquitous Computing, Entertainment, and Games Worshop, Tokyo (September 2005)
9. Girardin, F., Nova, N.: Getting Real with Ubiquitous Computing: the Impact of Discrepancies on Collaboration. eMinds 1 (2006)
10. Cheok, A., et al.: Human Pacman: a mobile, wide-area entertainment system based on physical, social, and ubiquitous computing. Personal and Ubiquitous Computing (11), 71–81 (2004)
11. Rashid, O., Bamford, W., Coulton, P., Edwards, R., Scheible, J.: PAC-LAN: mixed-reality gaming with RFID-enabled mobile phones. Comput. Entertain (2006)
12. Bohn, J.: The smart jigsaw puzzle assistant: Using RFID technology for building augmented real-world games. In: Workshop on Gaming Applications in Pervasive Computing Environments at Pervasive (2004)
13. Heumer, G., Gommlich, F., Müller, A., Jung, B.: Via mineralia - a pervasive museum exploration game. In: 4th International Symposium on Pervasive Gaming Applications, PerGames, pp. 159–160 (2007)
14. Flammer, I., Ka, W., Skraba, R.: Meet your heartbeat twin. In: Proceedings of 4th International Symposium on Pervasive Gaming Applications PerGames 2007, Salzburg, Austria, pp. 157–158 (June 2007)
15. Pellerin, R., Gressier-Soudan, E., Simatic, M.: uGASP: an OSGi based middleware enabling multiplayer ubiquitous gaming. In: International Conference on Pervasive Services, ICPS 2008 Demonstration Workshop, Sorento, Italy (July 2008)
16. Wozniewski, M., Settel, Z., Cooperstock, J.R.: A paradigm for physical interaction with sound in 3-D audio space. In: Proceedings of International Computer Music Conference (ICMC) (2006)
17. Puckette, M.: Pure Data. In: Proceedings of the International Computer Music Conference, San Francisco, pp. 269–272 (1996)
18. Geiger, G.: PDa: Real time signal processing and sound generation on handheld devices. In: International Computer Music Conference (ICMC) (2003)
19. Pellerin, R.: The MooDS protocol: a J2ME object-oriented communication protocol. In: Mobility 2007: Proceedings of the 4th international conference on mobile technology, applications, and systems, pp. 8–15. ACM, New York (2007)
20. Wright, M.: Open sound control 1.0 specification. Published by the Center For New Music and Audio Technology (CNMAT), UC Berkeley (2002)
21. Piekarski, W., Thomas, B.: Arquake: the outdoor augmented reality gaming system. Commun. ACM 45(1), 36–38 (2002)

# Author Index